E. A. Wallis Budge

The History of the Blessed Virgin Mary

and the history of the likeness of Christ

E. A. Wallis Budge

The History of the Blessed Virgin Mary
and the history of the likeness of Christ

ISBN/EAN: 9783337245825

Printed in Europe, USA, Canada, Australia, Japan

Cover: Foto ©ninafisch / pixelio.de

More available books at **www.hansebooks.com**

Luzac's

Semitic Text and Translation Series.

Vol. V.

I.

THE HISTORY
OF THE
BLESSED VIRGIN MARY.

II.

THE HISTORY
OF THE
LIKENESS OF CHRIST.

THE HISTORY
OF THE
BLESSED VIRGIN MARY

AND

THE HISTORY
OF THE
LIKENESS OF CHRIST
WHICH THE JEWS OF TIBERIAS MADE TO MOCK AT.

THE SYRIAC TEXTS EDITED WITH ENGLISH
TRANSLATIONS

BY

E. A. WALLIS BUDGE, M.A., Litt.D. D.Lit.,
KEEPER OF THE EGYPTIAN AND ASSYRIAN ANTIQUITIES IN THE BRITISH MUSEUM.

ENGLISH TRANSLATIONS.

London:
LUZAC AND Co.
1899.

[All Rights Reserved.]

PRINTED BY ADOLPHUS HOLZHAUSEN, VIENNA.

DEDICATED

TO

Lady Priestley,

WHO,
IN THE INTERVALS OF A BUSY LIFE SPENT IN THE
APPLICATION OF THE PRINCIPLES OF HYGIENE
TO THE WELL-BEING OF OUR RACE,
FINDS TIME TO INTEREST HERSELF
IN THE RELIGIOUS LITERATURE OF THE
ANCIENT PEOPLES OF THE EAST,
AND IN TRACING ITS INFLUENCE UPON THE BELIEFS
OF THE NATIONS OF OUR OWN TIME.

Preface.

In the following pages will be found translations of two curious and interesting works, which, though styled "Histories" by the Syrian translators, manifestly belong to the very large section of Syriac literature which contains the Apocrypha of the New Testament. The longer of the two texts is entitled "The History of the Blessed Virgin Mary", and contains the story of her Conception, Birth, Infancy, Annunciation, Death, and Assumption, and records a number of her miracles. Included in it is an account of the early life of our Lord, and a description of the miracles which were wrought by means of His swaddling-bands, and the water in which He had been washed, and by His word or touch. A perusal of the work will convince the reader that the object of the writer throughout has been to magnify the importance of the Virgin Mary, and to describe her miraculous power, in short, it represents the popular views which were held by devout but unlettered people concerning the earthly life of the Virgin and

Child. But the work, which in its present form is now published for the first time, has considerable value, for it is a tolerably full summary of a number of apocryphal books among which may be mentioned the Protevangelium of James,[1] the Gospel of the Pseudo-Matthew,[2] the Gospel of Thomas,[3] the Gospel of the Infancy,[4] the Gospel of the Nativity of Mary,[5] and the "Transitus", or Assumption of the Blessed Virgin Mary.[6] These and other books written in Greek and Latin were laid under contribution by the Syrian translator and editor, and as a result we have in the work before us a careful selection of the most important of the stories concerning the Virgin and Child which were current in Syria and Palestine as early as the end of the IVth century of our era, as well as some which were incorporated with them at a later date.

The attention of scholars was first called to the existence of a Syriac version of the apocryphal books which related to the birth and history of the Virgin and Child and to the Assumption of the Virgin Mary

[1] For the Greek text see Tischendorf, *Evangelia Apocrypha*, Leipzig 1876, pp. 1—50.

[2] For the Latin text see Tischendorf, *op. cit.*, pp. 51—112.

[3] For the Greek and Latin texts see Tischendorf, *op. cit.*, pp. 140—180.

[4] For the Arabic text see Thilo, *Codex Apocryphus*, Leipzig 1832, pp. 66—131.

[5] For the Latin text see Tischendorf, *op. cit.*, pp. 113—121.

[6] For a Greek and two Latin texts see Tischendorf, *Apocalypses Apocryphae*, pp. 95—136.

by the late Professor Wright, who published (1) a short fragment of the Protevangelium of James, (2) a short fragment of the Gospel of Thomas the Israelite, (3) the Letters of Herod and Pilate, (4) fragments of two recensions of the Assumption of the Virgin, and (5) fragments of the Obsequies of the Holy Virgin.[1] The contents of the first two fragments will be found to have been incorporated, with little change, in the "History of the Virgin" here given; but as they represent early forms of the works to which they belong I have collated Wright's texts with the manuscript Add. 14,484 and reprinted them in the Appendix to the text for purposes of comparison. In places our text reproduces, though in different words, and sometimes in quite different order, the incidents which are detailed in the fragments of the two recensions of the Assumption of the Blessed Virgin Mary published by Professor Wright, but for the Letters of Herod and Pilate, and for the fragments of the Obsequies it has no equivalent. As both our text and that found in the manuscript of the Royal Asiatic Society, from which I have printed a large number of variant readings, agree in omitting these, it seems as if they are not parts of the later recensions of the History of the Virgin Mary in Syriac.

Of the Syriac version of the Assumption of the Blessed Virgin Mary Professor Wright identified three

[1] *Contributions to the Apocryphal Literature of the New Testament*, London 1865.

editions or recensions. The first of these is represented by the fragment which he published from the British Museum Ms. Add. 14,484; this version seems to have been the earliest form of the work. The second is represented by the History of the Virgin Mary, "in six books," which he edited and translated in the "Journal of Sacred Literature", Vol. VI, pp. 417—448, January 1865, and Vol. VII, pp. 110—160, April 1865. In this recension the work has been considerably enlarged, in particular by the addition of a lengthy introduction which relates the pretended discovery of the book, and connecting its history with the church of Saint John at Ephesus and the monastery on Mount Sinai. The third recension is represented by the fragment found in the British Museum Ms. Add. 12,174 and in this form the work has been still farther enlarged, and carefully elaborated in all its details. Closely allied to it are the Arabic version of the Assumption of the Blessed Virgin Mary, published by Maximilian Enger,[1] and the Ethiopic version which is extant in several manuscripts. It is impossible to assign axact dates to these three recensions, but there is no doubt that the principal materials for the construction of the narrative were collected before the end of the IVth century. About this time and during the Vth century the history of the Virgin and Child must have been very widely known

[1] اخبار يوحنّا السليح فى نقلة امّ المسيح, *id est, Joannis Apostoli de Transitu Beatae Mariae Virginis Liber*, Elberfeld MDCCCLIV.

and read, for the apocryphal book called "Transitus, *i. e.*, Assumptio sanctae Mariae", was condemned, together with several other apocryphal works, by Bishop Gelasius and the Council in Rome A.D. 494.[1] Of the text which I have edited and translated in this work about one third is occupied with the history of the last days of the Virgin Mary upon earth and her Assumption. Many of the incidents and accounts of the miracles which were wrought by her are found in the third recension of the Syriac version, but the order in which they are given is not always the same. Incorporated in it are a number of later additions to the work, *e. g.*, the History of the Merchant and the Three Pearls (see within, pp. 155—158), and the History of Andrew the son of Andronicus, who was kept alive at the bottom of the sea by the Virgin Mary (see within, pp. 160—168). It will be noticed that several of the proper names have been corrupted, *e. g.*, Arbôlôs is written for Archelaus (p. 99); Bûzâ for Zeno (p. 82); Palônâ for Flavia (p. 137); Nûbkar for Yûkhapar, *i. e.*, Jochebed. The description of Tobia (κομητιανος), the father of Tabîthâ, has been corrupted into a proper name Ḳômnîṭôs (p. 99); and, as in the second recension of the Assumption of the Virgin Mary (see "Journal of Sacred Literature", Vol. VII, p. 134), Abgar, the king of Edessa, is made to address his complaint concerning the behaviour of the Jews to Christ to Sabi-

[1] See Labbe, *Concilia*, tom. V, col. 389.

nus, the procurator of the Emperor Tiberius Caesar, instead of to Olbinus.[1] Besides these our text offers a number of peculiarities which will reward the reader for a careful study of the work.

Concerning the "History of the Likeness of Christ, which the Jews of Tiberias made to mock at in the days of the Emperor Zeno", little need be said. It illustrates the curious belief in the power of pictures or figures to transform themselves, under certain conditions, into the living bodies of the beings whom they represented, which was current in Egypt some thousands of years before Christ and which probably passed from that country into Syria in the early period of the history of Christianity, and it reveals the existence of an unusual superstition among the Syrian Christians.

E. A. WALLIS BUDGE.

LONDON.
October 10th, 1899.

---

[1] See Duval, *La Littérature Syriaque*, Paris 1899, p. 113, note 2.

Contents.

	PAGE
I. THE HISTORY OF THE BLESSED VIRGIN MARY	3—168
THE PREFACE OF THE SYRIAN TRANSLATOR	1. 2
THE STORY OF YÔNÂKHÎR AND DÎNÂ .	3. 4
REUBEN PREVENTS YÔNÂKHÎR FROM MAKING HIS OFFERING	5
YÔNÂKHÎR DEPARTS TO THE DESERT	6
THE GRIEF AND LAMENTATION OF DÎNÂ	6—8
THE ANGEL OF THE LORD APPEARS TO DÎNÂ; THE BIRTH OF THE VIRGIN MARY FORETOLD. DÎNÂ'S NAME IS CHANGED TO ḤANNÂ	9
THE RETURN OF YÔNÂKHÎR	12
YÔNÂKHÎR AND ḤANNÂ GO TO JERUSALEM	13
THE BIRTH OF THE VIRGIN MARY	14
DESCRIPTION OF MARY'S CHAMBER .	15
YÔNÂKHÎR'S FEAST ...	15
BIRTH OF MARY'S SISTER PARÔGHÎTHÂ .	16
MARY ACCOMPANIED BY SEVEN VIRGINS GOES TO JERUSALEM	17
THE PRIESTS CAST LOTS FOR MARY.	17
MARY GOES TO LIVE IN ZADOK'S HOUSE	18
DEATH OF YÔNÂKHÎR AND OF ḤANNÂ	18
THE PRIESTS ASK THE LORD FOR DIRECTIONS ABOUT MARY'S FUTURE ...	19
MARY IS GIVEN TO JOSEPH, THE SON OF JACOB, THE SON OF MATTHAN . .	20
JOSEPH'S JOURNEY TO JERUSALEM	21

CONTENTS.

	PAGE
THE ARCHANGEL GABRIEL APPEARS TO MARY AND FORETELLS THE BIRTH OF JESUS	22
THE VISIT OF MARY TO ELIZABETH	25
RETURN OF JOSEPH WHO FINDS MARY WITH CHILD	26
GABRIEL APPEARS TO JOSEPH	28
THE PRIESTS CHIDE JOSEPH AND MARY	29
THE WATERS OF TRIAL	30
JOURNEY OF JOSEPH AND MARY TO BETHLEHEM	32
THE BIRTH OF JESUS	32
THE APPEARANCE OF THE STAR IN PERSIA	34
THE PERSIANS SET OUT FOR BETHLEHEM	36
HEROD MAKES ENQUIRIES OF THE PERSIAN KINGS	37
THE PERSIAN KINGS MAKE OFFERINGS TO JESUS	38
THE CIRCUMCISION OF JESUS	39
JESUS IS PRESENTED IN THE TEMPLE	40
SLAUGHTER OF THE CHILDREN BY HEROD	41
MURDER OF ZECHARIAH	42
JOSEPH, MARY, AND JESUS FLEE INTO EGYPT	44
THE BREAKING OF THE IDOLS OF EGYPT	47
THE SON OF THE PRIEST HEALED BY A SWADDLING-BAND OF JESUS	47
MARY DRIVES THE DEVIL OUT OF A WOMAN	50
THE BEWITCHED BRIDE	50
THE DEVIL IS DRIVEN AWAY FROM A RICH WOMAN	51
MARY HEALS A WOMAN WHO WAS A LEPER	52
MARY HEALS A CHILD WHO WAS A LEPER	53
STORY OF THE YOUNG MAN WHO HAD BEEN TURNED INTO A MULE	54—58
STORY OF THE THIEVES TITUS AND DUMACHUS	59
JOSEPH AND MARY AND JESUS RETURN TO BETHLEHEM	60
MARY CURES A CHILD WHO WAS SICK OF BOILS	60
MARY HEALS A CHILD OF A DISEASE IN HIS EYES	61
STORY OF THE CONCUBINES MARY AND ARZAMÎ	62—64
MARY RAISES THOMAS, SURNAMED DIDYMUS, FROM THE DEAD	65
MARY HEALS A WOMAN WHO WAS A LEPER	67
STORY OF THE BETROTHED MAIDEN WHO FELL SICK OF LEPROSY	68—69
MARY DRIVES A DEVIL AWAY FROM A WOMAN	70

CONTENTS.

	PAGE
THE CHILD JESUS CAUSES A DEVIL TO GO FORTH FROM THE BOY JUDAH, WHO WAS AFTERWARDS KNOWN AS JUDAS ISCARIOT	71
JESUS AT THE AGE OF FIVE YEARS GOES TO SCHOOL—HIS LIFE THERE ...	71—73
JESUS HEALS HIS BROTHER JAMES WHO HAD BEEN BITTEN BY A VIPER	73
JESUS DISCOURSES TO THE DOCTORS IN THE TEMPLE	73
JESUS GATHERS UP IN HIS GARMENT SPILLED WATER	75
JESUS LENGTHENS PLANKS OF WOOD WHICH WERE TOO SHORT	76
JESUS MAKES FIGURES OF HORSES, AND MARES, AND OXEN, AND ASSES, AND SPARROWS, WHICH MOVE AND EAT.	76
JESUS TURNS CHILDREN INTO GOATS.	77
THE STORY OF SIMON ZELOTES.	79
JESUS RELEASES A MAN FROM A SERPENT WHICH HAD BEEN COILED ROUND HIM FOR THREE YEARS	80
JESUS HEALS A YOUNG MAN WHO HAD BEEN BEATEN SORELY	81
JESUS RAISES THE CHILD BÛZÂ FROM THE DEAD	82
THE STORY OF NATHANIEL	83
JESUS RAISES THE SON OF THE WIDOW OF NAIN FROM THE DEAD	83—85
THE BAPTISM OF CHRIST BY JOHN	85
JESUS TURNS WATER INTO WINE AT CANA OF GALILEE	86
JESUS IS TEMPTED OF THE DEVIL.	87
THE RAISING OF THE DAUGHTER OF JAIRUS	89
CRUCIFIXION OF CHRIST ON FRIDAY, THE 30TH DAY OF ÂDÂR, ANNO ALEX. 336	89
JOSEPH IS SHUT UP IN PRISON	90
JESUS RISES FROM THE DEAD	91
THE MARIES VISIT THE GRAVE OF JESUS AND MEET HIM.	92
THE PHARISEES AND SADDUCEES DISPUTE ABOUT THE RESURRECTION OF JESUS.	93
THE ELEVEN DISCIPLES SEE JESUS IN GALILEE	95
THE ASCENSION OF JESUS.	96
MARY DWELLS IN JERUSALEM, AND THE JEWS PLOT TO SLAY HER.	97
VISIT OF GABRIEL TO MARY	98
LETTER OF ABGAR TO SABINUS, PREFECT OF TIBERIUS.	100

CONTENTS.

	PAGE
MARY PRAYS THAT SHE MAY SEE THE APOSTLES BEFORE SHE DIES	102
JOHN THE LESS, SIMON PETER, PAUL, THOMAS, MATTHEW, BARTHOLOMEW, AND JAMES THE APOSTLE VISIT MARY IN BETHLEHEM	106
PHILIP, SIMON ZELOTES, LUKE, ANDREW, AND MARK VISIT MARY IN BETHLEHEM	108
THE PATRIARCHS AND THE CHERUBIM AND SERAPHIM VISIT MARY	110
MARY HEALS THE SON OF THE JUDGE	114—116
DEATH OF MARY ANNO ALEX. 342.	117
THE JEWS BRIBE YÔPHANÂ TO CARRY OFF HER BODY	119
THE BURIAL OF MARY	121
THE COMMEMORATION FESTIVALS OF MARY.	125
THE HISTORY OF THE OBSEQUIES OF MARY BY JOHN THE LESS.	126
THE MIRACLES OF MARY:—	
1. THE HEALING OF THE WOMAN OF BEYRÛT	136
2. THE HEALING OF NÛBKAR WHO WAS A LEPER.	136
3. THE HEALING OF ABÎGÊL	137
4. THE RIGHT EYE OF PALÔNÂ IS RESTORED.	137
5. TWO DEVILS ARE DRIVEN OUT OF THE LADY MALCÔ	137
6. THE HEALING OF THE MAN WITH ELEPHANTIASIS	137
THREE THOUSAND EIGHT HUNDRED SICK FOLK ARE MADE WHOLE	138
THE DISPUTE BETWEEN CHRISTIANS AND JEWS	144
THE MIRACLES OF MARY:—	
1. MARY SAVES NINETY-FIVE SHIPS FROM DESTRUCTION.	154
2. MARY DELIVERS TRAVELLERS FROM ROBBERS.	154
3. MARY SAVES A CHILD FROM DROWNING IN A WELL	154
4. MARY HEALES A MAN WHO HAD BEEN SICK FOR TWENTY YEARS	154
5. MARY SAVES A DROWNING CREW	155
6. MARY SAVES A MERCHANT THREE TIMES FROM DROWNING	155
7. MARY DELIVERS TWO WOMEN WHO WERE ATTACKED BY A SERPENT	158
8. MARY RESTORES A PURSE CONTAINING ONE THOUSAND DÎNÂRS TO ITS OWNER.	158
9. THE STORY OF ANDREW THE SON OF ANDRONICUS.	160—167

CONTENTS.

II. THE HISTORY OF THE LIKENESS OF CHRIST WHICH
THE JEWS OF TIBERIAS MADE TO MOCK AT   171—246

	PAGE
PHILOTHEUS SETS OUT ON HIS TRAVELS AND VISITS THE HOLY PLACES OF PALESTINE	173
THE MESSENGER OF GOD EXPLAINS WHY THE COUNTRY HAD BEEN LAID WASTE	174
THE JEWS HIRE A PAINTER TO PAINT A LIKENESS OF CHRIST UPON A PANEL OF WOOD	185
THE JEWS SET UP THE LIKENESS IN THE TEMPLE AND MOCK AT IT	186
A JEW PIERCES IT WITH A SPEAR AND BLOOD AND WATER FLOW FORTH FROM IT	186
A BLIND MAN SMEARS SOME OF THE WATER AND BLOOD UPON HIS EYES AND IS MADE TO SE	187
A PARALYTIC IS HEALED BY THE WATER AND BLOOD	193
CONSPIRACY OF THE PRIESTS	194
CONVERSION OF THE DOORKEEPER OF THE CHAMBER WHEREIN THE LIKENESS WAS PLACED	198
THE LIKENESS IS TAKEN UP INTO HEAVEN	200
THE MAN WITH THE WITHERED ARM IS MADE WHOLE	201
TUMULT AMONG THE PEOPLE WHO THREATEN TO FORCE THE DOOR OF THE CHAMBER WHEREIN THE LIKENESS WAS PLACED	204
THE JEWS BRIBE THE GOVERNOR OF TIBERIAS	205
THE PARALYTIC SEEKS HIS BROTHER JUDAH	206
THE TWO BROTHERS ARE BAPTIZED	212
THEY RAISE A YOUNG MAN FROM THE DEAD	214
THEY CAST A DEVIL OUT OF A MAN	216
JUDAH CASTS A DEVIL OUT OF A YOUNG WOMAN	223
HE HEALS A SAMARITAN WOMAN	229
JUDAH AND HIS COMPANIONS ARE CAST INTO PRISON	232
THEY RESTORE THE SIGHT OF THE BLIND COUNCILLOR	236
THEY RESTORE THE SIGHT OF THE GOVERNOR'S SON	241
CONVERSION OF THE GOVERNOR	244
WARNED BY EUTYCHUS JUDAH AND HIS COMPANIONS LEAVE THE CITY	244
THEY GO TO CILICIA WHERE THEY BUILD A MONASTERY AND DWELL	245

PREFACE OF THE SYRIAN TRANSLATOR.

My brethren, wise men, and men of understanding, and men of knowledge, are wont to hide the treasures which they have laid up from every man, and also from their children and from their heirs, as long as they are young children. And thus are they in the habit of doing in respect of their children, even though they be their heirs who have the expectation of inheriting their possessions, until they have become grown men, and can enter into the understanding of things which are written, and know how to [distinguish] between good and evil. Then, at length, do they reveal and shew unto them the treasures which they have laid up. In this wise also hath the Creator, who made and stablished the universe by His grace, acted towards our mortal race in His unspeakable wisdom, for He hath first of all trained us in doctrine like young children who study carefully the alphabet, and who then pass on to the Psalms, from which they go on to the other Books of the Bible, and then to the interpretation thereof. Even thus hath God acted towards us in His wisdom. For aforetime He hid from us the treasure of heavenly life, which was concealed by His knowledge behind the curtains of His Manhood, which sprang from the House of David.

And he hid the mystery of his dispensation from every man. But to those who were righteous, and to the Prophets, and to the kings who were his friends, and who kept his commandments, he taught it. And to these he secretly gave signs by means of divers visions and sundry similitudes, concerning the treasure of the new life which was concealed in our mortal race, and which was about to be revealed at the end of times, and from which both spiritual and corporeal beings were to be enriched with possessions which cannot be described.

BY THE MIGHT OF OUR LORD JESUS CHRIST WE BEGIN
TO WRITE THE HISTORY OF OUR BLESSED LADY MARY,
THE MOTHER OF CHRIST[1]. O LORD, IN THY MERCY,
HELP ME! AMEN.

And it came to pass that when the time which was decreed[2] by the knowledge of God had arrived, He made the divine presence[3] of His Godhead to abide in the house of a just and righteous man, whose family was descended from the House of David. Now this man was called Yônâkhîr,[4] and he was the son of Mâthan (Matthan), the son of Elî'âzâr (Eleazar),[5] of the tribe of Solomon, the son of David. And there was born unto Matthan, the son of Eleazar, | a son, and he called him Jacob; and Jacob, the son of Mat-

---

[1] B The holy Virgin, the Mother of Christ our Redeemer. (B = the Royal Asiatic Society's MS. containing the History of the Virgin Mary.)
[2] Literally, "cut".
[3] Syr. ܫܟܝܢܬܐ i. e., שְׁכִינָה. According to the Rabbis the "Shechinah" represented the glorious majesty of the Almighty; but some of them called the Holy Spirit "Shechinah", קראו ר"זל לרוח הקודש שכינה. See Eisenmenger, Entdecktes Judenthum, I, p. 268.
[4] I. e., Ἰωαχείμ, Joachim.
[5] See St. Matthew I. 15.

than, took a wife whose name was Âstâ,[1] but he died, leaving behind him neither seed nor heir. Then Hêlî,[2] the son of Maṭṭath,[3] of the tribe of Nathan[4] the son of David, took his wife, and she bore him a son, who was called according to the Law, Joseph the son of Jacob, but who was in truth the son of Hêlî.[5] And there was born unto Nathan,[4] the son of Eleazar, another son, and he called his name Yônâkhîr the son of Matthan; and God enriched him exceedingly with flocks and herds, and with possessions, and with great wealth, but he was childless.

Now this[6] man was of Bethlehem of Judah, and his name was Zadok, and the name of his wife was Dînâ (Dinah); and they were both righteous before God, and they walked in all His laws of life. And this Zadok, who was surnamed Yônâkhîr, was a nobleman, and he was exceedingly rich, and he made offerings unto the Lord God of Israel, and said, "The "portion which I am bound by the Law to offer up "on my own behalf unto the Lord shall be an offer-

---

[1] Or Estâ (?).
[2] See St. Luke III. 23.
[3] Var. Maṭathath.
[4] Var. Matthan.
[5] Joseph legally the son of David, rightly the son of Hêlî.
[6] In *B* the text reads:—"And one day he had a matter of dispute "with one of his kinsmen who reproached Yônâkhîr by reason of his "childlessness; and Yônâkhîr was exceedingly grieved, and he rose "up and went to his house, being very sad and sorrowful; and he said "unto Dînâ his wife, Behold, all this house is left in thy hands," etc. The MS. *A* agrees with the Greek and Latin texts in attributing the cause of Yônâkhîr's departure to the words of one Reuben, who might, of course, have been a kinsman of his.

"ing of propitiation for myself; this portion is more than everything, therefore let it stand on behalf of the whole nation."[1]

And[2] it came to pass that when the great day of the Lord drew nigh, and the children of Israel were offering up their offerings, Rûbhîl (Reuben)[3] | came nigh unto Yônâkhîr and said, "Thou hast no power to be the first to make thine offerings, for thou hast no seed in Israel." And Yônâkhîr answered and said unto him, "Indeed I am one by myself, for I have not stablished seed in Israel." And when he had made enquiries he found that all the righteous men had stablished seed in Israel; but he remembered the patriarch Abraham, unto whom in his last days God had given a son, that is to say, the son of promise—Isaac.[4]

Then Yônâkhîr was sad, and exceedingly distressed, and he went down and entered into his house, being very sorrowful.[5] And he said unto his wife

---

[1] The Greek runs (see Tischendorf, *Evangelia Apocrypha*, 1876, p. 1):—καὶ προσέφερε τὰ δῶρα αὐτοῦ διπλᾶ, λέγων· ἔσται τῆς περιουσίας μου παντὶ τῷ λαῷ, καὶ τὸ τῆς ἀφέσεώς μου κυρίῳ εἰς ἱλασμὸν ἐμοί. The point seems to be that he gave away two thirds of his income, as we may see from the Pseudo-Matthew:—quascumque possidere videbatur tres partes faciebat: unam partem dabat viduis, orphanis, peregrinis atque pauperibus; alteram vero partem colentibus deum; tertiam partem sibi et omni domui suae reservabat. (See Tischendorf, *op. cit.*, p. 54.)

[2] Pseudo-Matthew, Chap. II, begins here.

[3] Pseudo-Matthew has "scriba templi nomine Ruben".

[4] See Genesis XV. 4; XVII. 16; XVIII. 10; XXI. 2.

[5] In the Greek and Latin texts Joachim goes to the desert directly: καὶ οὐκ ἐφάνη τῇ γυναικὶ αὐτοῦ· ἀλλ᾽ ἔδωκεν ἑαυτὸν εἰς τὴν ἔρημον κ. τ. λ. "et non est reversus in domum suam, sed abiit ad pecora sua."

Dînâ, "Behold, I leave all this house in thy hands;" and he left his wife, and went forth into a desert place. And he pitched an habitation there by himself, and he fasted there forty days and forty nights, and made supplication unto God Almighty, saying, "I will neither give sleep unto mine eyes, nor slum- "ber unto mine eyelids, until the Lord shall be re- "conciled unto me, and shall make my disgrace to "pass away from among the children of men; and "my prayer itself shall be unto me a consolation."[1] And thus he remained forty days and forty nights in watching, and fasting, and prayer, and sighing, and weeping, and making supplication unto God.

And Dînâ,[2] the wife of Yônâkhîr, dwelt in grief, and she beat her breasts, saying, "It is meet that I "should weep, for among the daughters of Israel there "is none like | unto me; and in all the house of Jacob "there is no childless woman except myself. Even "Yônâkhîr, my own husband, has forsaken me[3] and "fled from me, and among all created beings there

---

[1] An inexact rendering of καὶ ἔσται μου ἡ εὐχὴ βρῶμα καὶ πόμα. For what follows in the Syriac of this Chapter the Greek has no equivalent.

[2] The second Chapter of the Protevangelium of Jacob contains a conversation between Dînâ, who is, however, called Ἄννα, and her maid Judith. The maid wished her to put on festal attire in honour of the "great day of the Lord", and to lay aside the garments of grief; and finally, she put off the garments of grief, and arraying herself in her bridal attire she went to walk in her garden.

[3] Yônâkhîr left her for five months, and she says: — "Ecce enim "quinque menses transeunt et virum meum non video. Et nescio "utrum mortuus sit, ut vel sepulturam illi fecissem." Pseudo-Matthew, Chapter II.

"is none who resembleth me." And being in sore grief, she went forth with weeping and sighing into the garden which they had. And it came to pass that as she was walking about hither and thither in the garden, and was weeping bitterly, and sighing, and lamenting, she said, "O Lord God of my fathers, "bless me, even me, Thy sinful handmaiden, just as "Thou didst bless our mother Sarah, and didst give "her a son in her old age, even Isaac."[1] And these and many other such like things did she say as she wept with lamentation and tears, and she stretched out her hands [to heaven], for it was a grievously bitter thing unto her; and she made supplication unto God, and fixed her weeping eyes intently [upon heaven].[2] And as she looked she saw in a tree a sparrows' nest wherein there were young birds and their mother was hovering about over them and giving them food. And when she saw them she lifted up her voice with bitter sobs before the Lord, and she made entreaty unto Him, saying, "O Lord God, "what sin hath thine handmaiden sinned before Thee? "Or in what have my fathers done wickedly | in Thy "sight? For behold, I, even I, only am a reproach "in the house of Jacob, and a mockery in the house "of Israel. For the people make a mock of me, and "they treat me as a stranger, and they spurn me. "But though the children of men cast me away, it is "not meet that Thou, O Lord, shouldst cast me away

Page 8

---

[1] Protevangelium, Chapter II ends here.
[2] Protevangelium, Chapter III begins with the words, καὶ ἀτενίσασα εἰς τὸν οὐρανὸν εἶδε καλιάν; there is no equivalent in the Greek text for much of the prayer which follows in the Syriac text.

"from Thy face, for Thou art the hope of all those "who are about to perish, and the comforter of all "those who are afflicted; and all those who put their "hope in Thee, and trust in Thee, are never put to "shame. O Lord God, Thou great and mighty One, "Thy handmaiden is not even like unto this sparrow, "for behold, the bird hath young ones, and she is "fruitful, and bringeth forth, and giveth them food, "and reareth her young before Thee. O Lord God, "let not Thy handmaiden be before Thee like this "ground which is trodden upon by the feet of every "creature that Thou hast made; yet even unto it hast "Thou in Thy grace given the power to conceive, "and to bring forth, and to make trees bearing fruit, "and to bring to maturity before Thee crops of grain "and herbs. And, moreover, behold the beasts, and "the things which creep, and the winged fowl, and "the birds, and everything which Thou in Thy grace "hast made, each according to its kind conceiveth, "and beareth, and bringeth its offspring to ma-"turity before Thee. O my Lord, why hast Thou "made me a woman? And why hast Thou made me "a reproach and a mockery unto all those who bring "forth children in Israel? And if it be, O my Lord, "that my sin and the sin of my fathers be great be-"fore Thee, do Thou pardon and forgive us by Thy "grace. What | is the iniquity of all creation com-"pared with the overwhelming mercy of Thy grace? "And if our iniquity be great, and our sin much, "of Thy mercy¹ cast Thou both of them away from

---

¹ Reading with *B* ܡܢܠܘܬ ܪܚܡܐ.

"Thee like a pebble into the sea. O Lord, hearken
"Thou unto the prayer of Thy sinful handmaiden, and
"cast Thou me not away from before Thee; moreover,
"accept the petition which I have brought unto Thee."
And it came to pass that as her hands were
stretched out to heaven, and as she was gazing in-
tently at the nest and the young ones of the spar-
row[1] which were therein, and was praying, and was
saying these words and others like unto them, behold,[2] the angel of the Lord came unto her. And
he answered and said unto her, "Peace be unto thee,
"O woman, fear thou not, for thou hast found mercy
"with the Lord, and He hath heard thy prayer, and
"hath received thy petition; and His mercy hath par-
"doned thee and been gracious unto thee. And from
"now and henceforth thy name shall not be called
"Dînâ, but Ḥannâ, for the mercy of the Lord hath
"been gracious unto thee. And He will give thee
"conception, and thou shalt bring forth a child like
"all [other] women. For behold, thou shalt conceive,
"and shalt bring forth a daughter, and thou shalt
"call her name Mary; from her shall spring the Light
"of creation and Him for Whom the worlds wait, and
"He shall be the consolation of His people Israel.
"And behold, at the appointed time I will announce
"to thy husband Yônâkhîr concerning thy conception,
"and behold, he will return unto thee in great joy."[3]

---

[1] See the variant text in Tischendorf's footnote (*op. cit.*, p. 8) καὶ ταῦτα λέγουσα ἀφορᾷ εἰς τὸ δένδρον, καὶ θεασαμένη στρουθὸν, κ. τ. λ.

[2] Protevangelium, Chapter IV begins here.

[3] The angel's speech is very much shorter in the Greek:—ἐπή-κουσε κύριος τῆς δεήσεώς σου, καὶ συλλήψει καὶ γεννήσεις, καὶ λαληθήσεται

And Ḥannâ answered and said unto the angel who had spoken these things | unto her, "The Lord liveth, "and His word liveth; whatsoever He giveth unto "me will I give that it may live before Him."[1] Then was the angel hidden from her sight; and she was full of grace.

And she returned unto her house from the garden, being glad and rejoicing. Then the women who were with her there answered and said unto her, "Dînâ, "what is thy news? When thou didst go forth from "us thou wast weeping, but now thou art rejoicing "and dost laugh." And she made answer unto them with gladness, and spake unto them, saying, "[I re-"joice] because God hath been gracious unto me, "and because He hath visited me according to His "mercy. And He hath given me a message of glad "tidings by the hand of His angel, who hath said "unto me, 'Thou shalt conceive, and thou shalt give "birth unto a child like all other women; and now, "henceforth thy name shall not be called Dînâ but "Ḥannâ',[2] for His mercy hath been gracious unto me.

τὸ σπέρμα σου ἐν ὅλῃ τῇ οἰκουμένῃ. In the Pseudo-Matthew it is shorter still, and is different:—Noli timere Anna, quoniam in consilio dei est germen tuum; et quod ex te natum fuerit, erit in admirationem omnibus seculis usque in finem.

[1] In the Greek ζῇ κύριος ὁ Θεός μου, ἐὰν γεννήσω εἴτε ἄρρεν εἴτε θῆλυ, προσάξω αὐτὸ δῶρον κυρίῳ τῷ Θεῷ μου, καὶ ἔσται λειτουργοῦν αὐτῷ πάσας τὰς ἡμέρας τῆς ζωῆς αὐτοῦ. For what follows in the Syriac of this paragraph the Greek has no equivalent.

[2] The writer is here playing upon the root ܢܡ "to be merciful", and the name Ḥannâ ܚܢܢ which is explained to mean ܪܚܡ, i. e., "mercy".

"Moreover, the angel gave me a sign and said unto "me, 'This shall be a sure sign unto thee. Behold, "thy husband Yônâkhîr shall return unto thee from "his pastures'."

And it came to pass that whilst she was saying these things unto the women who were with her in the house, behold, two | men came there from pasturing their flocks, and they brought unto her a message, saying, "Behold, thy husband Yônâkhîr cometh from "his pasture, for the angel of the Lord appeared "unto him where he was abiding and gave him a "message, saying, 'Rise up, O Yônâkhîr, the son of "Matthan, the son of David, and go to thy house, "for the Lord hath heard thy prayer, and He hath "received thy petition; and thy wife Dînâ shall con-"ceive like all other women. Therefore her name "shall not henceforth be called Dînâ, but Ḥannâ; for "the Lord hath been gracious unto her, and hath put "away from her the reproach of the children of men'."[1] Then Yônâkhîr rose up and took from his flocks fat beasts for offering up by fire,[2] and he-goats without blemish upon them, and he took also from his herd fat oxen which had never been under the yoke, and offered them up as offerings unto the Lord.

---

[1] In the Greek the angel's speech is much shorter:—'Ιωακείμ, 'Ιωακείμ, ἐπήκουσε κύριος ὁ Θεὸς τῆς δεήσεώς σου· κατάβηθι ἐντεῦθεν· ἰδοὺ γὰρ ἡ γυνή σου Ἄννα ἐν γάστρι λήψεται. In the Pseudo-Matthew the conversation between Yônâkhîr and the angel is a long one, and differs considerably from that given in the Greek and Syriac texts. See Pseudo-Matthew, Chapter III (Tischendorf, *op. cit.*, p. 57).

[2] In the Protevangelium Yônâkhîr offers ten pure and spotless lambs unto the Lord, twelve calves for the priests and clergy, and one hundred goats for the people.

And when he had come nigh his house,[1] behold Ḥannâ his wife met him at the door. And when she saw her husband she ran to salute him with joy and laughter, and said unto him, "Rejoice and be glad, "O Yônâkhîr, for God hath put away my reproach "from among the children of men. And He hath given "unto me the power to conceive, and to bring forth "children like all other women; and blessed art thou "also, for the Lord hath become reconciled unto thee, "and He hath blessed thee. | And now I know that "God hath remembered me, and that He hath blessed "me, His handmaiden. For I was childless, but He "hath answered me even as He answered Sarah our "mother, unto whom He announced and gave Isaac; "to me likewise hath He given the power to con- "ceive and to bring forth children like all other wo- "men."[2] Then Yônâkhîr went into his house and took his rest.[3]

---

[1] ܣܚܘܪ ܒܝܬܗ, literally, "round about his house". According to Pseudo-Matthew, Yônâkhîr and his men took thirty days to come home from the mountains, (Cumque triginta dies ambularent et essent jam prope), and the angel of the Lord told Ḥannâ to go to the "Golden Gate" [at Jerusalem] to meet her husband (Vade ad portam quae aurea vocatur et occurre viro tuo). In the Protevangelium Ḥannâ seems to stand at the door of her house and not to have gone to Jerusalem, καὶ ἰδοὺ Ἰωακεὶμ ἧκε μετὰ τῶν ποιμνίων αὐτοῦ, καὶ ἔστη Ἄννα πρὸς τὴν πύλην καὶ εἶδε τὸν Ἰωακεὶμ ἐρχόμενον, κ. τ. λ.

[2] This long speech is based upon the Greek νῦν οἶδα ὅτι κύριος ὁ θεὸς εὐλόγησέ με σφόδρα· ἰδοὺ γὰρ ἡ χήρα οὐκέτι χήρα, καὶ ἡ ἄτεκνος ἐν γαστρὶ λήψομαι; Pseudo-Matthew is shorter still:—"Vidua eram, "et ecce jam non sum; sterilis eram, et ecce jam concepi."

[3] According to the Greek for the first day, ἀνεπαύσατο τὴν πρώτην ἡμέραν.

And¹ it came to pass after a few days² that he and Ḥannâ his wife went up to Jerusalem to offer up offerings unto the Lord. And Yônâkhîr made a vow concerning himself, and said, "If the Lord God ap-"peareth unto me at the time when the priest is offer-"ing up the offering on my behalf to the Lord, then "shall I know that God hath become reconciled unto "me, and that He hath put away³ my sins." Now when he had gone into Jerusalem, the priests receiv-ed him gladly, for he was a man of high degree and well known in Israel; and he was very rich and had goods and possessions in abundance, and when he went into Jerusalem much people came to do him honour and to visit him.

And it came to pass, when the high priest drew nigh to offer up the offering on behalf of Yônâkhîr, that Yônâkhîr had his eyes fixed intently upon him, and he saw between his eyes (*i. e.*, on his forehead), a little spot of light wherein was written, | "God "hath received thy sacrifices and thy offerings, and "He hath heard thy prayer and thy supplication; and "the Lord hath answered the petitions of thy heart "as concerning Dînâ thy wife, and hath put away "your reproach from among the children of men."⁴ Then Yônâkhîr said unto himself, "Now know I that "the Lord God hath become reconciled unto me, and

---

¹ Protevangelium Chapter V begins here.
² The Greek has Τῇ δὲ ἐπαύριον προσέφερε τὰ δῶρα αὐτοῦ.
³ Read ܐܥܒܪ.
⁴ There is nothing like this in the Greek or Latin texts. The Greek has, καὶ προσέφερεν τὰ δῶρα αὐτοῦ Ἰωακείμ καὶ προσεῖχεν τῷ πετάλῳ τοῦ ἱερέως, ὡς ἐπέβη ἐπὶ τὸ θυσιαστήριον κυρίου, καὶ οὐκ εἶδεν ἁμαρτίαν ἐν ἑαυτῷ.

"that He hath put away my sins, and hath forgiven "my transgressions." So he went down from Jerusalem, having given to the full alms and oblations both to God and to the poor. And it came to pass that when the days of Ḥannâ his wife were fulfilled that she should bring forth, she gave birth to a daughter, and called her name Mary. And Ḥannâ said, "Blessed be my soul, and glory be "to the Lord God Who hath remembered me, and hath "put away for me my reproach from among the chil-"dren of men[1]." And[2] when the days of her purification were accomplished, Yônâkhîr offered up an offering on her behalf. And he said unto Ḥannâ his wife, "Blessed be the Lord Who hath given us this "blessed fruit, although it be not a male child; there-"fore let us give praise unto the Lord God, and re-"joice in Him, even as did Abraham and Sarah for "Isaac." So he offered up offerings on her behalf, and he gave gifts to the poor.

And[3] it came to pass that when the child was one year[4] old, her mother made her to stand upon the ground to see if she was able to walk or not; and having set her up there, the child stood up firmly, and walked to her mother's apron[5]. And Ḥannâ took her in her arms, and kissed her, and said, "As the "Lord God of Israel liveth, I will not let thee walk

---

[1] In the Greek, ἐμεγαλύνθη ἡ ψυχή μου ἐν τῇ ἡμέρᾳ ταύτῃ.
[2] For what follows in this paragraph the Greek has no equivalent.
[3] Protevangelium Chapter VI begins here.
[4] In the Greek, γενομένης δὲ αὐτῆς ἐξαμηνιαίου.
[5] Gr. καὶ ἑπτὰ βήματα περιπατήσασα.

"upon this earth until I have taken thee up to the
"temple of the Lord, even as | I vowed unto Him." Page 14
And Ḥannâ cried unto her husband Yônâkhîr and
said unto him, "Build thou a chamber for Mary our
"daughter, so that she may abide therein until she
"hath grown somewhat, and we can carry her up to
"Jerusalem, where she may dwell before the Lord,
"even as we have promised unto Him." So Yônâkhîr
her father built for his daughter a beautiful chamber
wherein was a shrine;¹ and they strewed the ground
with costly silken stuffs, saying, "She shall not walk
"upon the earth until she hath gone up to the temple
"of the Lord." ²

And it came to pass that when Mary was three³
years old, Yônâkhîr her father made a great feast⁴,
and he invited the priests, and the Levites, and much
people thereunto; and Ḥannâ also invited many virgins from among the daughters of Israel, and she
filled Mary's chamber with them. And they brought
Mary to the seat where the priests were sitting that
they might bless her; and the priests did bless her,
and they spake, as in prophecy, saying, "The Lord
"God of our fathers bless this maiden, and grant
"unto her a noble, and exalted, and glorious name,
"for ever and ever, throughout all generations; and
"that from her may spring Him for Whom the na-

---

¹ Gr. καὶ ἐποίησεν ἁγίασμα ἐν τῷ κοιτῶνι αὐτῆς.
² Evidently a reflection of Ḥannâ's speech; there is nothing like it in the Greek.
³ Gr. ἐγένετο δὲ πρῶτος ἐνιαυτὸς τῇ παιδί.
⁴ ܩܘܒܠܐ, literally, "reception"; the Greek has ἐποίησεν Ἰωακείμ δοχὴν μεγάλην.

"tions wait." And [all] the people cried out, "Amen".¹ Then Ḥannâ her mother took the child, and went out praising and glorifying God, and saying, "Blessed "be the Lord God of Israel Who hath given unto "me the fruit of righteousness." And Mary continued to grow, and to become strong in the grace of God.

Page 15   And² it came to pass that when Mary was ten | years³ old her parents said, "Let us take her up "to the temple of the Lord that she may dwell be"fore Him, even as we have vowed";⁴ but Dînâ her mother said unto Yônâkhîr her father, "Let us wait "until she knoweth herself,⁵ before we will take her "up⁶." Now, in those days Ḥannâ conceived, and she brought forth a daughter, and called her name Parôghîthâ (*i. e.* "pullet") saying, "Mary shall belong to "the Lord, and Parôghîthâ shall be a delight unto us "in her stead"; so Yônâkhîr and Ḥannâ rejoiced in Parôghîthâ their daughter.⁷

And it came to pass that when Mary was twelve years⁸ old, her parents invited seven virgins to go

---

¹ Gr. γένοιτο γένοιτο, ἀμήν. Ḥannâ then, according to the Greek, took the child to the chief priests, and they also blessed her; but for the text of this passage and that of her song of triumph in which she calls upon the Twelve Tribes of Israel to hear that Ḥannâ giveth suck, the Syriac has no equivalent.

² Protevangelium Chapter VII begins here.

³ Gr. Τῇ δὲ παιδὶ προσετίθεντο οἱ μῆνες αὐτῆς.

⁴ The Greek adds, μήπως ἀποστείλῃ ὁ δεσπότης ἐφ' ἡμᾶς καὶ ἀπρόσδεκτον γένηται τὸ δῶρον ἡμῶν.

⁵ Read ܡܪܗ.

⁶ Gr. ἀναμείνωμεν τὸ τρίτον ἔτος, ὅπως μὴ ζητήσει ἡ παῖς πατέρα ἢ μητέρα.

⁷ There is no equivalent for this passage in the Greek.

⁸ Gr. καὶ ἐγένετο τριετὴς ἡ παῖς.

up with them to Jerusalem, and they put lamps into the hands of each of them; and they took Mary up to the temple of the Lord. And the priests received Mary, and the high-priest, as in prophecy, spake unto her, saying, "The Lord God of Israel shall bless thy "name, Mary, for in thee hath He revealed the re- "demption of the Hebrew nation, and of the Gen- "tiles also in the last days."[1] And God made grace and mercy to dwell in Mary, and the priests, and the Levites, and the people of Israel loved her; and they meditated upon her by day and by night.

And[2] the priests said unto each other, | "Come, "let us cast lots for Mary, and let us see unto whom "she shall belong." Now Mary was constant in prayer in the temple of the Lord, and one taught her the Law; and she was obedient unto the commandments of the Lord, and unto His judgments and His laws. So they cast lots for Mary, and the lot fell upon Zadok the priest; now Zadok was aged and, with Sham'î his wife, was full of days. And it came to pass that when the lot fell upon Zadok, the priests, and the Levites, and all who were there cried out, saying, "Righteous art Thou, O Lord, and Thy judg- "ments are most right." Then the high-priest said unto Zadok, "Behold, God hath given unto thee a "daughter according to the law, and thou hadst neither "son nor child. Behold, the Lord hath prepared for "you a daughter, that is to say, Mary; guard ye her

---

[1] In the Greek no mention is made of the Gentiles.
[2] See Protevangelium, Chapter VIII, and Pseudo-Matthew, Chapter VI. For the greater part of this and the two following paragraphs the Greek has no equivalent.

"diligently, and teach her to go into and to come
"forth from the temple of the Lord." And Zadok and
his wife Sham'î bowed down and worshipped, saying,
"Blessed be the Lord God of Israel Who hath been
"pleased to do this thing for us." And they called
Mary the daughter of Zadok, according to the law
of the Lord, but she was rightly and strictly the
daughter of Yônâkhîr by promise.

// Then Yônâkhîr gave much money unto Zadok the
priest, that he might build a chamber for Mary like unto
that which she had in her father's house. And he distributed many gifts among the poor in Jerusalem, for he
had much riches, and he and his wife Hannâ went down
from Jerusalem to Bethlehem rejoicing, and they were
full of gladness, having paid their just oblations to
the house of the Lord. And they went up each year
to the house of the Lord, and walked blamelessly.

And it came to pass that when twelve years were
ended, Yônâkhîr and his wife Hannâ died. And his
house and possessions were divided among those who
were to inherit them, and they were distributed and
gone; and when Mary was fourteen years old, Sham'î
the wife of Zadok died also.

/ Then Zadok came unto the chief priests and said
unto them, "Mary, the daughter whom the Lord
"hath given me, hath become a woman, and I am
"an old man and my wife is dead. Come now, let
"us enquire of the Lord, and let us see what He
"will say unto us concerning Mary, and whether we
"shall give her in marriage or not."[1] Then the high-

---

[1] In the Protevangelium the priests hold a council to discuss
Mary's future when she has lived in the temple for twelve years, and

priest[1] rose up and put on the apparel set apart for prayer,[2] wherein the high-priest was wont to approach the Holy of Holies, and he prayed and entreated the Lord concerning Mary, saying, "What shall we do "with her?" And the angel of the Lord appeared unto the high-priest on the right side of the altar of incense, and he answered and said unto him, "Let the trumpet be sounded, and let the Hebrews "who are in Jerusalem be gathered together, that "is to say, those of the tribe of Judah, and espec- "ially those of the house of David; and let Mary be "given unto the man in whom I shall shew the sign." And the high-priest went forth and said unto the people, "The Lord hath said, Let the trumpet be "sounded, and let the men of the tribe of Judah "and of the house of David be gathered together; "and let them come into the temple until it be full so "that they may see what the Lord saith concerning "Mary."

And[3] it came to pass that when they were gathered together, Joseph was found with them; and as they were assembled, and were waiting to see what would take place, behold a snow-white dove went forth from the sanctuary, and alighted upon the top of Joseph's staff, and then flew upon his head, after which it went back and entered into the temple and

Page 18

---

it is they, and not Zadok, who ask the high-priest to enquire of the Lord concerning her.

[1] By name, Zacharias.
[2] Gr. τὸν δωδεκακώδωνα.
[3] See Protevangelium, Chapter IX, and Pseudo-Matthew, Chapter VIII.

into the sanctuary. Then the people¹ cried out with a great cry, saying, "God is righteous in all His "ways. For there is no man here who is so closely "akin unto Mary as Joseph, and it is meet that she "should belong to him." Now they did not know the mystery which was hidden in the matter. And Joseph was an old man, and he had a wife who was herself called Mary, and by her he had two sons, Jacob and Jose. And Joseph said unto the chief priests, "How is it possible for me to take this wife? For I "am an old man, and my wife is the mother of sons "and of daughters."² And the chief | priests answered and said unto Joseph, "This thing is from before the "Lord, and it is He Who hath set her apart and hath "given her unto thee; and among the children of Israel "there is none who is nearer in kinship unto her than "thou, neither by race, nor by family succession." Now Joseph was the son of Jacob, and the son of Matthan, of the one according to the law, and of the other according to what was true, and Mary was the daughter of Yônâkhîr, the son of Matthan; thus Mary and Joseph were each the child of the other's uncle.³

So Joseph took Mary and brought her to his house, and stablished her dwelling-place therein. And he

---

¹ In the Greek the people are not mentioned, but the high-priest says to Joseph, σὺ κεκλήρωσαι τὴν παρθένον κυρίου παραλαβεῖν εἰς τήρησιν ἑαυτῷ: the Syriac here, as in other places, agrees generally with Pseudo-Matthew.

² Gr. υἱοὺς ἔχω καὶ πρεσβύτης εἰμί, αὕτη δὲ νεᾶνις· μήπως περίγελος γένωμαι τοῖς υἱοῖς Ἰσραήλ. In answer to Joseph's objections Zacharias bids him remember how God punished Korah, Dathan, and Abiram for disputing His will.

³ There is no equivalent for this passage in the Greek.

answered and said unto her, "Behold now, thou hast "been reared in the house of the Lord, and the Lord "hath set thee apart, and hath given thee unto me. "See thou, and dwell thou here, and guard thou thine "integrity whilst I go and finish the building which "I have begun; then will I come and take thee thither." And Mary answered and said unto him, "Let the will "of the Lord be fulfilled as concerning His hand- "maiden, and more than what she can possibly ask." So Joseph went to Bethlehem to finish the house which he had begun to build.

And[1] it came to pass in those days that the chief priests wished to make a curtain (or veil) for the temple. And they sent and brought virgins[2] to weave it, and they appointed Mary to help them to weave it;[3] then Mary rose up and went to the house of the Lord.[4]

---

[1] Protevangelium Chapter X begins here.

[2] The virgins were seven in number, καὶ εὗρον ἑπτὰ παρθένους. In Pseudo-Matthew the virgins are five in number, and they seem to have been given to Mary as companions until her marriage by the advice of Abiathar the high-priest, "Et respondens Abiathar "pontifex dixit, Virgines quidem ad solatium ejus dabuntur." Their names were Rebecca, Sephora, Susanna, Abigea, and Zahel.

[3] The seven coloured stuffs to be woven were τὸ χρυσίον καὶ τὸ ἀμίαντον καὶ τὴν βύσσον καὶ τὸ σηρικὸν καὶ τὸ ὑακίνθινον καὶ τὸ κόκ- κινον καὶ τὴν ἀληθινὴν πορφύραν. According to Pseudo-Matthew the weaving of the purple came to Mary after lots had been cast to find out which colour each virgin should weave, and in consequence her companions, as in jest, began to call her "Queen of the virgins"; an angel appeared and rebuked them, on which they begged his forgiveness and asked him to pray for them.

[4] In the Greek Mary is said to have taken the purple and scarlet and to have gone to her own house. At the end of the Xth Chapter it is stated that Zacharias, the high-priest, became silent, and that his place was filled by Samuel.

And[1] in the three hundred and third year of Alexander, on the thirty-first day of the month Âdâr,[2] on the first day of the week, at the third hour of the day, whilst Mary was sitting by herself in the great house of God, Gabriel, the angel of the Lord, appeared[3] unto her in the form of a venerable old man, so that she might not flee from him. And he said unto her, "Peace be unto thee, O thou wo-"man who art full of grace, our Lord is with thee, "O thou who art blessed among women!"[4] And when Mary saw Gabriel[5] she was greatly disturbed and she meditated what this salutation might be. And the angel Gabriel answered and said unto her, "Fear thou not, "O Mary, for thou hast found grace and mercy with "God. Behold, I announce unto thee tidings of a "great joy, the Lord having sent me unto thee so "to do. And behold, thou shalt receive conception, "and thou shalt bear a son, and thou shalt call his "name Jesus. And this thy son shall be great."[6] And Mary answered and said unto the angel, "How can "this thing be? And how can I bear a son seeing "that I have known no man?"[7] And the angel an-

---

[1] See Protevangelium, Chapter XI, and Pseudo-Matthew, Chapter IX.

[2] For ܐܕܪ, read ܐܕܪ.

[3] According to the Greek, Mary had taken a water jar and gone forth to draw water when she heard the angel's voice.

[4] In the Greek, Mary, having looked to the right and the left for the voice, goes back to her house, sets down the jar, and having taken the purple to cover herself, sits down upon her seat.

[5] Gr. ἄγγελος κυρίου.

[6] There is no equivalent for this sentence in the Greek.

[7] Gr. εἰ ἐγὼ συλλήψομαι ἀπὸ κυρίου Θεοῦ ζῶντος, καὶ γεννήσω ὡς πᾶσα γυνὴ γεννᾷ.

swered and said unto her, "The Holy Spirit shall
"come, and the power of the Highest shall over-
"shadow thee; therefore he that shall be born of thee
"shall be holy; and the child shall be called the son
"of the Highest."[1] And Mary answered and said unto
the angel, "A thing like unto this, that is to say,
"virgins | giving birth unto children without union   Page 21
"with man, hath never been heard of from the days
"of the beginning of the world."
And[2] Gabriel answered and said unto her, "The
"prophets prophesied concerning thee in the spirit,
"and concerning thy bringing forth did they speak
"in their revelations. Moses, the first of the prophets,
"depicted the type of thee by means of the rock
"from which he made water to flow down,[3] and
"Aaron the priest by means of the rod which he
"made to blossom;[4] and Jeremiah called thee the
"woman-earth;[5] and Gideon surnamed thee the fleece[6]
"which received the dew from on high; and Daniel
"taught the mystery of thee by means of the rock
"which he saw and which had been hewn from the
"mountain without hands;[7] and Isaiah spake openly
"of thee, saying, 'Behold, a virgin shall conceive, and
"shall bear a son, and his name shall be called Im-

---

[1] The Greek adds καὶ καλέσεις τὸ ὄνομα αὐτοῦ Ἰησοῦν· αὐτὸς γὰρ σώσει τὸν λαὸν αὐτοῦ ἀπὸ τῶν ἁμαρτιῶν αὐτῶν.
[2] The following paragraph has no equivalent in the Greek and Latin texts.
[3] See Numbers XX. 8—11.   [4] See Numbers XVII.
[5] The variant reading is ܟܐܢܘ ܐܪܥܐ, literally, "perforated earth". The allusion seems to be to the words of Jeremiah XXXI. 22. . ܟܐܢܘܗܝ ܒܢܘܟ ܒܐܪܥܐ . ܐܪܥܐ ܚܕܬܐ ܒܪܐ ܡܪܝܐ
[6] See Judges VI. 37—39.   [7] See Daniel II. 35—45.

"manuel."[1] Moreover, this shall be a sign unto thee "in thy days: thy kinswoman Elizabeth, even she, "shall conceive a son, and she shall give birth unto "him in her old age; and behold she is now in "her sixth month. And from thee the True Light "willeth to rise upon the world." And Mary answered and said unto Gabriel, "Behold, I am the "handmaiden of the Lord; let it be to me according "to thy word."[2]

Then straightway great joy dwelt in Mary, and all her body was glorified and became like light. And at that moment Mary saw the angelic hosts glorifying God, and ascribing praise unto herself, and proclaiming hope for mortals. And their hosts came round about Mary | like the troops and horsemen of a king when he cometh and taketh up his abode in his palace; and, having followed in his train to the palace, then return from the door thereof with joy and gladness. And when Mary saw them, great fear and joy came upon her, and she began to glorify God in the Hebrew tongue, saying, "Praise be unto the "Lord of the world and of created things, Who, though "the earth is full of the daughters of kings, hath "chosen to make His habitation in the poor abode "of His handmaiden and hath willed that light shall "rise upon the world out of her sinfulness;"[3] and

---

[1] See Isaiah VII. 14.

[2] Protevangelium Chapter XI ends with the words γένοιτό μοι κατὰ τὸ ῥῆμά σου.

[3] There is no equivalent for the above in the Greek. Protevangelium Chapter XII begins with the words Καὶ ἐποίησεν τὴν πορφύραν καὶ τὸ κόκκινον, καὶ ἀπήγαγεν τῷ ἱερεῖ.

she ceased not to glorify her Lord continually. And besides being constant in her praise, she worked always at the curtain (or veil), which the high-priest had delivered unto her. And when she had finished it, she carried it to the temple to the chief priests, who blessed her, and said unto her, "The Lord thy "God shall magnify thy name, and shall make thee "to be a woman blessed among all the families of "the earth." And Mary returned to her house in great joy.

And it came to pass that Mary sent unto Joseph at Bethlehem, saying, "I wish to see Elizabeth my "kinswoman"; and Joseph gave her his consent for her to go, and taking her women with her she went there.[1] And it came to pass that when she went in to Elizabeth, and saluted her, John leaped in Elizabeth's womb, and did homage to his Lord. And Elizabeth answered and said unto Mary, "Peace be "unto thee, O blessed woman, thou bearer of great "riches, for behold, as soon as thy salutation fell "upon my ears the child leaped in my womb; | "blessed be thou who art held to be worthy of such "a gift." And Mary began to praise the Lord her God, saying, "My soul doth magnify the Lord, and "my spirit hath rejoiced in God Who giveth me life, "and Who hath regarded the lowliness of His hand-"maiden;"[2] and the two women, Mary and Elizabeth,

---

[1] No mention of Joseph's permission being asked is made in the Greek, which reads, χαρὰν δὲ λαβοῦσα Μαριὰμ ἀπίει πρὸς Ἐλισάβετ.

[2] In the Greek Mary says, τίς εἰμι ἐγώ, κύριε, ὅτι πᾶσαι αἱ γενεαὶ τῆς γῆς εὐλογοῦσιν με.

began to glorify the Lord. And Mary abode with Elizabeth for about three months.[1]

And Elizabeth began to persuade Mary, saying, "Rise up, and get thee to thy house, for it is im-"possible for thee to stand and to minister unto me "whilst I am ill in childbed, and it is impossible for "the mother of the servant to sleep upon a bed whilst "the mother of the Lord standeth ministering unto "her. Rise up, and get thee to thy house, and do "honour to the gift which hath come unto thee; for "nothing which is created can abide it." So Mary rose up and returned to her house with the hope of the gift which she bore.

And[2] it came to pass, when it was the fifth month[3] with Mary, that Joseph came from his village Bethlehem, having finished the building of his house.[4] And when he saw that Mary was with child, he began to rub his hands together, and to smite his face, and to weep bitterly, saying, "Woe is me, for how can "I look up to the Lord God, and with what coun-"tenance can I behold the children of Israel? I took "thee,[5] O Mary, a virgin from the house of the Lord, "but I have not guarded thee; behold, through that "of which I never had any fear at all | I have fallen

---

[1] Protevangelium Chapter XII ends with the statement that as the child grew Mary became greatly afraid, and went home and hid herself from the children of Israel; at this time she was sixteen years old.

[2] Protevangelium Chapter XIII begins here.

[3] Gr. Ἐγένετο δὲ αὐτῇ ἕκτος μήν.

[4] ܒܝܬܐ is a large house, or palace.

[5] Gr. τί δὲ εὔξομαι περὶ τῆς κόρης ταύτης; ὅτι παρθένον παρέλαβον αὐτήν, κ. τ. λ.

"into trouble. Who is it that hath led thee astray,
"O pure virgin, and hath corrupted thee, and hath
"destroyed thee, and hath wrought this wickedness
"in thee? and who hath led captive thy mind?"[1] And
Joseph continued to chide Mary, saying, "Who hath
"led thee astray in such wise that thou hast forgotten
"the covenant which thou didst stablish with me be-
"fore the Lord?"[2] Then Mary answered and said
unto Joseph with tears, "As the Lord God of Israel
"liveth, I am pure, and no man hath known me."
Then Joseph answered and said unto her, "And this
"which is in thy womb, whence is it? For behold,
"thou art big with child.[3] If[4] I hide this matter con-
"cerning thee it will be a sin unto me; and if I reveal
"it unto the children of Israel I fear lest they stone
"thee, and lest I shall find that I have delivered inno-
"cent blood to the judgment of death. What I shall
"do I know not. To leave thee and to flee would be

---

[1] In the Greek Joseph is made to compare himself unto Adam, for just as in the hour of Adam's glory the serpent came and finding Eve alone seduced her, so some fiend has come and led Mary astray during his absence.

[2] Read ܪܒܝܬ ܩܘܕܫܐ. The variant Syriac text has, "Which I stablished with thee when thou wert pure, and thou wast reared in the house of the holy of holies of the Lord." The Greek has ἡ ἀνατραφεῖσα εἰς τὰ ἅγια τῶν ἁγίων, κ. τ. λ., so we must read ܕܒܝܬܐܪܐ instead of ܕܒܝܬܐܪܐ.

[3] In the Greek Joseph's speech ends here, and Mary answers, ζῇ κύριος ὁ Θεός μου καθότι οὐ γινώσκω πόθεν ἐστίν μοι; thus ends the Chapter. See Pseudo-Matthew, Chapter X, wherein Mary's companions vouch for her spotless conduct, saying, "Nam custodita "est a deo, semper in oratione nobiscum permansit; cotidie cum "ea angelus domini loquitur, cotidie de manu angeli escam accipit. "Quomodo fieri potest ut sit aliquod peccatum in ea?"

[4] See Protevangelium Chapter XIV.

"a reproach unto me in Israel; but leave me, [and "take] what thou shouldst take [with thee] and depart "in peace, and the secret shall not be revealed by me." And Joseph continued to chide Mary with these words, and with many others like unto them, until the night Page 25 came on. | And when Joseph had fallen asleep in the night by reason of the anxious thoughts which he had in his mind, that is to say, what he should do with Mary, and whether he should send her away or not, behold, the angel Gabriel appeared unto him and said unto him, "Joseph, son of David, "be not doubtful concerning Mary thy betrothed.[1] "For behold, He for Whom the eyes of all created "things look, and whose advent they await, hath made "his habitation in Mary thy betrothed.[2] And, Joseph, "canst thou not believe this? The priests, and the "kings, and the prophets, and the governors of Is- "rael waited in the expectation of seeing Him among "their daughters and sisters, but they saw Him not. "Wilt thou, then, be in doubt concerning Mary thy "betrothed? Wilt thou not hearken unto what Isaiah "saith in his prophecy,[3] 'Behold, the virgin shall

---

[1] In B, "Why is thy mind doubtful concerning Mary?"

[2] In B, "Behold, Him for Whom the righteous men were looking, "and Whom prophets and priests waited to see in their houses,— "but they saw Him not, and were not held to be worthy to see "Him – hath gone unto thy poverty and hath entered in and taken "up His abode there. And thou, Joseph, the son of David, art "angry with Mary because she hath been held to be worthy that "He Whom the nobles, and governors, and kings of Israel, ex- "pected to see in their houses or among their sisters, should enter "into thy betrothed and make His abode therein, and dost blas- "pheme."

[3] Isaiah VII. 14.

"conceive, and shall bear a son, and his name shall
"be called Emmanuel'? Behold now, He hath made
"His abode in thy betrothed. Rejoice and be glad,
"and pay honour [unto Him] even as a servant payeth
"honour unto his master, so that thou mayest not be
"a stranger unto the treasury of life which hath made
"its habitation in thy betrothed."[1] And when Joseph
woke from his sleep, he did homage unto Mary, and
he besought her forgiveness, and said unto her, "In
"very truth thou art Mary;" and from that night onwards she was like the light in his sight.[2]

And[3] when the morning had come, Joseph went
out to pray in the temple, for he was a famous man
among the children of Israel. And when the priests
saw him they called unto him, and said, "Joseph,
"what hast thou done? Thou hast taken Mary to
"wife and hast not called us to the wedding feast."
And Joseph said unto the priests, "I know not what
"ye say." Then the priests sent and brought Mary,
and the high-priest said unto her, "What is this that
"thou hast done? Thou wast brought up in the Holy
"of Holies of God, and thou hast heard the sound
"of the angels' praises three times." And Mary answered and said with tears, "As the Lord God of

---

[1] In the Greek the angel's speech is very much shorter.

[2] A very free rendering of καὶ ἐφύλασσεν αὐτήν.

[3] See Protevangelium, Chapter XV. In the Greek the scribe Annas comes to Joseph's house to enquire why he has not appeared at the meeting of the priests, and Joseph excuses himself on the ground of fatigue; the scribe then seeing Mary perceives that she is with child, and goes straightway and reports the matter to the priests, who despatch messengers to enquire into the truth of the scribe's report.

"Israel liveth, I am pure, and no man hath at any "time known me." And the high-priest, after the manner of prophecy, said unto her, "Art thou, then, "about to give birth unto the Messiah? But how can "we believe thy words? For thou art great with child, "and yet thou sayest, | 'No man hath known me.' "Thou and Joseph have hidden the day of your mar- "riage from the priests of the Lord. But I know that "it is not thou who hast done amiss, and that it is "Joseph who hath done this thing." And Mary said unto the high-priest, "As the Lord liveth, I have not "known any man carnally, neither Joseph nor any "other man." Then the high-priest said unto her, "Thou liest; for thou sayest 'I know not man', and "yet thou art great with child."

Then[1] the priests said unto the high priest, "The "judgment is hidden from men; make them drink the "water of trial, and thus seek out the matter; and it "will make their sins to rebuke them before the chil- "dren of men." So they made Joseph to drink of the water first of all, and they took him up to the moun- tain,[2] and brought him down again; and he was un-

---

[1] See Protevangelium, Chapter XVI. In the Greek the priest calls upon Joseph to restore the virgin whom he had taken from the temple of the Lord, and it is he who makes the offer to drink the water of trial ποτιῶ ὑμᾶς τὸ ὕδωρ τῆς ἐλέγξεως κυρίου.

[2] Gr. καὶ ἔπεμψεν αὐτὸν εἰς τὴν ὀρεινήν. In Pseudo-Matthew, Chapter XII, no mention is made of the going to the mountain, but the person who had drunk the water was obliged to walk seven times round the altar in the Temple, after which God would make a sign to appear in his face. "Vocatus est autem "et Joseph ad altare, et data est ei aqua potationis domini: quam "si gustasset homo mentiens et septies circuisset altare, dabat deus "signum aliquod in facie ejus. Cum ergo bibisset securus Joseph

injured, and was sound and well. Then the priests said unto Mary, "Reveal the truth; but if thou wilt "not do so, then thy blood be upon thine own head." And Mary said, "He who knoweth hidden things "knoweth that I know not man;" and the priests said, "Of what advantage is this vain labour to us? Let "us make her drink the water of trial, and judgment "shall come by the hand of God, and not by our "hands." So they made her to drink the water, and they took her up to the mountain, and they brought her down again; and she was sound and well. Then all the people cried out and said, "In very truth God "hath wrought a new thing in our days. A woman "who hath not known man is great with child, and "yet is innocent in the judgment before God."[1] And the fear of Mary came into the hearts of many, and Joseph ministered unto her as a servant.

And[2] it came to pass in the three hundred and fourth year of Alexander[3] that the registration [ordered by] Caesar Augustus took place, wherein every man was to register himself in his country, and in his city; and Joseph took Mary[4] to go to his city

Page 28

---

et girasset altare, nullum signum peccati apparuit in eo." On the "water of jealousy" see Numbers V. 11 ff.

[1] In the Greek the priest dismisses them with the words, εἰ κύριος ὁ Θεὸς οὐκ ἐφανέρωσε τὰ ἁμαρτήματα ὑμῶν, οὐδὲ ἐγὼ κρίνω ὑμᾶς.

[2] See Protevangelium, Chapter XVII.

[3] In the Greek no date is given for the registration.

[4] In the Greek Joseph is puzzled how to inscribe Mary, ταύτην δὲ τὴν παῖδα τί ποιήσω; πῶς αὐτὴν ἀπογράψομαι; γυναῖκα ἐμήν; αἰσχύνομαι. ἀλλὰ θυγατέρα; ἀλλ᾽ οἴδασιν πάντες οἱ υἱοὶ Ἰσραὴλ ὅτι οὐκ ἔστι μου θυγάτηρ. In the end he sets her upon an ass and sends her on before, whilst he and Simon follow behind.

Bethlehem. And as he and Mary were journeying along the road, he saw that Mary's face was sometimes sad, and sometimes glad. And Joseph answered and said unto Mary, "What aileth thee, O Mary?" And Mary said unto Joseph, "O Joseph, I see two "distinct things which are full of wonder for me. I see "the nation of Israel, which though being in the light, "weepeth and mourneth, and I see that it is like unto "a blind man that seeth not the sun. And I see the "Gentiles, who are uncircumcised, and who dwell in "darkness, and I see that light springeth up upon "them and round about them; and behold, they re-"joice and are glad, even as is the blind man whose "eyes have been opened and he seeth the light."[1]

And it came to pass that when they drew nigh unto Bethlehem, Mary said unto Joseph, "Joseph, the "hour | for my giving birth hath come, and the pains "of childbirth will not let me reach the city; come, "let us go into this cave."[2] Now, it was the time of sunset when they entered the cave. And Joseph ran to bring a woman to be with Mary,[3] but behold, whilst

---

[1] Mary's answer is much shorter in the Greek. See also Pseudo-Matthew, Chapter XIII; where we have, "Duos populos video ante "me, unum flentem et alium gaudentem." Joseph having answered somewhat abruptly, "Sede et tene te in jumento tuo et noli super-"flua verba loqui," is rebuked by an angel.

[2] See Protevangelium, Chapter XVIII.

[3] Gr. καὶ ἐξελθὼν ἐζήτει μαῖαν Ἑβραίαν. As Joseph was going about seeking for the woman he saw the pole of heaven standing still, and the upper heights of heaven astonished, and the birds stopping in full flight. And workmen were sitting at their table but not eating; those with food in their mouths swallowed it not, and those who had their hands raised to their mouths kept them still in mid-air. The sheep were scattered about in the fields,

he was running, it happened that a certain old Hebrew woman was on her way down from Jerusalem to Bethlehem. And Joseph said unto her, "Come, thou "blessed old woman, and go into this cave wherein "there is a woman who is giving birth unto a child." And when the old woman and Joseph had gone into the cave, the sun had set, and they had nothing in the cave [to give them light].¹ But when they had gone in, they saw that the cave was full of light, like [that of] the sun, and that Mary was giving her child suck—now he had been wrapped in swaddling-clothes and had been laid in a manger.² And whilst they were wondering at the light, certain shepherds came and made a great fire, and the heavenly hosts

---

but were standing still; and when a shepherd lifted his staff to smite them his hand remained in the air motionless. The goats also stood on the edge of the stream with the water touching their mouths, and yet they drank not. There is no equivalent in the Syriac for these statements.

¹ Compare Pseudo-Matthew, Chapter XIII, "et praecepit de-"scendere de animali Mariam et ingredi in speluncam subterraneam, "in qua lux non fuit unquam sed semper tenebrae, quia lumen diei "penitus non habebat. Ad ingressum vero Mariae coepit tota spe-"lunca splendorem habere, et quasi sol ibi esset ita tota fulgorem "lucis ostendere; et quasi esset ibi hora diei sexta, ita speluncam "lux divina illustravit; nec in die nec in nocte lux ibi divina de-"fuit quamdiu ibi Maria fuit".

² In the XIXth Chapter of Protevangelium two midwives are mentioned, and one of them is called Salome; in Pseudo-Matthew (Chapter XIII) Joseph is said to have brought two who were called Zelomi and Salome. Zelomi declares to Salome that a virgin hath brought forth a child (παρθένος ἐγέννησεν ὃ οὐ χωρεῖ ἡ φύσιν αὐτῆς—virgo concepit, virgo peperit, virgo permansit), but Salome will not believe it; and when she goes into the cave to Mary, and touches her with her hand, her hand is straightway burnt off from her body. Salome then prays to God Who sends

appeared, singing hymns and praising God.[1] Now at that moment the cave became a type of the Church which is above, for the mouths of beings of fire, and the lips of beings of earth were praising and celebrating the birth of the Messiah. | And when the old woman saw the wonderful thing which had been wrought, she cried out and said, "I praise the God "of Israel, for mine eyes have this day seen a great "wonder in the birth of the Redeemer of all."[2]

And on that night a Watcher[3] was sent into Persia, and he shewed himself unto the Persians in the form of an exceedingly brilliant star, which lit up the whole region of their country. Now all the people

---

His angel to her and tells her through him to go to the Child and to take Him in her arms; she does so and her hand is straightway made whole. Solomon of Baṣra mentions Salome only, and says, "The heretics say that she was called Ḥadyôk, but they err from the truth" (see my *Book of the Bee*, p. 80); but elsewhere we are told that Ḥadyôk was the name of her son, the dealer in unguents and spices (see Payne Smith, *Thesaurus*, Col. 1202, at the foot). The MS. *B* says that the old woman who was going down from Jerusalem to Bethlehem was a Samaritan ܐܘܪܝܬܐ (see p. 29, note 7).

[1] Compare Pseudo-Matthew, Chapter XIII. "Nam et pastores "ovium asserebant se angelos vidisse in medio nocte hymnum dicen- "tes, deum caeli laudantes et benedicentes," etc. According to Solomon of Baṣra the names of the shepherds who entered the cave were Asher, Zebulon, Justus, Nicodemus, Joseph, Barshabba, and Jose; *Book of the Bee*, p. 81. A great fiery star also stood over the cave from the evening until the morning, the like of which for size had never been seen since the beginning of the world.

[2] On the third day after the birth of Christ Mary left the cave and brought Him into a stable where an ox and an ass worshipped Him; see Pseudo-Matthew, Chapter XIV.

[3] "Watchers" is the name given to a class of angels; see Duval, *Bar Bahlule*, Col. 1432.

of Persia were celebrating a great festival, wherein they were worshipping the fire and the stars, on the twenty-fifth day of the first Khânûn,[1] which is the day of the festival of the birth of Christ; and all the Magians were arrayed in their festal apparel, and they were proudly celebrating their festival, when suddenly a great light shone upon them. And they left their kings, and their feasting, and their pleasures, and their houses, and they went forth to see what the light was; and they saw a fiery star,[2] which was like unto the great sun in its light, standing over Persia. Then their kings cried out unto their priests, saying, "What is this sign which we see?" And involuntarily they answered, as in prophecy, saying, "The "King of kings | is born, and the God of gods, and "the Light of light. And this star is one of our gods "who hath come to inform us concerning His birth, "so that we may go and offer unto Him offerings, "and pay homage unto Him." And all the governors, and the judges, and the generals said unto their priests, "What offerings are meet to go with us?" And the priests said unto them, "Gold, and myrrh, "and frankincense." So three men, who were kings,[3]

[1] *I. e.*, كانون الاول = December; the latter Khânûn كانون الاخر = January.
[2] According to the "Cave of Treasures" a star appeared unto the Magi two years before Christ was born; within it was a maiden carrying a child with a crown upon his head. Another legend says that the star was like an eagle having within it the form of a young child, and above him the sign of the cross. See Sandys, *Christmas Carols*, p. LXXXIII ff.; Bezold, *Schatzhöhle*, p. 56; and my *Book of the Bee*, p. 83.
[3] According to Solomon of Baṣra *twelve* Persian kings brought offerings. Zarwândâd, Hôrmîzdâd, Gûshnâsâph, and Arshakh brought

and sons of the kings of Persia, took, as in a mystery, one three pounds of myrrh, and another three pounds of gold, and another three pounds of frankincense; and having arrayed themselves in their costly apparel, with their crowns on their heads, and their treasures in their hands, they went forth from their country at cock-crow, along with the nine men who were with them. And they began to travel along the road, and to follow after the star which had appeared unto them, when that same angel who took from Jerusalem [to Babylon] the prophet Habakkuk,[1] and who carried food to Daniel the prophet when he had been cast into the den of lions in Babylon, by the power of the Holy Spirit carried the kings of Persia to Jerusalem. They set out from Persia | at cock-crow, and at day-break they entered into Jerusalem. And they asked the people of Jerusalem, saying, "Where "was the King born? for we have come to see Him." And[2] when the people of Jerusalem saw them, they trembled and were afraid, and they carried a report

---

gold; Zarwândâd, Îryâhô, Arṭaḥshisht, and Ashtôn'âbôdân brought myrrh; and Mêhârôḳ, Aḥshîresh, Ṣardâlâḥ, and Merôdâch brought frankincense. See *Book of the Bee*, p. 85.

[1] The allusion is to *Bel and the Dragon*, vv. 33—39, according to which Habakkuk, who was in Judea, had made pottage and broken bread in a bowl to take to the reapers. The angel of the Lord met him and told him to take the food to Daniel in Babylon, and when he replied that he had never seen Babylon, and did not know where the den of lions was, the angel took him by the hair of his head and set him in Babylon over the den. When Daniel had eaten the angel set Habakkuk back in his own place. This story is also repeated by Pseudo-Dorotheus and Pseudo-Epiphanius, and by other writers who copied from them.

[2] See *Protevangelium*, Chapter XXI.

of them to Herod the king. And Herod the king sent and called the kings of Persia, and had them brought in before him, and he asked them, saying, "Whence are ye? Whence have ye come? Whom seek "ye?" And they made answer, saying, "We seek the "king who is born in Judea, in the district of Jerusa- "lem, for one of our gods gave a sign to us and told "us concerning his birth, so that we might offer unto "him offerings and homage." Then at the sight of the sons of the Persian kings was Herod afraid, for he saw them with their crowns upon their heads, and their treasures in their hands, and [knew that] they were seeking for the king who had been born in Judea. And Herod and every one who was with him trem- bled at the sight of the sons of the kings, and he said, "The power of the king who moved you to "come to do honour unto him is great, and indeed, "he must be a king, and the king of kings; go ye "and seek him, and when ye have found him, come "and shew me, that I also may go and do homage "unto him." And Herod, having formed in his heart the evil design of killing the king | whilst he was a child, and the kings of Persia with him, said, "Behold, "all creation is subject unto me."

Then the kings went forth from his presence, and they saw the star going on before them until it came and stood above the cave; and then the star chang- ed itself and became like unto a pillar of light that reached from the earth to the heavens. And they went into the cave, and they found Mary, and Joseph, and the Child, wrapped in swaddling-clothes and laid in a manger; and they did homage unto Him, and offered their offerings,[1] and they saluted Joseph and Mary. And Joseph and Mary were wondering at the three kings of Persia, for with their crowns upon their heads they were kneeling upon their knees and were paying homage to the Child, without asking any questions concerning Him. Then Joseph and Mary asked them, saying, "Whence are ye?" And they answered and said unto them, "We come from Persia." And Joseph said unto them, "When did ye set out "from Persia?" And they said, "There was a festi- "val in the evening, and after we had eaten and "drunk, one of our gods said unto us, 'Rise up, and "go, and offer up offerings to the King Who hath "been born in Judea.' Now, as we were setting out "to come, the cock crew. We set out from | Persia "at cock-crow, and now, at the third hour of the "day, we have reached you." And Mary took one of the swaddling-bands of Jesus, and gave it unto them; and they took it from her in faith as a most exalted gift. And when the night of the fifth day of the week after the birth of the Child was come, the Watcher who, in the form of a star, had brought the Persians there arrived; and they set out on their road following him. And whilst they were talking together concerning the cause of their coming, they arrived in their own country at the time of the first meal of the day. And Persia rejoiced at their arrival, and marvelled.

---

[1] Gr. καὶ ἐξέβαλον . . . . . χρυσὸν καὶ λίβανον καὶ σμύρραν. The Chapter ends with the statement that an angel warned the Persians not to go back into Judea, and has no equivalent for the rest of this paragraph in the Syriac.

And it came to pass that when the morning was come, and the day had become light, the kings and priests were gathered together and they said unto them, "How did ye go? How did ye come? What "did ye do? And what have ye brought for us?" And the sons of the kings shewed them the swaddling-band which Mary had given them. Then the kings and priests made for them a festival of Magianism, and they cast the swaddling-band into the fire of which they were worshippers; and the swaddling-band took the form of the fire. And when the fire had been put out, they brought out the swaddling-band, which was like the snow and was firmer than it was before. Then they took | it and kissed it, and laid it upon their eyes, and said, "In very truth, and beyond "all doubt, this is a garment of the God of gods; "for the fire of our gods was unable to consume "it." And they received it in faith and with great honour.[1]

And it came to pass that when the eight days for the circumcision of the Child had been fulfilled, they circumcised Him in the cave in which he had been born.[2] And the woman who had been with them on the day of his birth, now the name of that old woman was called Shâlôm, took away with her that which had been cut off from him. And this woman had a son[3]

Page 35

---

[1] See Evangelium Infantiae, Chapter VIII. (Tischendorf, p. 184).

[2] On the sixth day of the week Mary and the Child went into Bethlehem, where they spent the Sabbath; see Pseudo-Matthew, Chapter XV.

[3] His name was Ḥadyôk ܚܕܝܘܟ, and he is described as ܪܒܝܠ and ܪܣܘܡܐ i. e., a druggist and scent maker.

who was a maker of perfumes and scented unguents, and she placed that which had been cut off[1] from Jesus in a flask of the most precious and costly ointment, and she enjoined her son strictly, and said unto him, "Take heed, O my son, that thou sell not "this flask of ointment unless the buyers thereof will "give thee three hundred dînârs of gold for it." Now it was this flask of ointment which Mary the sinful woman bought, and she poured it out over the head of our Lord.

And it came to pass that when Jesus was ten days old,[2] they took Him up to the temple of Jerusalem to present Him before the Lord, and to offer up offerings on His behalf, according to what is written in the law of Moses, "Every male that openeth the womb "shall be called holy unto the Lord."[3] Now, if Mary, and Joseph, and the child were in the cave ten days, it is most certainly true | that the Magians came from Persia in one night, and that they went back to their own country in another night. And on the eleventh day after the birth of the Child, that is to say, on the day of the Sabbath, they went forth to carry him to the temple. And it came to pass that when Mary came to the door of the courtyard of the temple, the old man Simeon, with the eye of the Holy Spirit,

---

[1] Compare, Sumsitque anus illa Hebraea pelliculam istam, dicunt vero alii eam sumsisse nervum umbilicarem, eamque in ampulla oleo nardini vetusti recondidit. See Evangelium Infantiae, Chapter V. (Tischendorf, p. 183.)

[2] Compare, Decem diebus post Hierosolymam eum transtulerunt, et quadragesimo a nativitate die templo illatum coram domino stiterunt, etc. Evang. Infantiae, Chapter V.

[3] See Exodus XIII. 2.

THE WRATH OF HEROD. 41

saw that she was like unto a pillar of light,[1] and that she was carrying in her arms a wonderful Child Who was wrapped in swaddling-bands of fire and was not consumed. And whilst Simeon was marvelling at Mary, he saw the hosts of the angels standing round about her and the Child, and they were ascribing honour unto them, and they were like unto the companies of soldiers that compass kings round about. And when Simeon had seen this sight, he ran towards Mary, and stretching out his arms to her he said, "Give me the "Child." And he took Him in his arms and said, "Lord, "let now Thy servant depart in peace, according to "Thy word. For mine eyes have seen Thy great "mercy." And Anna the prophetess was also there, and she too saw the vision, and believed; and she stood up giving praise unto God, and ascribing praise unto Mary.

And it came to pass that when Herod saw that he had been mocked by the Magians[2] who had tarried long and had not returned to him, he was filled with rage, and sent and brought the wise men, | and asked Page 37 them, saying, "Where is the Christ born?" And they said unto him, "In Bethlehem of Judea"; and he determined to slay Jesus.[3]

---

[1] Tum vidit illum Simeon senex instar columnae lucis refulgentem, etc. Evang. Infantiae, Chapter VI.

[2] See Protevangelium, Chapter XXII; Pseudo-Matthew, Chapter XVII; and Evang. Infantiae, Chapter IX.

[3] In the Greek Herod orders that all children "two years old and under" shall be slain; compare St. Matthew II. 16. Some say that he slew 2000 children, and some say 1800; see my *Book of the Bee*, p. 86. Mary hid Jesus by wrapping Him up in rags, and laying Him in the manger of the cattle.

[Here comes in the MS. *A* the following passage, which is wanting in *B*.]

And when Elizabeth heard that John was sought for, she took him and went up into the mountain, but she had no place there wherein to hide him. And, with a sigh, she said unto the mountain, "O mountain of God, "receive thou a mother with her son"; and straightway the mountain opened and received her. And the mountain made light to shine upon them, for the angel of the Lord was with them.

And[1] Herod sent some of his body-guard[2] to Zechariah the priest, and they said unto him, "Where is "thy son?" And Zechariah said unto them, "I am a "servant of the Lord my God, and I am in His house "continually; I know not where my son is." And the body-guard went and told Herod. And when Herod heard these words he was angry and said, "Is then "the son of a priest about to reign over Israel?" And again he sent his body-guard [unto Zechariah], and he told [them to say] unto him, "Shew us truly where thy "son is. If [thou wilt] not [do so] then thou knowest "that thy blood shall be under thine own hands."[3] So the body-guard went and told Zechariah these things. And Zechariah said, "God shall bear witness that thou "hast poured out my blood,[4] and the Lord shall re"ceive my spirit; for thou hast shed innocent blood "which hath committed no wrong." Now Zechariah

---

[1] See Protevangelium, Chapter XXIII.
[2] Gr. καὶ ἀπέστειλεν ὑπηρέτας.
[3] Gr. οἶδας γὰρ ὅτι τὸ αἷμά σου ὑπὸ τὴν χεῖρά μου ἐστίν. We should, therefore, in the Syriac read ܬܝܕ ܐܝܕܝ.
[4] Gr. μάρτυς εἰμὶ τοῦ Θεοῦ, εἰ ἐκχέεις μου τὸ αἷμα.

was slain¹ about the time of dawn, and the children of Israel knew not of it.

And² it came to pass that at the time of the burnt-offering of propitiation, the priests came, but the wonted blessing of Zechariah did not give them the sign; and the priests stood there waiting to ask for peace in prayer, and to praise the Lord [until Zechariah should come]. And when he continued to tarry, fear fell upon them all. And one of them ventured to enter into | the   Page 38
sanctuary, and he saw on the side of the altar of the Lord blood which had been shed and had become clotted.³ And a voice was heard which said, "Zechariah "hath been slain, and his blood shall not be washed "away until the avenger cometh." And when they heard these words they were afraid, and they went out and told the priests what they had seen and heard; and they all cried out and rent their garments.⁴ Now the body of Zechariah was not found, but they found his blood which was clotted and had become like a stone.⁵ And the priests wept and mourned for Zechariah three days; and after three days they took thought concerning whom they should raise up in his

---

¹ The Syriac does not say where Zechariah was slain, but the *Book of the Bee* (p. 86) says "between the steps (ܟܣܛܐܝܠܡܐ = κατάστρωμα) and the altar". Tischendorf's text has, περὶ τὸ διάφαυμα ἐφονεύθη Ζαχαρίας. The ܟܣܛܐܝܠܡܐ is explained as "the raised platform which is before the door of the altar." See Duval, *Bar Bahlule*, col. 1815.
² See Protevangelium, Chapter XXIV.
³ Gr. αἷμα πεπηγός.
⁴ Apparently a misunderstanding of the Greek, καὶ τὰ φατνώματα τοῦ ναοῦ ὀλόλυξαν, καὶ αὐτοὶ περιεσχίσαντο ἀπὸ ἄνωθεν ἕως κάτω.
⁵ Gr. λίθον γεγενημένον. For ܠܐܒܢܐ, read ܐܒܢܐ

place. And the lot fell upon Simeon, the priest unto
whom it had been revealed by the Holy Spirit that he
should not see death until he had seen the Lord in the
flesh.[1]

And an angel appeared unto Joseph,[2] and said unto
him, "Arise, take the young Child and His mother and
"go to Egypt;" so Joseph and Mary arose at cock-
crow.[3] And whilst[4] Joseph was thinking how he should
arrive there, he found himself at day-break in the

---

[1] Here ends the Protevangelium of James, as far as the narrative of the Virgin's history is concerned.

[2] The angel appeared unto him one day before the slaughter
of the children.

[3] Here and onwards the Syriac agrees closely with the Arabic
Gospel of the Infancy; for the Arabic text see Thilo, *Codex Apocryphus*, p. 66 ff., where it is printed with a page for page Latin
translation. See also the Latin rendering in Tischendorf, *Evangelia
Apocrypha*, p. 181 ff.

[4] According to Pseudo-Matthew, Chapter XVIII, Joseph and
Mary on their road to Egypt take shelter in a cave, when suddenly
the three boys and the girl who were with them shriek out in
terror at the sight of a number of dragons with which the cave
is filled. Thereupon Jesus leaves his mother's bosom, and stands
on His feet before the dragons, which straightway adore Him and
depart. Thus was fulfilled the verse (Psalm CXLVIII. 7), "Lau-
"date dominum de terra dracones, dracones et omnes abyssi." On
their way through the desert (see Chap. XIX) lions accompanied
Joseph and Mary and shewed them their way, going in front of
them for the purpose; and they bowed their heads to Jesus. They
never interfered with or injured the sheep and cattle which Joseph
had with him, and thus was fulfilled the verse (Isaiah LXV. 25),
"Lupi cum agnis pascentur, leo et bos simul paleas vescentur."
During the journey Mary sat down to rest under a palm by reason
of the heat, and looking up, and seeing dates at the top of the
tree, she wished Joseph to get her some; Joseph was, however,
more occupied with thought concerning their want of water, especially as the height of the tree made it impossible for him to reach

middle of the land of Egypt,[1] near a mighty village. Now there was in that village a certain idol in which a rebellious devil dwelt, and all the Egyptians sacrificed unto him, and offered up offerings, and poured out libations unto him. And there was a certain priest with whom that devil used to speak from out of the idol, and everything which the Egyptians wished to ask of their gods they went and told that priest; and he gave them the | answers which their gods had made. Now this priest had an only son who was thirty[2] years old, and a multitude of devils dwelt in him; and they wrought all manner of evil things upon him. And when

---

the dates. At this moment Jesus ordered the palm to bend down its crown to Mary, who gathered dates therefrom, and when He had given the command the tree unbent itself and stood straight; out of its roots also there flowed "fontes aquarum limpidissimi et frigidi et dulcissimi nimis". The following day Jesus decreed that a branch of the palm should be taken by His angels and planted in the paradise of His Father (see Chap. XXI). In the XXIInd Chapter Pseudo-Matthew tells us that one day Joseph complained to Jesus of the great heat, and suggested that they should journey from town to town along the sea-shore. In answer Jesus promised that He would shorten the journey for them, and that they should travel in one day the distance which would ordinarily require thirty days to perform; having said these words they began to see the mountains of Egypt. Soon after this, with great joy they arrived on the borders of Hermopolis, in a district called Sotina. The Hermopolis here refered to is, of course, the Hermopolis Parva of the Greeks, and the Temäit en Heru of the Egyptian inscriptions, which was situated on the left bank of the Canopic arm of the Nile. See J. de Rougé, *Géog. Ancienne de la Basse Égypte*, pp. 30, 102.

[1] See Evang. Infantiae, Chapter X, and Pseudo-Matthew, Chapter XXIII.

[2] Evang. Infantiae, "Erat huic sacerdoti filius triennis."

they came upon him he used to rend his garments, and then he would stand up naked, and go forth, and stone the people with stones. And belonging to this idol's temple there was a place in which the poor might be received;[1] and Joseph and Mary came there and went in thither to sleep. And whilst they were alighting in the place for strangers, there was a movement and quaking throughout all the land of Egypt, and all the idols fell down from their pedestals and were broken in pieces. Then all the priests and nobles of Egypt gathered themselves together unto that priest, and they asked him, saying, "What is the reason of "this earthquake which hath taken place in our land, "for all our gods are broken in pieces?" And the priest said unto them, "There is a secret and hidden god "who hath a son, like unto himself, concealed within "his bosom; the footstep of his son hath fallen upon "the land of Egypt,[2] which hath quaked at the might "and terror of his glorious splendour, and therefore all "the gods have fallen down and have been broken in "pieces."[3] And all the Egyptians gathered themselves

---

[1] Syr. ܒܝܬ ܐܟܣܢܝܐ = ξενοδοχεῖον. The Arabic text (Thilo, p. 74, l. 12) has بِيمَارِسْتَان, bimârastan, "hospital"; but a khân or public guest-house is what is meant, and no reference to a place where sick folk were treated is intended.

[2] The Syriac is here not an accurate rendering of the Arabic.

[3] According to Pseudo-Matthew there were three hundred and sixty-five gods in the temple, all of which fell down and were broken in pieces before Christ; therein the writer saw a fulfilment of the prophecy in Isaiah XIX. 1. On the behaviour of Affrodosius, the captain of the guard of the city of Hermopolis, and of how he adored Jesus, and took Him in his arms, see Pseudo-Matthew, Chapter XXIV.

together to that priest, and they accepted his counsel that they should make to themselves [a figure of] the hidden and secret god.

And it came to pass that whem Mary and Joseph were in the place for strangers, the son of the priest entered therein, | and all the people fled from before him. And he came and took up one of the swaddling-bands of Jesus which Mary had washed and had thrown on the wall [to dry]; and having taken it up he threw it over his head. Then straightway the devils began to go forth from his mouth in the form of ravens which flew away exceedingly quickly, and others passed out of his body¹ in the forms of snakes. And the young man was healed immediately, and he glorified God. And when the priest saw his son, he asked him, saying, "What hath happened unto thee, O my son? "And by what means hast thou become whole? And "who hath made thee whole this day?" Then the young man said unto his father, "The child who is with the "woman who is lodging in the place for receiving "strangers. I took a swaddling-band of her son, and "threw it on my head, and straightway the devils be-"gan to go forth and to flee from me." And the priest said unto his son, "Peradventure, my son, this is the "son of the god who hath come and hath entered into "the land of Egypt, and hath broken the gods [there-"of]." And herein was fulfilled that which is written, "Out of Egypt have I called my son."²

---

¹ The Arabic (Evangelium Infantiae) has يخرجون من فمه شبه الغربان ومثال الحيات; there is, then, no authority for the Syr. ܡܢ ܚܩܦܗܘܢ.

² See Evang. Infantiae, Chapter XII.

Now when Joseph and Mary heard | these things they were afraid. And Joseph and Mary spake unto each other, saying, "In the land of Judea Herod sought "to slay Jesus, and on account of us he sent and slew "all the children who were in Bethlehem and in all the "borders thereof; if now the Egyptians hear from this "priest concerning their gods, they will burn us in the "fire." And the rumour reached Pharaoh the king of Egypt, and he sent for Him (*i. e.*, the Child), and found Him not; and he made all the people of the city to go forth, one by one, to learn concerning the Child. And as our Lord drew nigh unto the gate of the city, the two images of the gods which were fixed, one on each side of the gate of the city, cried out, saying, "This is the "King of kings, and the Son of the hidden God." Then Pharaoh wished to slay the Child, but Lazarus[1] became surety for Him; and Joseph and Mary escaped, and they went forth from that place and departed.

And[2] it came to pass that on the road upon which they were travelling there were thieves, and they had bound many people, and stripped them of their possessions, and slain them. And when Joseph and Mary drew nigh unto the neighbourhood of the thieves, a voice came unto the thieves, before they came up to them, and they heard terrible sounds like unto the noise of [the procession of] a passing king; and they heard the sound of drums, | and of captains of hosts,

---

[1] According to Solomon of Baṣra Lazarus was an official of the king of Egypt, and the friendship which existed between Christ and himself dated from the time when he made himself surety to the king of Egypt for Christ. See my *Book of the Bee*, p. 87.
[2] See Evang. Infantiae, Chapter XIII.

...nd of the neighing of horses; and the thieves, by reason of the fear which fell upon them, left everything and fled. Then those who were bound in fetters in the place where the thieves had been rose up, and untied each other, and each one of them took that which belonged to him. And when Joseph and Mary came up [to them] the thieves asked them, saying, "Where 'did you see the governor? for behold, the sound of 'him came unto us, and those who have plundered 'us heard it, and have fled from before him." Then Joseph said unto them, "Behold, he is coming on behind us."

And[1] when Joseph and Mary had passed over to a certain village, behold, there was there a certain poor woman who went out[2] to drink water. And she saw the Evil One in the form of a young man, and he threw out her hands to lay hold upon him, but she was not able touch him;[3] and he entered in unto her and dwelt in her. And the woman would not let any clothes stay upon her, and the Evil One used to make her stand up naked and uncovered as on the day on which she was born; and when they threw her in chains, she used to break them. And the Evil One was wont then to bring her forth naked to the crossroads, and to the graveyards, when she threw stones at every one who beheld | her; and the inhabitants of the district suffered many things by reason of her, and the people prayed that she might die. And it came to pass that when Joseph and Mary had come,

---
[1] See Evang. Infantiae, Chapter XIV.
[2] The Arabic adds "in the night", فى الليل.
[3] Here the Syriac varies from the Arabic.

and had entered into that village, Mary saw the poor woman sitting down and gathering stones, being naked; and as she looked upon her, her compassion for her revealed itself. And Mary took one of the swaddling-bands of Jesus, and threw it upon her, and straightway the Evil One left her, and fled away in the form of a vigorous young man, who murmured, and said, "Fie¹ upon thee, Mary, and fie upon thy Son"; and he fled away, and Mary saw him no more. Then the woman became ashamed as in days of old, and she covered her nakedness with the swaddling-band of Jesus,² and she ran to her relatives, and put on her clothes, and told them what Mary had done for her. Now her parents were the lords of that village, and they received Joseph and Mary with great honour. And³ when the morning was come and Joseph and Mary went forth to go on their way, they furnished them with food and accompanied them a distance on their way. And when the evening was come they entered into a village where a marriage-feast was being celebrated,⁴ but by reason of the evil acts and the agency of devils, and the sorceries of wicked men, the tongue and the hearing of the bride had become fettered. And when Mary had entered into their midst,

---

¹ Arab. وبذلة.
² There is no authority for this in the Arabic.
³ See Evang. Infantiae, Chapter XV.
⁴ *B*, "And they went to a certain village and entered therein "at sunset. And many people were seen to be gathered together, "and there was among them a bride whose speech had been fet-"tered by the agency of devils, and by the sorceries of evil men; "the speech of her tongue and the hearing of her ears were fet-"tered."

having Jesus | in her bosom, the bride saw her and Page 44
an towards her; and she stretched out her hands towards our Lord, and she carried Him in her arms, and embraced Him, and kissed Him, and breathed in the odour of His body,[1] and straightway her tongue and her hearing were unloosed, and she could speak and could hear, and she glorified God that healing had come to her. And that night there was great rejoicing among the inhabitants of that village, for they thought that God had entered in and had made His abode in their houses.

So[2] Joseph and Mary remained there for three days in great honour; and when they went forth therefrom, the people of the village provided them with food, and accompanied them on their way joyfully.

And when they came to another village to pass the night therein, they found in it a large number of people. Now a certain woman of noble family, and of high rank, who belonged to this village, had gone down to the river to wash her clothes, | and whilst she Page 45 was washing she looked about to see that there was no man round about her; and having thrown off her garments, she was swimming about in the water when the Evil One leapt out in the form of a serpent and encircled her body.[3] And when she came to Mary and saw the Child Whom she was carrying, she ran quickly to meet her, and said unto her, "Give me the Child

---

[1] Arab. وجنبته وحملته ولزمته وقبلته فتصاعدته راجة جسمه (Thilo, p. 80).
[2] See Evang. Infantiae, Chapter XVI.
[3] The Arabic is fuller: ووثب عليها واستدار على بطنها وكلما جا الليل كان يتطاول عليه.

"that I may love Him"; and she took Him and kissed Him. And it came to pass that when the Evil One breathed in the odour of Jesus,[1] he straightway loosed his hold upon her, and came down from her body, and fled; and he was never more seen. And when the people that were there saw what had been done they all glorified God; and the woman herself made a feast for Joseph and Mary.

And[2] when the morning had come, the woman prepared some scented water for Mary to wash Jesus in; and whilst she was washing Him, behold, a certain poor young woman, who was as white as snow with leprosy, was sitting with them in the courtyard. And when she saw Mary, and that healing had come to that woman, she also came in faith, and took some of the water in which Jesus had bathed, and washed | herself in it. Then straightway was she cleansed from her leprosy, and she glorified our Lord. And the people of the village likened Joseph and Mary unto gods, and did not consider them to be human folk; and they went about with them, shewing great honour unto them. Then the young woman did homage to Joseph and Mary, and said unto them, "I entreat you, O my parents and masters, to "hearken unto me, for I would become as a daughter "and as a serving woman unto you, and would go "with you; for I have neither father nor mother."[3]

And[4] they permitted her, and she went with them. And they arrived at a certain village wherein was a

---

[1] Arab. فلما قرب منها استروخا ... عنها.
[2] See Evang. Infantiae, Chapter XVII.
[3] The Arabic has only: وسالتهم ان ياخذوها معهم.
[4] See Evang. Infantiae, Chapter XVIII.

mighty governor who had an outer courtyard to his house; and in this courtyard strangers were allowed to lodge, and Mary and Joseph went and took up their abode there. And the young woman [their servant] went to the wife of the governor, and she found her sighing and weeping sorrowfully. And she said unto her, "Mistress, why weepest thou?" And the governor's wife said unto her, "I weep because my sor-
"row is sore unto him, and it cannot be revealed." And the young woman said unto her, "If thou wilt re-
"veal it unto me, perhaps thou wilt be able | to find "a remedy for thyself." And the wife of the gover- *Page 47* nor said unto her, "I am the wife of this governor "who is,—see that thou keep the matter secret,—a "rich man. And I lived with him a long time, but "had no children by him until now, when a son was "born unto me; and he is a leper." And when his father saw him he said unto me, "Give him to the "nurse to bring up, in a place a long way off from "us, so that it may not be known that he is our son; "or, kill him. And if thou dost not do this thing, I "will never live with thee again, and I will never see "thee again. And my pain is great. Ah, woe is me "through my husband, and woe is me through my "son!" Then the young woman said unto her, "If I "can find healing for thy son, thou shalt neither weep "nor suffer pain. I whom thou seest was once a leper "woman, but God visited me in [the form of] Jesus, "the Son of Mary, and I was cleansed." And the governor's wife said unto her, "In what country is "He?" And the young woman said unto her, "He is "nigh; for behold, He is in thy courtyard." And the

governor's wife said unto her, "Where?" And the young woman said | unto her, "Behold, Joseph, and "Mary with her Son, are lodging in thy courtyard." And the governor's wife said unto her, "Shew me "how thou thyself wast healed through Jesus, the Son "of Mary, according as thou hast said." And the young woman said unto her, "His mother made ready "a bath for Him, and washed Him in the waters there- "of; and I also washed myself in the waters which "had been upon His body, and I became clean." Then the wife of the governor rose up with the young woman, the daughter of Mary, and she brought Joseph and Mary into her house with great honour, and she made a feast for them and for many people with them.

And when the morning was come, Mary made ready a bath of scented water, and washed Jesus therein, and the wife of the governor brought her son, and washed him in the water in which Jesus had been washed; and straightway he was cleansed of his leprosy. Then his mother glorified God and said, "Bless- "ed is the woman who brought thee forth, O Jesus, "Who, with the water in which Thy body hath been "washed, healest children like unto Thyself." And she gave Mary a great and precious gift, and set | them on their way in peace.

And[1] it came to pass that when they had come to a certain village, and had gone in there to pass the night, they entered into the house of a man for whom a marriage-feast had been made; but he was bound

---

[1] See Evang. Infantiae, Chapter XIX.

[and kept from] his wife,[1] and he was unloosed[2] on that very night which they spent in his house. Now, when the morning had come, Joseph and Mary wished to set out on their way, but the man and his wife would not let them, and they kept that day with great gladness.

And[3] early on the morrow Joseph and Mary set out on their journey, and they arrived at another village where they wished to lodge for the night. And behold, three women were coming forth from the cemetery weeping, and Mary saw that they wept. And she said unto the young woman that was with her, "Ask these "women why they weep? and say unto them, 'What "news have ye?'" And the young woman asked them, but they would not reveal unto her the reason of their weeping. Then they asked the young woman, and said unto her, "Whence come ye? And whither go ye? for "the sun is about to set." And the young woman said unto them, "We are wayfarers, and are seeking for a "place wherein to pass the night." Then the women said unto her, "Come, pass ye the night with us"; so they went with them. Now the women had a certain new and handsome house wherein they had much furniture; and they took Joseph and Mary there, because the season was winter. And the young woman, Mary's servant, went into their presence, and found them weeping and uttering cries of grief. And the women had near them a mule upon which cloths and trappings of the costliest and finest silks were laid, and food of

---

[1] The Syriac ܡܢ ܐܢܬܬܗ ܗܘܐ ܐܣܝܪ translates the Arabic وهو صربوط عن زوجته.
[2] Arab. حُلَّ رِباطُه.
[3] See Evang. Infantiae, Chapter XX.

sesame¹ was set before him; and the women were stroking him, and kissing him, and weeping.² Then the young woman said unto those women, "Mistresses, "what is the affair of this mule?"³ And with weeping the women answered and said unto her, "This mule "that thou seest is our brother, and is of our flesh.⁴ "Our parents died and left us great riches, and we "were wishing to take a wife for him, and to make a "marriage feast for him;⁵ but certain women who were "sorceresses⁶ worked spells upon him, and he was "thereby turned into this mule which we know is our "brother. And we have not left any man who hath any "knowledge | whatsoever whom we have not brought "unto him, but he hath not been benefited thereby,⁷ "and each time that an attack of grief cometh upon us "we go to the cemetery of our parents and weep."⁸

Page 51

---

¹ Arab. وعليه جل ديباج وبين يديه سمسم.

² *B* has, "a mule upon which precious stuffs were spread, and "food of sesame was in front of him, and they were kissing him, "and pouring out water for him."

³ The Arabic has, فقالت لهن تلك الصبية يا سيداتي ما خبر هذا البغل (Thilo, p. 86), but for خبر read خبر "news".

⁴ *B*, "son of our mother"; Arabic اخونا من امنا.

⁵ They had no other brother: وكان لنا هذا الاخ لا غير.

⁶ *B*, "This hath happened to us through the agency of evil "women and sorceresses. We were sleeping [one night], and the "door of the court-yard and the door of the house were shut, "and when it was dawn we saw that it was not our brother who "was with us, but this mule."

⁷ Arab. وما تركنا فى الدنيا احدا من المعلمين والسحرة والمعزمين الا واحضرناهم ولم يفدنا شيا البتة.

⁸ *B*, "And when we are afflicted we go with our mother, and "weep at the grave of our father"; so also in the Arabic, but ونعود "and we return", is not translated in the Syriac.

And[1] when the young woman heard these words she said unto them, "Rejoice in our Lord, for ye have "found healing for your brother in your own court-"yard." Then the women said unto her, "How?" And the young woman said unto them, "I whom ye see was "once a leper woman. And a certain woman, who was "called Mary, and who had with her a little Son, whose "name was Jesus,[2] came to the place where I was; and "the mother of the Child made ready water in which to "wash Him, and when she had done so, I took in faith "the water in which He had been washed, and I wash-"ed in it, and I became clean, even as ye see me. He "hath healed many, and I know that He can heal your "brother also. But go ye to His mother, and bring her "into your house, and reveal unto her the secret which "is in your hearts, and entreat her to have mercy upon "you." And when the women had heard the words of the young woman they went forth after Mary, and they brought her into their house; and they sat down before her, shedding tears | and making supplication unto her, and saying, "O Lady Mary, have compassion "upon thy handmaidens, for we have no place where "we may lay our head,[3] and we have neither father, "nor mother, nor brother; this mule is our brother, but "he hath been destroyed, therefore do thou have pity "upon us." Then was Mary grieved for them, and she took our Lord and set Him on the back of the mule,

---

[1] See Evang. Infantiae, Chapter XXI.
[2] B, "This woman who hath with her a little son who is call-"ed Jesus."
[3] Arab. فما بقى لنا كبير ولا ريـــس ولا اب. The words ܚܕܐ ܡܚܣܢ ܐܚܝ are a mistranslation.

and she and the women shed tears. And Mary said, "May the mighty power which is hidden in Thee, O "Jesus my Son, visit this mule, and make him to be a "man again even as he was in the days of old." And straightway whilst they were looking at the mule he was transformed, and became a man, even a young man, as he was aforetime. And the young man and his sisters fell down upon the ground and did homage to Mary, and they carried Jesus about in their arms, and were kissing Him, and saying, "Blessed be the "woman that gave Thee birth, O Jesus, and the eyes "which have seen Thee." Then[1] the sisters began to say unto each other, "Our brother has been restored, "but he would not have been except for this young "woman[2] who made known[3] to us | concerning Mary "and Jesus. Now, our brother hath no wife, therefore "let us take this young woman, and let her be his "wife." And the women spake unto Mary and persuaded her concerning the young woman, and she gave her to them, and they made a marriage-feast for their brother.[4] Thus the matter of their brother was straightened, and gladness took the place of sorrow, and the women changed[5] their cries of woe into songs of

---

[1] See Evang. Infantiae, Chapter XXII.
[2] For ܪܒܘܠܐ read ܪܒܘܠܐ.
[3] *B*, "The sisters said to their mother, '[Our brother] hath "been restored and hath become a man, and his restoration hath "taken place through this young woman who made known'," etc.
[4] *B*, "And the women made a marriage-feast for their brother, "and there was great rejoicing, and these women and the young "woman had joy instead of grief."
[5] *B*, "And the women changed their sorrow to gladness, and "their cries of grief to songs of praise. For their riches were great,

praise; and the women were saying, "Jesus the Son
"of Mary hath changed mourning into rejoicing." And
Joseph and Mary stayed with them ten days; and they
departed from them in peace. And the women having
accompanied them some distance returned weeping,
and especially the young woman who had been Mary's
servant.

And when Joseph and Mary had gone on their way,
they arrived in a desert country, wherein they heard
that thieves lived; and they wished to pass by night
through the district where the thieves were. And whilst
they were journeying, behold, they came upon two |
thieves[1] [called]. Titus and Dumachus, who had been
detached from their companions, and had been set to
guard the road. And when the thieves saw Joseph and
Mary, Titus said to Dumachus, "Let them pass on
"their way, and say nothing about it to our compa-
"nions,[2] and I will give thee my share, four $\zeta\hat{u}\zeta\acute{e}$".[3] And
Titus gave Dumachus his belt as a pledge that he
would keep silence, and would not reveal the matter
to his companions. And Mary blessed Titus and said
unto him, "The mercy of God shall be gracious unto
"thee, and shall make thee worthy of the forgiveness
"of sins." Now these are the two men who were cru-

Page 54

"and their brother being restored they brought out chains, and
"adorned themselves beautifully, and they rejoiced, and danced,
"and sang, saying, 'Jesus, the son of David, changeth sorrow to
"joy'."

[1] B, "They saw two thieves asleep by the wayside." See
Evang. Infantiae, Chapter XXIII.

[2] B, "That they plunder them [not]." In the Arabic text Dumachus refused to agree to this suggestion.

[3] In the Arabic, "forty dirhams".

cified with our Lord, Titus on the right, and Dumachus[1] on the left.[2]

And it came to pass that when Joseph and Mary had arrived in the country of Judea they were afraid to go into Bethlehem; for Archelaus had become king in Judea in the stead of Herod the king his father. It is a very marvellous thing, O my brethren, but they were carrying round about from place to place the Pacifier of the worlds, and of created things as if, He had neither a house nor a shelter.[3] Then the angel of the Lord appeared unto Joseph in a dream, and said unto him, "Arise, go into Bethlehem[4] to thy house."

And[5] when he had gone into his house, a sickness and boils and blains broke out that summer among the children, and very many of them | died. And a certain

---

[1] In the Arabic Mary tells Titus that God shall give him a place of honour on His right hand, and shall forgive him his sins, whereupon Jesus speaks and declares that, thirty years later, the Jews shall crucify Him, and shall lift up these two thieves with Him on crosses, Titus on the right hand and Dumachus on the left, and that after that day Titus shall go before Him into Paradise. After this Mary and Jesus journey on to the city of idols, which, as soon as they approach, become changed into heaps of sand.

[2] Here the Arabic text has two short Chapters (XXIV and XXV) for which the Syriac has no equivalent. In the XXIVth we are told that Mary came to the village of Maṭariyyeh, and washed the Child's shirt in the fountain there; from His sweat which she sprinkled there sprang the famous balsam trees. In the XXVth Chapter the Holy Family come to Memphis and see Pharaoh; they live in Egypt for three years, during which time Jesus works many miracles which are nowhere fully recorded.

[3] Arab., عجباه كيف يحمل ويطاف فى البلاد صاحب البلاد (Thilo, p. 94).

[4] Arab., Nazareth.

[5] See Evang. Infantiae, Chapter XXVII.

believing woman had a son who was sick,¹ and he was nigh unto death. And she came unto Mary whilst she was washing Jesus, and she said, "O my Lady Mary, "my son is grievously sick." And Mary said unto her, "Wait until Jesus be washed, and then take the water "in which my Son hath been washed, and go and bathe "thy son in it; and may God visit him." And the woman took the water, and went and washed her son in it, and when she had wrapped him up she put him to sleep; and he woke up sound and well. And the woman glorified God and Jesus for the recovery of her son.

And² a certain woman who was a neighbour of her whose son had been healed, said unto her, "My son is "grievously sick. His eyes are blinded with pain, and "the throbbing in them ceaseth not either by night or "by day." And the woman whose son had been made whole said unto her, "My son also | was grievously "[sick],³ and was nigher⁴ unto death than life; and I "went in to Mary, the mother of Jesus, and took the "water in which Jesus had been washed, and washed "my son in it, and then I wrapped him up, and put him "to sleep; and he woke up relieved and well. And, "behold, thou canst see him." And when the woman heard these things she also went to Mary. And she waited until Mary had washed Jesus, and then she took the water in faith, and washed the eyes of her son; and the throbbing ceased from them, and he slept like a dead man, because he had not slept at all for many

---

¹ For ܩܢܝܐܘ read ܩܢܝܐܘ.
² See Evang. Infantiae, Chapter XXVIII.
³ B adds ܐܠܝܨܐ "tortured".
⁴ B has the better reading.

days.[1] And when he awoke he stood up, and he was healed and his eyes were opened. And his mother was glad, and she glorified God. Then she took him in her arms and went to Mary,[2] who said unto her, "See that thou tell no man."

And[3] there were there two women who were concubines,[4] and each of them had a son,[5] and both sons were sick.[6] Now one of the women was called | Mary, and her son was called Cleophas.[7] And she went to Mary, the mother of Jesus, and gave her[8] a beautiful cloak; and Mary gave her one of the swaddling-bands of Jesus; and the mother of Cleophas made from it apparel[9] wherein she dressed her son, and he was made whole. But the son of her companion[10] Arzamî died, and anger against her fellow-concubine Mary laid hold upon her, for she was jealous because her own son had died, whilst that of Mary was alive. Now the two women Mary and Arzamî used to minister in their houses each a week at a time. And it came to pass that when the week of Mary had come, she made the

---

[1] *B*, "because he had been in pain for many days". There is no Arabic equivalent for these words.

[2] *B*, adds, "and revealed unto her the whole matter as it had taken place." Arab. وكشفت لها كلما جرى.

[3] See Evang. Infantiae, Chapter XXIX.

[4] Arab. امرانان لزوج واحد "two wives belonging to one husband".

[5] Literally, "the two of them had two sons".

[6] Arab. وقفوا, "and they were sick of fever".

[7] Arab. قليوفا.

[8] *B*, "and gave her a beautiful cloak, and asked her for one "of the swaddling-bands of Jesus".

[9] Literally, "tunic" or "shirt"; ܟܘܬܝܢܐ and ܟܘܬܝܢܐ here = Arab. قميصا.

[10] Literally, "rival", Arab. ضرة.

oven hot, and went to fetch the dough [to bake] for bread.¹ And when Arzamî saw that there was no one there looking on at her, she ran and seized Mary's child, and cast him into the oven, and then went away from the place. And when the mother of Cleophas came back [and looked in], she saw her son sitting in the furnace and playing in the midst thereof; for the fire had become extinguished, and the furnace was as cold as snow, and as if fire had not been in it.² Then Mary, the mother of Cleophas, took her son in her arms, and went to Mary, the mother of Jesus, and spake unto her | and revealed the matter. And Mary said unto her, "Hold thy peace and tell no man; for "this will be to thy advantage."³

And it came to pass that when the week of Arzamî came, she went to fetch water from the well, and she found Cleophas by the side of it; and seeing that there was no one there to observe her, she took the child and threw him into the well, and then went home to her house. And when the people came to draw water from the well, they saw the child sitting⁴ upon the water and crowing joyfully and laughing; and they went down [into the well] and brought him up, and many marvelled. And his mother took him and went to

Page 58

---

¹ She left her son Cleophas by the oven. وكان ابنها هذا قليبوفا قد تركته عند التنور.

² B adds, "And Mary knew that it was her fellow-concubine "who had cast [him] into the furnace", which represents the Arabic فعلمت امه ان ضرتها التى رمته فى النار.

³ Arab. فانى اخاف عليك من اذاعته, "for I have fear on account "of thee if thou make it known."

⁴ The Arabic has وهو جالس فوق الما, and has no equivalent for the Syriac ܘܡܬܓܚܟ ܘܡܦܨܚ.

Mary, the mother[1] of Jesus, weeping and said [unto her], "See, O my mother, behold, Arzamî hath cast "him into the well, and she will certainly kill him [one "day]." And Mary said unto her, "Hold thy peace, for, "behold, the Lord will now work deliverance, and "judgment, and vengeance for thee." And it came to pass that Arzamî went to draw water from that well, and the rope passed between her legs, and she fell down into the well; and they went down and brought her up with her head split open, and her bones broken, and she was dead. And in her was fulfilled that which is written by David,"[2] "He dug a well and made it "deep, and fell into the pit which he had made."

And[3] after these things, behold, there was a certain woman who had two sons that were twins, and they were both very sick; and one of them died, and the other was nigh unto death. And his mother took him in her arms and came weeping to Mary, the mother of Jesus, and said unto her, "O my Lady Mary, help me. "I had two sons that were twins; one of them is al- "ready dead, and the other is dying." And holding her child in her arms she wept and said, "O[4] Lover "of men, Thou just and merciful One, deal Thou right- "eous judgment unto Thy servant. Thou gavest me "two sons; let one be Thine, and let the other be[5] "mine;" and she wept bitterly. Then was Mary sad on

---

[1] Read, with *B*, ܡܢܪܟ.
[2] Psalm VII. 15.
[3] See Evang. Infantiae, Chapter XXX.
[4] *B*, "Thou art the Lover of men, and art not unmerciful; and "Thou art the good, and not the cruel Being".
[5] Read ܕܐܡܝ.

her account, and she said unto her, "Place thy son in "the bed of Jesus." Now his eyes were closed and he was nigher unto death than life. But when Mary had wrapped him in the swaddling-bands of Jesus, he inhaled from them the breath of life,[1] and he opened his eyes, and cried out for his mother, saying, "Mother, "mother, give me the breast." So his mother gave | him the breast and he sucked. And his mother answered and said unto Mary, "Now know I that the power "of God dwelleth in thee, and that thou didst give "birth unto the Son of God, for children like unto "Him are made whole by the odour of Him." And this child was Thomas who was called Didymus.[2]

And[3] after this a certain beggar-woman who was a leper came to Mary, the mother of Jesus, and said unto her, "O my Lady Mary, help me." And Mary said unto her, "What help dost thou seek? Is it gold, "or silver, or the cleansing of thy body from leprosy "and scab?" And the young woman said unto her, "Woe is me, for who is able to give me this thing?" And Mary said unto her, "Wait a little until Jesus hath "gone up out of the water of His bath, and I have "wrapped Him up and placed Him in His bed." [So the woman waited as Mary had said] Then Mary said unto her, "Take this water, and wash thy whole body "therewith;" and when she had washed she became clean, and she glorified God.

---

[1] B "He inhaled from them new life".
[2] In the Arabic the child is said to have been called Bartholomew, برتولما. On Thomas, who was surnamed Didymus, see St. John XI. 16; XX. 24; XXI. 2; Acts I. 13.
[3] See Evang. Infantiae, XXX.

And[1] having stayed with Mary three days she went on her way. And it came to pass that she arrived at a certain village wherein was a governor, who had a daughter | that was betrothed to another governor of another country; but the mark of leprosy having appeared in her forehead like a star, the governor would not take her[2] to wife because of the mark which was in her. And her mother began to weep over her with bitter tears, and the maiden also wept for herself. And it came to pass that when the beggar-woman came to them, she found them weeping, and she said unto them, "What is the cause of your weeping?" And they said unto her, "Our grief[3] is too great to reveal to "men." And the beggar-woman said unto them, "If ye "will reveal to me your sorrow, peradventure the heal- "ing may be found for it here." Then the women told her of the mark of leprosy which was in their daughter's forehead. And the beggar-woman said unto them, "I whom ye new see was once a leper.[4] And having "gone to Bethlehem, I came to a certain woman who "was called Mary, and who had a Son named Jesus. "Now this Jesus is the Son of God. And when Mary "saw me she was very sorry for me, and she gave "me the water in which the body of her Son had been "washed; and I washed my whole body therein, and "I became clean."[5] Then the women said unto the

---

[1] See Evang. Infantiae, Chapter XXXI.
[2] Literally, "they would not take her".
[3] Read ܐܪܟܐ.
[4] B, "I who now stand before you was once a leper covered "with scabs".
[5] B adds, "even as ye see".

beggar-woman, "Rise up, [and come] with us, and "shew us where Mary is." So the three of them rose up and went to Bethlehem having with them gifts and costly presents for Mary; and when they had gone into her house, and had shewn her the mark of leprosy, she said unto them, "May the might of Jesus abide "with you." Then she gave to the daughter of the governor some water in which Jesus had been washed; and the girl washed herself therein and was cleansed from that moment. And she took a mirror¹ and looked at herself therein, and she saw that she had become cleansed from that moment. And the women returned to their village glorifying God. And it came to pass that when he who had been betrothed unto the maiden heard that she had been made clean, he made ready the wedding feast and took her to wife.

And behold² there was a young woman of noble family who was possessed of a devil, and he was wont to appear and to come [to her] in the form of a mighty serpent³ which was about to swallow her;⁴ and all her body used to burn with heat,⁵ and she became like a dead woman. And whenever she saw him coming from a distance | she used to clasp tightly her head with her hands, and say,⁶ "Woe is me! Woe is me! for "there is none who can deliver me from this adver-

---

¹ In the Arabic text there is no mention of the mirror.
² See Evang. Infantiae, Chapter XXXIII.
³ Read ܪܚܫܐ.
⁴ Arab. ويهم ان يبتلعها.
⁵ Arab. وكان يمص جميع دمها, "and he used to suck out all "her blood"; the reading of B is ܡܨܐ.
⁶ B, "and shriek out, saying".

5*

"sary." And her parents used to weep before her, and every one who heard her voice was sorry on her account; and all who saw her used to weep, especially when she wept and said, "O my parents, O my bre "thren, is there none to deliver me from this slayer?" And when the daughter of the governor who had been healed of her leprosy heard her voice, she went up to the roof,[2] and she saw the young woman with her hands clasped tightly over her head and weeping, and many people weeping before her. And she said unto her husband,[3] "What is the matter with this young "woman?"[4] And he revealed to her the matter of the young woman. And the wife of the governor said unto him, "Hath this young woman no parents?" And he said unto her, "She hath both father and mother.' Then she said unto him, "Send[5] and call her mother "unto me." And he sent and called her mother. And when the mother had come into her presence, she

Page 64 said | unto her, "Is the young woman who is thus tor "tured thy daughter?" And she said unto her, "Yea.' And the wife of the governor said unto her, "Dos "thou wish her to be made whole?" And the mother of the young woman said unto her, "Yea." Then the

---

[1] *B*, "And many people used to gather together about her, and "they wept and groaned before her more and more as she wept" [saying,] "Is there" etc.

[2] *B*, "up on to the roof of the house".

[3] *I. e.*, the husband of the woman that was possessed of the devil. Arab. وقالت لزوج هذه المجنونة.

[4] Arab. ما لامراتك, "What is the matter with thy wife?", or "What is there to thy wife?" The Latin renderings are not exact here.

[5] *B*, "I conjure thee by the living God send" etc.

wife of the governor said unto her, "Take heed and "keep this secret of mine hidden carefully.¹ Rise up, "and take thy daughter, and go to Bethlehem,² and "enquire for a woman who is called Mary, the mother "of Jesus, and reveal unto her thy business, and, be- "hold, thy daughter will be made whole, and thou "shalt come from her with joy."³ So the woman rose up, and took her daughter and went to Bethlehem; and she went to Mary, and made known to her [her business]. And Mary gave unto her the water in which the body of Jesus had been washed,⁴ and she washed the body of the young woman therein. And Mary gave unto her one of the swaddling-bands of Jesus, and said unto her, "When thou seest thine enemy coming, "throw this swaddling-band over thy head."

And they set forth to come into | their village.⁵ Now the day arrived for the adversary of the young woman to come. And when the young woman saw that he was coming, she was afraid of him, and said to her mother, "Mother, behold the adversary cometh, and "I am greatly afraid of him." And her mother said unto her, "Remain thou, O my daughter, near the "water that we may see what he will do unto thee."⁶

---

¹ In the Arabic the wife of the governor tells the mother that she herself had once been a leper, and that Mary, the mother of Jesus, had healed her.
² B adds, "the city of David the great king".
³ Reading with B.
⁴ Literally, "the water of the body of Jesus".
⁵ See Evang. Infantiae, Chapter XXXIV.
⁶ In the Arabic the mother tells her daughter to put away fear from her and to let the devil come nigh unto her, when she must set the swaddling-band of Jesus before him.

And the young woman saw that he was coming in the form of a mighty serpent, and that he was of most horrible appearance; and she perceived that all her body was trembling. And when he drew nigh unto her she saw that darts of fire were going forth from the swaddling-band of Jesus which was upon her head, and that they were smiting him in his face; and he shrieked and cried out with fearful outcries, and fled, and was destroyed, and was nevermore seen. Then had the young woman rest, and she passed from tribulation to happiness, and she gave glory unto our Lord; and from that day onwards she nevermore saw that horrible sight.

And[1] it came to pass that when Jesus was three years old there was a certain woman [in that village] who had a son who was called Judah, and he was afflicted with a devil that vexed him. And when this devil came upon him he used to bite[2] every one who was nigh unto him; and when he saw that there was no one near him, he would tear the flesh of his own arms and members. And when his mother heard that Jesus had healed many [sick] folk, she brought her son unto Him. Now the brethren of Jesus, James[3] and Joses, had taken Him [out] and were playing with Him. And Judah came and sat by the right[4] side of

---

[1] See Evang. Infantiae, Chapter XXXV. The Arabic makes no mention of the age of Jesus.

[2] Read ܕܢܫ.

[3] See St. Matthew XIII. 55.

[4] In the Arabic Judah is made to attempt to bite Jesus, but not being allowed to do so, he smites Him on the left side, whereat Jesus weeps; at this moment the devil leaves Judah in the form of a mad dog.

Jesus, and straightway the devil that vexed him went forth from him in the form of a mad dog; and many folk were looking on. Now this man was the disciple who was called Judas Iscariot. It was he who smote[1] our Lord, and it was he who betrayed our Lord; and in the place in which he smote Him the Jews smote our Lord with a spear.

And[2] it came to pass that when Jesus was five years old Joseph took Him to school to Zacchaeus the scribe. Then Zacchaeus the scribe began to say unto him, "Alphâ, Bîṭâ", that is to say, "Âlaph, Bêth", and he told Him to answer and to say [these words] after him. | But Jesus was silent, and the scribe became angry, and smote the Child, and straightway the scribe died. Then Joseph came and took away the Child [from school], and as he was on the road [home], a certain boy ran and threw stones at Jesus. And Jesus said unto the boy, "Thou shalt never return from this "road;" and immediately the boy fell down and died. And those who saw Him cried out and said, "Where "was this Child born?"

And Joseph said, "Who will be able to give in- "struction to such a child as this?" And the Child Jesus answered and said unto the scribe, "The words "which thou hast just spoken I have listened unto "diligently; but I am a stranger unto them [just as "I am] a stranger unto you, even though I am with "you and among you, and honour according to the "flesh I have not. But thou art under the law, and

---

[1] Literally, "bit"; the Arabic has ضرب.
[2] See Evang. Pseudo-Matthew, Chapters XXXI and XXXVIII.

"under the law thou shalt remain, Before thy father "was brought forth, I had My being. Thou thinkest "within thyself that thou art My father, for thou "knowest not whence I have been brought forth, nor "whence I have come. But I am One by Myself, and "I know you truly, both when ye were brought forth, "and how long time ye have to live, and to remain "in this world." And when they heard these words they marvelled and were astonished. And another scribe said unto Joseph, "Deliver Jesus unto me, and "I will teach Him." And the scribe began to instruct Jesus, and said unto Him, "Alphâ;" and Jesus said, "Alphâ." And the scribe said, "Bîṭâ", and Jesus said unto him, "What is Alphâ? And again I say "unto thee, What is Bîṭâ?" And the scribe was angry and smote Him, and straightway he fell down and died. Then the Child Jesus went to His people. Then Joseph cried unto Mary His mother and said unto her, "Thou shalt not let this Child go outside "the house lest those who smite Him die."

Then another scribe said unto Joseph, "Deliver "Jesus unto me, and I will teach Him by coaxing "Him;" so Joseph took Him to the scribe. Then Jesus took | the roll, and read,[1] but He read not the things which were written therein; but He opened His mouth and spake by the Spirit.[2] And when the scribe heard these things he went down and sat upon the ground;

---

[1] See Evang. Pseudo-Matthew, Chapter XXXIX.

[2] Pseudo-Matthew, "sed in spiritu dei vivi loquebatur, tanquam "si de fonte vivo torrens aquae egrederetur et fons semper per- "maneret".

and wonder and astonishment laid hold upon him by reason of the things which he heard from the Child. Now great multitudes of people were gathered together there; and Jesus opened His mouth and spake so that they might wonder and be astonished. Then Joseph ran and came there because he was afraid lest this scribe also would strike Jesus, and would also die. And the scribe said unto Joseph, "Thou "didst not deliver a disciple unto me, but a Master "and a Doctor;" so Joseph took Him and brought Him to his house.

And again Joseph sent the Child, together with James his son, into the vineyard. And as they were walking along a certain venomous viper bit James, but Jesus drew nigh and blew a breath upon the wound, and it was made whole; and the viper dried up, but James was healed and lived.

And again on a certain day Jesus was sitting in the temple among the doctors, when one of them said unto Him, "Âlaph." And Jesus said, "Âlaph." And the doctor said unto Him, "Bêth." And Jesus said unto the doctor, "Tell me the explanation of "'Âlaph', and I will tell thee the explanation of 'Bêth'." And the doctor said unto Him, "I do not know." And Jesus said unto them, "Ye hypocrites! For how can "those who do nor know 'Âlaph, Bêth' give instruction? "First of all teach [Me] what Âlaph is, and then I "will believe you concerning [what ye say] of Bêth." Then the Child began to enquire of the teacher concerning the forms of each of the letters of the alphabet, and why the first letter had angles, and why the sides [of the others] were close together and were pointed, and were gathered in over each other, and were extended, and were ornamented; and why the tops of them were spread out, and square, and hiding themselves, and were turning back; and why their sides were double, and bending over, and were fixed in the form of the Trinity.[1] Then the teacher was astonished, and his mind reeled at the words of the Child, and at the names which He pronounced, and at the greatness of the power which was hidden in His questioning. Then the doctors cried out and said, "Oh, oh, it is not right for this Child to be "upon the earth; in very truth this Child is able to "set fire to fire, and we think that He must have "been born before the Flood which took place in the "time of Noah. What womb received this Child? Or "what mother reared Him? We are not able to bear "Him. We thought that a disciple had come to us, "but He is found to be a doctor." And Jesus said unto them, "Ye marvel at My smallness, but ye are "smaller than I in your minds." And the first teacher said, "He entreated us to instruct Him! O my bowels, "I cannot bear it! I must flee from the village, for

---

[1] "Et coepit Jesus singularum litterarum nomina interrogare, et "dixit: Dicat magister legis, prima littera quid sit, vel quare tri- "angulos habeat multos, gradatos, subacutos, mediatos, obductos, "productos, erectos, stratos, curvistratos." Pseudo-Matthew, Chapter XXXI. According to the Gospel of the Infancy (Chapter XXXVIII) Joseph was not a very skilful workman: "Quoties ergo "Josepho aliquid operis sui sive cubito sive spithama longius aut "brevius, latius vel angustius faciendum erat, dominus Jesus ma- "num suam versus illud extendebat, quo facto tale quale volebat "Josephus fiebat, neque ipsi opus erat quicquam manu sua facere: "non erat enim Josephus artis fabrilis admodum peritus."

"I cannot bear to look upon the little Child. I am "overcome! Even at the beginning I did not know "what He said, but now my mind hath become fool-"ish by reason of the ordering of His speech, and "by reason of the beauty of His words. This Child "must be something mighty; He is either God, or He "is an angel. What I shall say unto Him I know not." Then the Child Jesus laughed, and said unto them, "Indeed I laugh with you."[1]

And[2] it came to pass that the mother of Jesus sent Him to the well to draw water, and by reason of the press of the multitude of people[3] that were there the water-bottle was struck and was broken. Then Jesus spread out the garment which He had on Him, and He gathered up the water, and carried it to his mother. And Mary marvelled at the matter, and kept it in her heart.

Now Joseph[4] was a carpenter, and he was wishing to make a bed, but one of the planks thereof was smaller in measure than its fellow.[5] Then Jesus took hold of one end of it, and said to Joseph, "Take "thou hold of the other end of it," and Jesus having stretched Himself out on it made it equal in length

---

[1] In Pseudo-Matthew the speech of Jesus is much longer.
[2] See Pseudo-Matthew, Chapter XXXIII. This miracle took place when Jesus was six years old.
[3] Pseudo-Matthew, "quidam ex infantibus impegerit eum."
[4] See Pseudo-Matthew, Chapter XXXVII.
[5] Pseudo-Matthew, "contigit ut quidam juvenis illi faciendum "grabatum cubitorum sex demandaret. Et jussit Joseph puero suo "incidere lignum seca ferrea secundum mensuram quam miserat. "Qui non servavit definitum sibi modum; sed fecit unum lignum "brevius altero." The rest of the story is much fuller in the Latin.

to its fellow. And Joseph said, "Do now according "to Thy desire."

And it came to pass at another time that Jesus went out and sowed a bushel of wheat, and it produced a hundred measures of wheat; and He gave them to the dwellers in the village.

| And[1] it came to pass that when Jesus was about seven years old, He and the children who were His companions made figures in clay of horses, and mares, and oxen, and asses; and each child was saying, "Mine "is more beautiful than thine." Then Jesus said unto them, "If I command these My figures they will walk." And the other children said unto Him, "If Thou canst "do this thing then must Thou be the Son of the Crea- "tor." And Jesus gave them the word of command, and they walked; and Jesus said unto them, "Come," and they came. And Jesus formed sparrows, and spake unto them and they flew in the air; and when He gave them the word of command, they also alighted upon the ground. And He made figures of asses also, and having set chopped straw and barley before them they ate, and they drank water. And the children went and made known to their parents everything that Jesus was doing, and they admonished them not to play with Jesus the Son of Mary.[2]

And[3] it came to pass that Jesus went out one day

---

[1] See Evang. Infantiae, Chapter XXXVI.

[2] The Syriac version makes no mention of the episode of the dyer's shop which is related in the Gospel of the Infancy, Chapter XXXVII, and it has no equivalents for Chapters XXXVIII and XXXIX.

[3] See Evang. Infantiae, Chapter XL.

and saw a company of children playing together, and
He went after them, but they fled before Him, and
went into a furnace. And Jesus came after them,
and stood by the door [of a house], and said unto the Page 71
women who were sitting there, "Where are the children
"who came in here before Me?" And the women said
unto Jesus, "No children came here." Then Jesus
said unto them, "Then what are the beings that are
"inside the house?" And the women said unto Him,
"They are goats." And Jesus said unto them, "Let
"the goats which are in the furnace go out to their
"shepherds;" and there came forth from the furnace
goats which leaped round about Jesus, and skipped
joyfully. And when the women had seen what had
taken place, they wondered, and great fear laid hold
upon them. Then the women rose up and did homage
unto Jesus, and they made supplication unto Him,
saying, "O Jesus, Thou Son of Mary, Thou good
"Shepherd of Israel, have compassion upon Thine
"handmaidens; for Thou didst come to heal and not
"to destroy." And Jesus answered and said unto them,
"Verily the children of Israel are like unto the Black
"folk among the nations,[1] for the Black ones seize
"the outer side of the flock and harass their Shep-
"herd; even thus are the people of Israel." Then the
women said unto Him, "Thy disciples could never
"hide themselves away from Thee, and they could
"never harass thee; for they perform Thy will, and

---

[1] Arab., "the children of Israel are among the nations like
"[the people] of the Sûdân," ان بنى اسرايل فى الشعوب هـــم
كالسودان. The Arabic has no equivalent for the latter part of
Jesus' speech.

"they fulfil Thy commandments." And Jesus gave the word of command and said unto the goats, "Come, "O ye children, My playfellows, and let us play to- Page 72 "gether." And straightway, | whilst these women were looking on, they were changed from the similitude of goats and became children again. And they went after Jesus and from that day the children were not able to flee from Jesus; and their parents admonished them, saying, "See that ye do everything that Jesus, the "Son of Mary, commandeth you to do."

And[1] it came to pass that when it was the month of Îyâr, Jesus gathered together the children, and said unto them, "[Let us make unto ourselves a king]."[2] And He set them upon the king's highway, and they spread their garments upon the ground, and they seated Jesus upon them; and they wove for him a garland of flowers like unto a crown, and they set [it] upon His head, and they stood before Him, a company[3] upon His right hand, and a company upon His left hand, like the companies of soldiers who stand before a king. And every one that passed along the road they brought unto Jesus, saying, "Come, and offer "salutation unto the king."

And[4] there came along certain people who had with them a youth who was fifteen years of age, and he was called Simon. Now he had seen a bird's nest[5] in

---

[1] See Evang. Infantiae, Chapter XLI.
[2] This sentence is added from *B*.
[3] Literally, "companies, companies". The reading of *B* follows the Arabic more closely:—ووقفو بين يديه عن يمينه ومن شماله
[4] See Evang. Infantiae, Chapter XLII.
[5] Arab., "partridge's nest", عش حجل.

a tree,¹ and, thinking that there were young ones in it, he stretched out his hand [to take it], and a serpent bit him; and his parents took him up to carry him to a physician at Jerusalem. And as they were journeying along the way the children that were with Jesus saw them; and they said unto the travellers, "Come and see what the King wants | from you, and Page 73 "cry peace unto Him." Now the parents of Simon were weeping because their child was in such an evil case; for his arm had become greatly inflamed and swollen. And when they had come to Jesus, He said unto them, "Why do ye weep?" And they said unto Him, "Be- "cause of this our son. He went to take some young "birds [from a nest], and a serpent bit him." And when Jesus saw them He had compassion upon them, and He drew nigh and took hold of Simon's hand, and said unto him, "Art thou ready to be My disciple?" And straightway his arm ceased from troubling, and it became as if the serpent had never bitten it. Now the youth was he who was called Simon Zelotes by the Apostles, on account of the nest of birds.²

And after this thing there came a certain man from Jerusalem, and the children went out and laid hold upon him, and said unto him, "Come, and cry peace "to our King." And when he had come Jesus saw that a serpent encircled his neck, and sometimes it choked him, and sometimes it allowed him to breathe freely.³

---

¹ He had gone up into the mountain with some other boys to fetch some word, ܚܛܒܐ ܠܝܓܝܒ ܐܠܓܒܠ ܐܠܝ ܐܠܨܒܝܐܢ ܡܥ ܐܢܛܠܩ.

² There is here a play on the words ܩܢܐ "nest", and ܩܢܢܐ "Zelotes".

³ Literally, "it set him free".

Then Jesus said unto him, "How long has this serpent "been on thy neck?" And the man said, "Three years." And Jesus said unto him, "Where did he [first] cling "to thee?" And the man said, "I treated him fairly "and well, but he hath rewarded me | evilly." And Jesus said unto him, "In what manner didst thou treat "him well? And how did he recompense thee evilly?" The man said unto him, "I found him in the winter "dried up by the cold, and I laid him in my bosom; "and when I went into [my] house, I put him in an "earthenware jar,[1] and fastened up the mouth thereof. "And it came to pass that when the summer had come, "I opened the mouth of the jar, and brought him out, "whereupon he leaped upon my neck and coiled him- "self round it. And he inflicteth severe pain upon me, "and I have not yet been able to deliver myself from "him." Then Jesus said unto him, "Thou hast behaved "badly and hast treated him badly, though thou knowest "it not. God created the serpent in the dust, so that he "might crawl about in the dust and live therein; and "sometimes he is cold and sometimes he is hot. Thou "shouldst have left him in the earth to come to life "[again], even as he was created by God to do; but "thou didst take him and put him in a jar without "food, and herein didst thou treat him badly". Then Jesus said unto the serpent, "Come down from this "man, and go and live in the earth;" and the serpent uncoiled himself, and came down from the man. And the man said unto Jesus, "Verily thou art a "King, and the King of kings; for every worker of

---

[1] *B*, "silver jar".

THE CHILD WHO FELL FROM THE ROOF. 81

"magic, and every rebellious creature is obedient unto "Thee."[1]

| And it came to pass after this thing that, behold, Page 75 a young man who had been lain upon an ass came to Jesus, and there was with him an old man who was supporting him and weeping. And Jesus saw him, and was sorry for him, and He said unto him, "What "aileth thee, O aged one, that thou weepest? And "what is the reason of thy weeping?" Then the old man said unto him, "How is it possible for me to help "weeping and choking myself with tears, for I have "no other son to work for me, and no one to give me "food, nor hath his mother who is an aged woman, "except this youth whom thou seest. Thieves fell upon "him, and stripped him, and dealt him many blows, "and beat him, and then left him like a dead man, "and went away." And Jesus had compassion upon that old man, and He laid His right hand upon the youth, and straightway he was healed of his sickness; and he came down off the ass, and walked away and went to his house.

And[2] it came to pass a few days afterwards that certain children were playing together upon a very high roof, and that one of them fell down and died; and the children said to one another, "Come, let us "say that he was thrown over by Jesus the Son of "Mary." Then were Jesus, and Mary, and Joseph seized for the murder of the child, and they carried

---

[1] *B*, "Thy kingdom is received by all the workers of magic and "by all the rebellious beings". A very much shorter form of this story appears to exist in Evang. Infantiae, Chapter XLIII.

[2] See Evang. Infantiae, Chapter XLIV.

them before the governor; and the children bore witness before the governor against Jesus, saying, "It was He who threw him down." And the governor said, "An eye for an eye, and a tooth for a tooth, "and a life for a life." And when they had delivered Jesus to the governor, He answered and said to the judge, "If I raise up this child, and he shall say "that I did not throw him off the roof, what wilt thou "do to those who have borne false witness against "me?" And the governor answered and said unto Jesus, "If Thou canst do this thing Thou shalt go forth "free, and they shall be condemned." Then Jesus said unto the child who was dead, "Bûzâ, Bûzâ,[1] was "it I who threw thee off the roof?" And the dead child answered and said, "God forbid! O my Lord "Jesus, Thou didst not throw me off the roof, for Thou "wast not there when they did it;[2] those who threw "me down have borne false witness against Thee." Then Jesus drew nigh and took Bûzâ by the hand, and raised him up on his feet; and the enemies of Jesus were put to shame, for all those who saw this marvelled and wondered, and ascribed glory unto God. And they said, "Verily God is with this Child; "what will become | of Him?" Now Jesus was twelve years old when He wrought this miracle.

Now when war broke out against the children, and they were about to be slain by Herod, the mother

---

[1] Arab., "O Zeno, O Zeno", يا زينون يا زينون.
[2] Arab., "O my Lord, Thou didst not throw me down; nay, "it was so and so who cast me down" يا سيدى ما رميتنى انت بل فلان الذى رمانى.

of Nathaniel took him, and set him¹ up in a fig-tree, and she covered him with the leaves thereof. And when he came to Jesus to see him, Jesus answered and said unto him, "Behold a child of Israel in whom, "verily, there is no guile." And Nathaniel said unto him, "Where didst Thou know me?" Then Jesus said unto him, "I saw thee before Philip called thee, when "thou wast under the fig-tree." And Nathaniel went and told his mother everything which Jesus had narrated unto him; and his mother said unto him, "Verily, "my son, this is the Messiah for Whom creation waiteth."

And it came to pass when Jesus was about twenty years old that He used to go continually into the synagogues, and ask the doctors questions, and He was also asked questions by them; and they were astonished at the words of grace which came forth from His mouth. And many said, "God speaketh by "the mouth of this young man, and he shall be great "in favour with God and man."

And it came to pass when Jesus was about thirty years old, and before He had been baptized by John, that He wrought this miracle in the city of Nain. The son of the governor | of Nain was dead. Now when his father died he left him, being a little child, to his mother; and his mother brought him up to take his father's place;² now his father was of noble and distinguished family,³ and no man dared to sit in his place. And all the people of Nain were subject

---

¹ Literally, "she hung him".
² Literally, "to be in his father's place".
³ *B*, "Because of the greatness, and sovereignty of his father, "and his exalted family."

unto the widow whilst they were waiting for the boy to grow up and to sit in his father's place, and to take his father's dominion. And when the son was two-and-twenty years old his mother betrothed unto him a bride, but when she wished to make the marriage-feast for him, he fell sick. And his mother brought many physicians unto him to heal him, but they were not able to do so. And great sorrow reigned over the city of Nain, and over the dominions thereof, by reason of the [sickness of the] young man whom they expected to become their prince and governor; and, behold, the young man lay under the yoke of death. And both men and women were suffering more pain than his mother. Now Jesus, Who knoweth all mysteries, knew of him also, but He did not wish to heal him; for He desired to shew forth His power in him so that the children of men might see and might believe in Him. And when the young man was dead, his mother prepared for him a place in which to lie outside | the graveyard. And it came to pass that as they were carrying the bier of the young man, and were going forth from the gate of the city—now there were many people there from every district and city—Jesus said unto them, "Put down the bier "upon the ground."[1] Then He took the young man by his hand, and said unto him, "I say unto thee, O "young man that sleepest, arise, and wake up." Then he awoke and stood up, and Jesus took him by his hand and set him upon his feet, and gave him to

---

[1] *B* adds, "And I will bring him to life. And when they had "lifted the young man down from the bier, He took him," etc.

his mother who, together with all those who were looking on, worshipped Him. And in order that [the people] might not think that the matter was one of error, Jesus said unto them, "Bring me one hundred "loaves of bread,[1] and eat all of you, and rejoice ye "with great gladness." And nations and peoples gave praise unto Him, and said, "Jesus, the Son of Mary, "changeth grief into gladness." And Jesus went into the city of Nain with them, and He healed all those who were sick therein.

Then certain people went from Nain unto John at the river Jordan, | and they testified before him and said, "We have seen Jesus Who cried unto a dead "man in the graveyard and made him to live again; "and, behold, He is now with him eating and drinking." And John sent two of his disciples unto Jesus, and said unto Him, "Art thou he that should come, "or must we look for another?"[2] And Jesus answered and said unto the disciples of John, "Go ye and "tell John everything which ye have seen and heard;" and they went and told everything which Jesus had done in Nain.

And it came to pass that in the three hundred and thirty-fourth year of Alexander, on the sixth day of the latter Kânûn,[3] Jesus came unto John to be baptized by him. And with the eye[4] of the Spirit

Page 80

---

[1] Literally, "one hundred tables"; for ܪܒܐ read ܐܪܒܐ. *B* reads, "Bring ye a table of bread".

[2] *B* adds, "Now one of them was Stephen, the deacon and "martyr, and [the other was] Ananias (see Acts IX. 10; XXII. 12) "who baptized Paul".

[3] *I. e.*, January.

[4] *B*, "by the might of the Spirit".

John saw Jesus as He was coming, and the heavens and the earth were filled with light from the face of Jesus, like unto that which cometh from a star that appeareth in the day-time; and the eyes[1] of beings of flesh were not able to look upon the splendour of Jesus. And John was afraid, and he began to make supplication unto Jesus, saying, "Master, all creation seek-"eth pardon from Thee, and it entreateth for pity. "Yet how | is it that Thou dost ask baptism from "me?" And Jesus said unto him, "For this have I "been sent, and for this have I come; perform, then, "and complete, and fulfil the work for which I have "been sent." And when Jesus went down to the baptism, John saw that the heavens were opened unto Him, and that the Spirit came down upon Him in the form of a white dove; and the voice of the Father was heard from above, saying, "This is My beloved "Son in Whom I am well pleased, hear ye Him." And great fear fell upon those who were there; and Jesus went up from the water and commanded His disciples that they should be baptized.

And it came to pass that three days after His baptism there was a feast in Cana of Galilee; and they invited Jesus, and His disciples, and His mother thereto. And when the guests had taken their places at the feast, they were lacking wine. Now Mary was relying upon the power of Jesus, and she said unto Him, "My Son Jesus, they have no wine." And He said unto her, "Woman, what have I to do with thee? "My hour is not yet come." And Mary said unto those

---

[1] Read ܥܝܢܐ, with *B*.

SATAN TEMPTS JESUS.

who ministered [unto them], "Whatsoever He telleth
"you to do, that do." And Jesus commanded | the Page 82
servants to fill the water-pots with water, and they
filled them to the brim. And Jesus said, "Pour out
"the water and give the guests to drink." And they
began to do so, beginning with the governor of the
feast. And when the governor of the feast had tast-
ed it, he said unto the bridegroom, "Every man first
"of all bringeth forth the good wine, and when the
"guests have drunk deeply thereof he then bringeth
"forth that which is less good; but thou hast kept
"the good wine until the last." And the bridegroom
said unto him, "I do not know whence cometh this
"wine." Then the chief cup-bearer answered and said
unto the governor of the feast, "Verily the bride-
"groom knoweth not, but we know that this wine
"was water, and that Jesus, the Son of Mary, changed
it into wine." And everyone who was there glorified God. This is the first miracle which Jesus wrought
after His baptism.

And it came to pass that when eleven days of the
latter Kânûn had passed after the feast of Cana,
Jesus went into the wilderness to wage war with
Satan; and when He had fasted eleven days, Satan
came unto Him to tempt Him, and to make war with
Him by means of the desire for bread. And Satan
said unto Jesus, "Why | fastest Thou? And why art Page 83
"Thou hungry? Make these stones bread, and eat,
"even as Thou hast made water into wine." And
Jesus answered Satan, saying, "Man liveth not by
"bread alone, but by every word which cometh forth
"from the mouth of God." And Satan and his power

were put to shame, and Jesus was victorious in this first strife.

And when the beginning of the month Shĕbâṭ had come, that is to say, the middle of the fast, Satan came to tempt Jesus, and to wage war with Him by means of the lust for money. And he fashioned and made up phantasms, and said unto Jesus, "The whole "world, and all that therein is, hath been delivered "unto me, and I can deliver it over and give it unto "whomsoever I please; if Thou wilt fall down and "worship me, I will give it unto Thee." And Jesus said unto him, "It is written,[1] Thou shalt worship the "Lord thy God, and Him only shalt thou serve." Thus Satan and his hosts that were looking on were put to shame, for Jesus had vanquished them in two strifes.

And it came to pass that when Jesus had fasted twenty days of the latter Kânûn, and twenty days of the month Shĕbâṭ, He went up at the end of His fast to the pinnacle of the temple of Jerusalem. And Satan came, and stood below Him on the ground, and answered and said unto Jesus, | "Cast Thyself "hence upon the ground, for it is written, 'He shall "give his angels charge concerning thee, to bear thee up "upon their arms, lest thy foot stumble upon a stone'." And Jesus answered and said unto him, "Get thee "behind me, Satan, for it is written, 'Thou shalt not "tempt the Lord thy God'." And Satan and his hosts were put to shame, for Jesus had conquered them in three strifes.

---

[1] Deuteronomy VI. 13; St. Matthew IV. 10.

Now after His fast He made the daughter of Jairus to live, and then He chose disciples to go with Him. Then He began to do those miracles which are written in His Gospel; yet the disciples did not write all of them, but only those which they saw with their own eyes and heard of with their own ears.

And it came to pass in the three hundred and thirty-sixth year of Alexander, that the priests, and Pharisees, and Sadducees became envious of Him; and they set Him up before Pilate to be judged. Now Pilate was innocent of His blood, for he found neither blemish nor sin in Him. And he delivered Him unto them amid a great tumult of people who were all crying out, and bearing testimony against Him, saying, "He is guilty of death." Thus they received His blood upon themselves and upon their children. And on the thirtieth day of the month Âdâr, on the day of the eve of the Sabbath, at the ninth hour, they crucified Him upon a cross with thieves. And when the sun had set, Joseph went to Pilate and asked for the body of Jesus, and he swathed it with clothes | made of precious stuffs, and he embalmed Him with myrrh and aloes. Now the myrrh was that which the Magians of Persia had brought prophetically, and it had been laid up by Mary, His mother, in the vessel in which they had brought it until that hour. So Joseph, having swathed the body of Jesus, laid it in his own grave, which was in a new cave which had been dug in his own garden. And the priests, and Sadducees, and Pharisees went to Pilate and said unto him, "O our Lord, this [Man] Whom "we have crucified was worthy of death, and He was

"deserving of the death of the cross, for He preach-
"ed concerning Himself, saying, 'I am a king'. And
"He was also worthy of death because He abrogat-
"ed the law of Moses, (now thou thyself dost know
"that God spake with Moses), and because He made
"Himself out to be God, and because He was pro-
"claiming concerning Himself, saying, 'I am a king.'
"On thy behalf and on thy account we killed Him.
"And He was wont to say, when He was alive, to
"His disciples, 'In three days I will rise again from
"the dead'. And now, O our Lord the king, set watch-
"men over His grave. And as for Joseph who reared
"him, bind him in fetters and shut him up in prison
"until the next three days are passed, lest Joseph
"and His disciples go | by night and steal Him and
"say, 'He hath gone forth from the grave and hath
"risen from the dead'; and the last error shall be greater
"than the first." Then Pilate said, "I am innocent of
"the blood of Jesus, the Son of Mary;" and they
said, "His blood be upon us, and upon our children."
And Pilate said unto them, "Since ye take upon
"yourselves His blood, His judgment also is given
"unto you. Go ye and take good heed unto Him,
"even as ye know how." And they went forth from
Pilate, having been put to shame.

And they took companies of soldiers from Pilate,[1]
and they went and seized Joseph and cast him into
prison;[2] and they sealed[3] the grave and set seventy

---

[1] *B* reads, "And guards and soldiers went forth from Pilate,
"and they went and took him".   [2] *B*, "fetters".

[3] *B*, "And they bound him in prison by himself, and they shut
"the door of the prison and sealed it".

men as watchmen over it, and they wove a plot[1] to kill Joseph in prison, and to burn the body of Joseph with fire. But these men who had been put to shame did not know that they themselves were about to become witnesses of the resurrection of Jesus by reason of their own shame of face. And they gathered themselves together and made themselves into two companies, the one consisting of scribes and Pharisees, and the other of Sadducees and Jews; now the Jews and Sadducees were the guardians of the body of Jesus, and the scribes and Pharisees were the guardians of the house of Joseph. And it came to pass that when it was the fourth watch | of the night of the first day of the week, which is the first day of the month Nîsân, a great earthquake took place, and the angels came down, company after company, to the grave of Jesus, which they surrounded like the soldiers who stand round about a king to do him honour. And behold the archangel Gabriel descended like lightning from heaven, and the guardians of the grave became like dead men through fear. And when Jesus rose from the grave, the angels bowed the knee and worshipped Him because of the victory which had come through Him to all the children of men, and because of the vivification which He had wrought by His hand for all the race of Adam, and because of the renewal of the companies of the angels. And the guardians saw that Jesus had risen from the grave, and that the sealings and the marks of the seals were not destroyed.

Page 87

---
[1] B, "against Joseph, saying, 'Let us slay Joseph secretly, on "the morning of the first day of the week in prison'" etc.

And Jesus went to Joseph whilst those who were guarding Joseph were keeping their watch, and they saw that a great light had risen upon them. And they saw the prison in which Joseph had been bound lifted up into the air about fifteen cubits, both the building and the seals thereof; and they saw Joseph standing upon the upper ground in the light of the appearance of Jesus. Now the face of Jesus was like unto the sun. And the fetters of Joseph fell from him, and Jesus said unto him whilst all the guardians were listening, "Get "thee to thy house, O Joseph;" and with the end of the speech of Jesus, Joseph and Jesus were hidden from before the eyes of the guardians. And they found the house standing upon the ground again with its door and with the fastenings of the seals [unbroken]. And the guardians of Joseph marvelled, and they said unto each other, "Verily this Jesus is the Christ for "Whose coming all creation waiteth." And Jesus returned to the garden, and was walking about in the midst thereof.

Then the guardians answered and said unto each other, "Rise up, and let us go to the city. Why should "we watch an empty grave? Behold, He Whom we watch is walking about in the garden." And their companions said unto them, "Let us wait a little, and see "what will happen." And behold some women were coming: Mary the mother of Jesus, and Mary the mother of Cleophas, and Mary the sister of Lazarus, and Mary the wife of Joseph, and Pĕrôghîthâ, the sister of Mary, who is the mother of John the Less. And when Jesus saw them He went to meet them, and they thought that He was the gardener belonging to the garden, and said unto him, "Master, what have the "guardians done with Jesus?" And Jesus said unto them, "I, even I, am He, for I have risen from the "grave and from the dead, even as I said unto you "aforetime; but go ye and tell My brethren and My "disciples to go to Galilee, and there shall they see "Me." So the women went back with great joy to the disciples; and they rejoiced and were exceeding glad.

And it came to pass that, when the guardians of the grave saw Jesus and [heard] the things which He spake unto the women, they left the grave and went into the city, and they were marvelling and saying, "Verily Jesus, the Son of Mary, is the Christ for Whom "creation waiteth." And when the dawn of the first day of the week had come, the scribes, and the Pharisees, and the Sadducees, and the Jews gathered themselves together, and the priests came and said unto the Jews, "Where is the body of Jesus?" And they said unto them, "Behold, [He is] in Galilee." Then the Pharisees and the scribes said unto the guardians, "We know that ye have taken a bribe from "the disciples of Jesus, and that ye have given His "body unto them, and that ye now proclaim with them "that He hath risen when He hath not risen. But we "know what it is meet to do unto you; we will deliver "you over to the hands of the judge who will take "away from you with stripes and punishments the bribe which ye have taken." Now the guardians of the grave of Jesus were Jews and Sadducees, and they told the scribes and Pharisees [who were the guardians of Joseph], that they had heard that Joseph had escaped from prison. And the Jews and Sadducees said unto

Page 89

the scribes and Pharisees, "Deliver over to us Joseph "whom we delivered over to you, that we may give "to you the body of Jesus, which | ye gave to us." And the scribes and Pharisees said, "Behold, Joseph "is in Ramah." And the Jews and Sadducees said, "Behold, Jesus is in Galilee." Then the Sadducees said unto the Pharisees, though they were not wishful so to do, "Ye say unto us that we have taken a bribe, "and that we have given away the body of Jesus; "but who hath removed from you Joseph, whom we "delivered over unto you? Give us the man whom "we delivered over unto you alive, and come and "take the dead and crucified body which ye gave unto "us." And the scribes said, though they were not wishful so to do, "O men and brethren, Joseph, whom "ye delivered over unto us, hath the dead Jesus, "[Whom] we received from your hands, taken out of "our hands." And the Sadducees said, "Now is certain "unto us that which we ourselves have said, 'Jesus "hath risen from the dead';" thus they themselves proclaimed concerning the resurrection of Jesus, and they became true witnesses through their own untrustworthiness. And strife and a great tumult broke out among them, and they fought one against the other. And when the priests saw the great tumult which had broken out among them, they made the bands of men on both sides to keep the peace. And they cried unto the guardians of the grave and the guardians of Joseph, and said unto them, "Know ye "what | ye are testifying against yourselves? Ye have "taken the Man, and ye have borne witness against Him that He was guilty of death; and ye have taken

"upon yourselves and upon your children His blood.
"And behold, ye have made yourselves guilty, and
"ye have made yourselves participators in innocent
"blood; and the government will seize you and will
"pillage your houses." And the Pharisees and Sadducees said, "What shall we do unto you? Ye say
"unto us, 'Ye have taken a bribe', but we have not
"taken a bribe, and we are not conscious of having
"done anything wrong; and ye do us harm. And we
"have told you the whole truth, even as it happen-
"ed." Then the priests said unto them, "Be ye silent
"now, and hold your peace about this matter, and
"take ye a bribe, and say ye unto every man, 'The
"'disciples of Jesus stole Him by night whilst we
"'were asleep'. And if this report be heard in the
"governor's presence we will persuade him that the
"matter was so, and to you will we cause no injury
"whatsoever." And so the priests spread abroad this
rumour among the Jews until this day.

Now the eleven disciples went to Galilee where
Jesus had appointed to meet them, and they saw Him,
and rejoiced exceedingly at the sight of Him, both
themselves and the women who had become His disciples, during the whole of the first day of the week.
And on the morning | of the second day of the week
they returned to the upper chamber in Jerusalem,[1]
where they had been from the first, even as Jesus
had commanded them; and Mary and those who believed on Christ were constant in prayer in the cave

---

[1] B, "They went back to Jerusalem through the operation of
"the Holy Spirit."

of the tomb of Jesus. And Jesus appeared unto the disciples in the upper chamber, the doors thereof being closed. And on the first day of the week which was after the Resurrection He appeared unto two disciples as they were going along the road; and He caused them to be certain[1] concerning His resurrection, and also Thomas by the touching of His side. And He used to visit His disciples continually, and He made them to be certain about Him, and He consoled them by the sight of Himself until the end of forty days.

And it came to pass on the fifth day of the week, on the tenth day of the month Îyâr, that He invited the disciples, and the women who had become His disciples, and sent them to the Mount of Olives, where He gave them spiritual commandments, and [ordered them] to remain in the upper chamber in Jerusalem for ten days, until they received the Holy Spirit; then were they to go forth and preach His Gospel among all nations. And whilst they were looking on, He separated himself from them, and ascended into heaven, and a cloud received Him and He was hidden from their eyes. And they went back [to Jerusalem being sorrowful, and they were weeping because He had been separated from them; and they remained ten | days in the upper chamber in Jerusalem. And it came to pass on the twentieth day of the month Îyâr, on the morning of the first day of the week, that the Spirit Pârâklîṭâ[2] descended upon

---

[1] Read ܀܀܀܀, and ܀܀܀܀ in note 8.
[2] "The Comforter, *which is* the Holy Ghost"; see St. John XIV. 26.

THE PLOT TO KILL MARY. 97

the disciples.[1] And the Apostles went forth to the four quarters of the earth and preached His Gospel.

And Mary[2] remained in Jerusalem, and she was constant in prayer in the cave in the grave of Jesus; and multitudes of women used to go about with her, and many sick folk were healed there.[3] Now when the unbelieving Jews saw that the Messiah had risen from the dead, and that He had ascended into heaven, and that He had sent the gift of the Spirit unto His disciples, and that they were preaching His Gospel unto the Nation[4] and unto the Gentiles, and that honour was being paid unto Mary, they became mad and inflamed with envy. And they gave a bribe to the judge, and they set watchmen over the cave of the grave of Jesus, so that the children of men might not go and pray there; and against the cave they heaped up many stones, and they closed it carefully. And they made crafty plans to kill Mary,[5] the mother of our Lord. And they commanded the watchmen who were keeping guard there that if Mary came to pray, one of their number was to come and inform them.

And it came to pass that when the eve of the Sabbath[6] had come, Mary went and offered up in-

---

[1] *B* adds, "and they received the gift, and they enriched many, "and many believed in our Lord." On that day, etc.

[2] See Tischendorf, *Johannis Liber de Dormitione Mariae*, Leipzig, 1866.

[3] *B* adds, "Mary was honoured by every man".

[4] *I. e.*, the Hebrew nation.

[5] *B* adds, "and to burn her with fire". In note 12 to the Syriac text for "omits" read "adds".

[6] Gr. Μιᾷ δὲ τῶν ἡμερῶν, παρασκευῆς οὔσης.

cense,[1] and prayed, and she saw that the sweet sme
ascended | into heaven, and that it went in throug
the door thereof. And behold the Watcher Gabrie
came down to her, and said unto her, "Peace b
"unto thee, O thou who art blessed among womer
"Thy prayer hath been received before God an
"thou thyself art blessed because thou art prepare
"to depart from this world unto never-ending life. A
"the very moment in which thou prayest upon th
"earth thou art answered in heaven; and every thin
"which thou askest shall be given unto thee." No
the women that were with Mary heard the voice o
the angel, but they did not see him. Then Mary re
turned from the grave in great joy, and she wa
greatly honoured by the women who were waitin
to see her on every side, and they were salutin
Mary's garments, and they were bowing down i
homage to her, and were kissing her feet; and th
women related in Jerusalem every thing which the ange
had spoken unto Mary.

Then the watchmen went unto the chief priests, an
said unto them, "Mary hath been with other women
"and hath prayed at the grave." And the chief priest
went to the governor, and gave him a bribe, and the
sent out heralds through all Jerusalem, saying, "Who
"soever shall pray at the grave of Jesus, whether i
"be man or | whether it be woman, his blood be upo
"his own head, and his death shall be[2] by stoning
"with stones." And they set watchmen over Mary

---

[1] Literally, "laid incense"; *B* adds, "on the fire".
[2] Read ܪܳܓܡܺܝܢ.

so that if they found her nigh unto the grave of Jesus they might stone her with stones. But Mary knew the guile of the Jews, and she left Jerusalem, and went to her house in Bethlehem; and the virgins who were the daughters of princes and nobles, and who ministered unto her, went with her. And one of these was the daughter[1] of Nicodemus[2] who became a disciple of Jesus; and [another was] Neshrî[3] the daughter of Gamaliel,[4] the chief of the synagogue, at whose feet Paul was brought up; and [another was] Ṭabîthâ, the daughter of Ḳômnîṭôs the Greek, the kinsman of Arbôlôs the king, who was of the family of the wicked Nero; and there were many other women with Mary whose names have not been written down. And they went about with Mary, saying, "We "will not separate from thee, O Mary, blessed mother, "except through death." And they used to say unto her, "How couldst thou conceive, and bring forth, "without union with man?" And they used to talk about the history of Jesus all day and all night long, and upon Him they used to meditate.

Now the believing folk who remained in Jerusalem were wont to give a bribe to the watchmen, and they used to go secretly and pray | at the grave of Jesus; and multitudes of sick people were healed there. And when the unbelieving Jews saw that mighty works were being wrought there, they gathered themselves together and made a plot. And they went and

---
[1] *B* has "daughter-in-law" (ܟܠܬܗ).
[2] See St. John III. 1; VII. 50; XIX. 39.
[3] Added from *B*.
[4] See Acts XXII. 3.

took the three crosses, and the nails, and the spear and the reed on which they gave Him the sponge of vinegar, and the crown of thorns which they had woven for Jesus, and they dug a hole in the ground and buried them in it. And they said, "Here are "buried the Book of Moses, and the box of manna, "and the rod of Aaron, and the mantle of Elijah;" and people went to the grave and took away some of the dust which was there, and all such as had diseases were healed. And when the unbelieving Jews saw that mighty works were being wrought at this place, they set watchmen who were not to let the people pray there, nor to take away dust from the place unless they each would confess and say, "I "have received healing through the Book of Moses, "and through the box of manna, and through the rod "of Aaron, and through the mantle of Elijah."

And it came to pass that after these things Abgar, the king of Edessa, heard of what the Jews had done unto Jesus, and he wished to go up against Jerusalem, and to destroy it, and to kill the children of Israel. And he meditated and wrote a letter[1] to Sabinus, | the prefect of the Emperor Tiberius, and he wrote therein, saying, "Abgar, the son of Mânî, the "king of Edessa, to thy Majesty the Emperor Tibe-"rius, greeting! Thou art the Emperor, and thou hast "dominion over Jerusalem. I entreat thee, therefore, "to pass sentence of punishment, and to take ven-"geance upon the Jews, the children of Jerusalem,

---

[1] See Abgar's letter and the answer of Tiberius Caesar printed in Phillips, *The Doctrine of Addai*, pp. 36, 37.

"because they have slain Jesus the Messiah, Who "was guilty of no offence and Who had done no- "thing wrong. On the contrary, He was a righteous "Man, and He raised the dead, and He opened the "eyes of the blind, and He cleansed the lepers, and "He did that which was good unto all the children "of men. But the Jews gathered themselves together, "and without the command of thy Majesty condemned "Him to death in their envy, and they crucified the "Man." And when Sabinus had read the letter which Abgar had sent him, he was exceedingly angry within himself, and he wished to go up against Jerusalem, and to destroy it with the edge of the sword, and to kill all the children of Israel. Then the Jews that were in Jerusalem heard of this, and they were afraid of him with an exceedingly great fear, and they collected rich and costly presents, and very many gifts, and they sent certain of the priests, and certain of | the Pharisees, with them unto him. And they wrote unto him, and sent letters, saying, "O lord "our Emperor, we waged war against this Jesus, and "we contended with Him on behalf of thee, and on "behalf of thy Majesty, because He used to pro- "claim concerning Himself, saying, 'I shall be king,' "and because He disturbed thy kingdom." And by this means and by the great gifts which they sent they quieted his impulse to go up against Jerusalem.

And it came to pass that the Apostles had gone into the four quarters of the world, but Mary remained in Jerusalem, mourning because of her separation from our Lord, and because of the remoteness of the Apostles from her and from the place where she was.

And she prayed unto God, and she put incense on the fire, and she lifted up her eyes, and she spread out her hands towards heaven, and said, "O Christ, "the Son of the Living God, hearken unto the prayer "of Thine handmaiden, and send unto me John the "Less, and the Apostles his companions, so that I "may see them and may be consoled by the sight "of them before the day of my departure; and I "will give thanks and worship Thy goodness."[1] And "straightway it was revealed unto the Apostles by "the holy Spirit, even unto each one of them in the "place wherein he was, that the mother of our Lord "was about to depart from this world to the life "which never endeth. And the | Holy Spirit made "known to them all in a revelation that on the morn- "ing of the morrow they should all be gathered to- "gether unto Mary.[2]

---

[1] See the passage in Tischendorf, *Liber de Dormitione Mariae*, p. 97, beginning κύριέ μου Ἰησοῦ Χριστέ, ὁ καταξιώσας διὰ τὴν ἄκραν ἀγαθότητά σου ἐξ ἐμοῦ τεχθῆναι, κ. τ. λ.

[2] For the text from p. 99, l. 2 to p. 107, l. 20, *B* has as the variant the following:—"And they came unto her, at the time of "dawn, each one of them from his country, by the operation of "the Holy Spirit, and they saluted Mary and did homage unto her, "and they saluted each other. Now when she saw them she did "homage and gave thanks unto our Lord. And she said unto "them, 'How have ye been received in this world?' And the Apostles "said unto her, 'We have been received wheresoever we have "'gone. Fear not, O blessed Mother, for the King Christ, Who "'sprang from thee, shall guard thee; and He shall take thee out "'from this world with great glory, and shall give thee happiness "'in the mansions of His kingdom.' And Mary said, 'I give thanks "'unto my Son Jesus for all the good things which He hath done "'for me, and still doeth.' Then the Apostles made known to Mary "concerning their coming unto her, which took place by the oper-

And it came to pass that in the morning the blessed woman Mary laid incense upon the fire, and she prayed and said, "O my Lord, behold the people of "the Jews wish to burn the body of Thine hand- "maiden, but fulfil not for them their desire; but my "desire for the coming of John the Less and of the "Apostles, his companions, do Thou fulfil." And as soon as her prayer was ended, the Holy Spirit revealed her wish unto John the Less whilst he was preaching in Ephesus; now many people were gathered together round about him. And straightway the Spirit urged him, and said unto him, "To-day | is "the last day of the mother of thy Lord upon earth, "and she is now about to depart from this world "unto everlasting rest, and she desireth earnestly to "see thee; arise, then, and go speedily, and see her "before she goeth out of the world." And it came to pass that whilst the Spirit was speaking unto him, he was seized bodily by the power of Christ, and with exceedingly great quickness and in the twinkling of an eye he found himself in the presence of the blessed woman. And when he saw her lying upon her death-bed he was sorrowful, and he saluted her, and he did homage before her in faith. And the blessed woman rejoiced exceedingly at his coming, and she said unto him, "O John, the hour hasten- "eth, and there is no opportunity for talking. Rise "up, make ready the censer, and put incense therein,

Page 100

"ation of the Holy Spirit. And she rejoiced at the sight of them, "and was comforted, and gave thanks unto our Lord; and the "Apostles gave thanks unto our Lord because He had gladdened "them by the sight of the blessed woman."

"for I am desiring to see all thy companions at the "same time as I see thee." Then the blessed woman straightened herself in her bed, and sat up, and she and John prayed together. And it came to pass as they were praying, that immediately the sweet smell of their censers had ascended, in that same moment the Holy Spirit made known [concerning the departure of Mary] unto all the Apostles, unto each one in the country wherein he was, the living in the places where they were, and the dead in their graves. And the Spirit made known unto each one of them in his country, saying, "The mother of thy Lord departeth "this day from this world. Arise, go, salute her, and "see her, and be blessed by her holiness." And as soon as the Spirit had revealed the matter unto each one of them, immediately he appeared in the presence of the holy woman.

Simon Peter, the chief of the Apostles, was teaching in Rome, where many people had been turned to the faith of God by his hand. And on the day when he was ending his discourse (now it was the time when he was about to break the Eucharist, when much people were gathered together to be blessed by him, and when he himself was offering the Offering, and at the time of the offering of the Offering, whilst he was kneeling before the altar,) the Holy Spirit revealed the matter unto him and said, "Leave thy "Offering in the hands | of those who shall complete "it, and arise, go, and salute the mother of thy Lord, "for this day she departeth from this world." And whilst the words were in the mouth of the Spirit, Simon Peter found himself in the presence of the blessed woman.

And Paul, the Apostle, the teacher of the Gentiles, after he had taught in various cities, and had turned many people unto Christ, went down to the city of Tiberias; and he preached unto and taught all the people that were therein. And on that day he was oppressed in his speech, and whilst he was among the congregation his mind was perturbed, and it was revealed unto him in a revelation, saying, "The mother "of thy Lord is about to depart this day from this "earthly life unto the life and happiness which are "everlasting." And when as yet the words of the Spirit were not ended, he found himself seized by the might of the Spirit, and carried away to the upper chamber where the blessed woman was lying.

And the apostle Thomas, after he had taught the Indians, and the Chinese, and the Cushites, and [the people of] all the islands near and far, having crossed the sea in his [journeys to] preach, was one day preaching in India, when the Spirit revealed Himself in his heart, saying, "O Thomas, rise up, and go unto "Jerusalem, and see the Virgin before she departeth "from the world; and tarry not overmuch, for the "distance is great". And whilst he was thinking upon this thing, straightway he found himself standing before the holy woman.

And Matthew, one of the Evangelists, after having preached the Gospel of the glad tidings of Jesus in Judea, and in all the country of Palestine, was minded to go and preach unto the other islands. And it came to pass that whilst he was travelling[1] on the

---

[1] For ܟܝ read ܟܝ.

sea in a ship, and was among the waves of the sea the Holy Spirit made known unto him concerning the approaching death of the lady of peace; and from the midst of the ship the Spirit seized him and brought him unto the Virgin.

And whilst Bartholomew was teaching in the city of Thebes,[1] the Spirit told him concerning the departure of the excellent woman; and he rose up quickly, and by the power of the Holy Spirit he was transported into Jerusalem unto the holy woman.

And James | the blessed Apostle, who was surnamed the brother of our Lord, was in Jerusalem. And whilst he was standing at his ministrations, the Spirit said unto him, "Go forth, and get thee gone "to Bethlehem, for the mother of our Redeemer shall "this day depart from the world; go thou, and be "blessed by her." And he went forth and departed, without having finished his ministrations, unto Bethlehem, and he saw the blessed woman.

O my brethren, that the Apostles who were alive, and who were gathered together by the might of our Lord, and who came, each one from the country wherein he was, in a moment, is indeed a most wonderful and marvellous thing, and one which the tongue cannot possibly tell. But it is a much more marvellous thing how the Apostles who had departed this life, and were dead and buried in their graves were brought to life in one moment; and how they were turned into living beings again; and how their bodies

---

[1] This name is probably a mistake; see my *Book of the Bee*, p. 106, note 3.

were renewed; and how they cast off the dust into which they had turned; and how they were changed from beings of corruption into beings of incorruption; and how they rose up, and went forth from their graves without thinking in their minds and saying, "What can this thing be?" For they did not meditate in their minds, saying, "What is this matter? And "for what reason are we removed from our graves?" Now, according to my opinion, they considered this removal to be the Resurrection, and they imagined that it was the quickening of the dead. But the Power which quickened them made them to understand that they must not delay, and that they must not imagine that the movement was the quickening of the dead, and that they must not think that it was the Resurrection. For it said unto them, "Ye have "come to life that ye may hear this message, 'The "'mother of your Lord is about to go forth from the "'world this day; rise up, and go forth out of your "'graves'." And as soon as they heard the word, the Spirit of the Lord seized them and bore them to the blessed Woman, and they were blessed by her.

First of all unto Philip was it said in the grave, "O Philip, rise up from among the dead, for the "mother of thy Lord looketh [for thee];" and the Spirit like a bird took him, and bore him away unto the blessed woman, and set him down by her side.

And Simon the Canaanite was dead also, but unto him likewise in the grave did the Spirit say, "The "mother of thy Lord expecteth thee; rise up, depart, and be blessed by her." And straightway he found himself by the side of the blessed woman.

And Luke, the Apostle, one of the Evangelists, who had taught in Alexandria had been slain there because of his preaching, and therein had his body been buried. And as he was lying in the grave, the Divine Power quickened him, and said unto him, "This day will the mother of thy Lord de-"part this life;" and whilst he was marvelling within himself, the nod of his Lord seized him, and carried him away and set him by the side of the couch of his Lady.

Andrew, the brother of the blessed Peter, died in Byzantium,[1] and being in the grave the Spirit quickened him, and took him to the holy woman.

Mark, the son of Simon Peter, had built a church in the city of Anzianzu, and having died his body was laid in it. And, though dead, he felt the motion of life, and the Spirit quickened him, and took him with power, and made him to come unto the place where the blessed and holy woman was.

Thus the living went forth from the places wherein they were, and the dead arose from out of their graves, and in one moment they were all gathered together; then straightway a chariot of light was yoked beneath them all, and by the might of the Spirit it bore them from afar off to the Virgin without labour and without weariness. And a cloud of light yoked itself unto the chariot beneath them, and they all sat thereon; and a pillar of light went before them. And the Archangel Gabriel ran before them, and Michael leaped before them and made smooth their

---

[1] Literally, "in this Byzantium".

way; and David the king went before the Apostles of the blessed One, holding his harp and singing psalms, until they arrived at the upper chamber in which the Lady Mary was reclining.

And it came to pass that when the Apostles arrived at the upper chamber, they did homage before her, the mother of their Lord. And they saluted their Lady, and they embraced her, and they kissed her, and they shewed love unto the blessed woman because they saw her still alive. And the blessed woman Mary straightened herself, and sat up on her couch, and rejoiced with an exceedingly | great joy Page 104
by reason of the coming of the Apostles. And she said unto them, "Come in peace, O ye Apostles of "Christ, come in peace, O ye servants of the High-"est; our heart is to you, O ye chosen ones of the "Blessed One! How have ye fared in the world? "How have ye taught? How have ye preached? How "have ye made disciples? Have ye brought the Gen-"tiles nigh unto your Lord? Have ye turned all the "people of the world into members of the household "of Christ?" And the Apostles said unto the blessed woman, "By the help of thy Son, and by the might "of thy prayer we have fared well. And we have "made disciples and baptized many; and we have "brought the world to the belief of our Lord, and "we have preached His Name in the four quarters "of the earth. There remain neither kings nor gover-"nors whom we have not brought under the yoke of "Christ; behold, His Name is preached and praised "from one end of the earth even unto the other." And when the blessed woman heard these things

she gave thanks unto the Lord, and blessed the Apostles.

Then the Lady Mary commanded John, and said unto him, "Put incense [on the fire], for, behold, all "creation is about to arrive." And it came to pass that when John had put incense [on the fire], and whilst the Apostles were standing up, behold the mother of the holy woman Mary entered, and bowed the knee, and did homage unto her, and saluted her. And after a little while Elizabeth also entered, and saluted her and sat down; and afterwards Anna the prophetess entered also. And then there arrived at the door of the upper chamber the chariot of the Patriarchs, and our father Adam alighted therefrom, and entered in and did homage to the holy woman Mary. And after him there came Seth, and he knelt upon his knees before her; and then Noah and Shem did homage unto her.

And next there came the chariot of the true believers, with Abraham the righteous man, and Isaac his son, and Jacob the true believer. And then there entered in the Heart of God, the prophet David, the good king, with his harp in his hand; and he did homage before the blessed woman, and he sat down to sing psalms in her honour and to celebrate her glory. And they all said unto her, "Peace be unto "thee, O blessed woman;" and they did homage before her with reverence, | and they bowed their heads before her, and were blessed by her.

And next there came a chariot which travelled along in a mass of fire, and the wheels thereof were of fire, and in it were seated all the prophets who had prophesied concerning the coming of Christ; and they, too, went into the chamber and saluted Mary.

And next there came a chariot which was one blaze of light, and in it there sat the martyrs who had been slain for the hope of the kingdom; and they entered into the chamber, and did homage before the glorious Virgin.

And next there came the chariot of the Cherubim and of the Seraphim, and they did homage before her; there remained upon earth not a single righteous man, living or dead, who did not come to do honour to her departure; and there was not a spirit in heaven that tarried in coming to accompany her with honour.

And after a little time the holy woman said unto John and unto all the Apostles, "Burn incense, and "go forth to meet your Lord, for, behold, He com- "eth". Then straightway were the heavens shaken, and the doors of the firmament were opened wide, and the earth reeled by reason of its quaking, and the hosts of heaven went forth through the gate of the firmament, glorifying the name of their King; and they were carrying trumpets, and they were singing psalms sweetly, and were praising His glory. And they were drawn up in companies, and the various squadrons of angels were ready to accompany their Lord as He went forth. Then suddenly thousands and tens of thousands of spiritual beings ran and took up their positions like pillars round about the upper chamber, and there came down from above an ark of fire and flame which overshadowed the blessed woman. And next there appeared the glorious chariot which bore within it Enoch, and Elijah, and Moses;

and they came in and did homage unto the holy woman, and then they went forth to await their Lord. And next there appeared twelve legions of angels holding trumpets in their hands, and they blew blasts upon the horns, and they sounded their trumpets loudly. And it came to pass that at the blast of the horns and trumpets our Lord Christ revealed Himself, and He was arrayed in a garment of glory, and He bore | in His hands the emblem of the Cross. And all creation shone by reason of His splendour, and all created things ran to salute Him; and they all did homage before His chariot which was brilliant with fire and with flame. And they all surrounded the chariot with shouts and with acclamations; and the chariot descended and alighted by the side of the place where the blessed woman was. And when the holy woman saw Him, she recovered her strength, and stood up, and blessed Him, and did homage unto Him. And our Lord cried unto His mother in that hour, and said unto her, "Mary!" And she made answer unto Him, saying, "This is too great for me, "O my Lord and Teacher. But I have greatly longed to see Thee." And He said unto her, "Behold "[Me]." And when she had looked and had seen Him, her soul rejoiced, for she saw upon Him glory and goodness which the mouth and tongue [of man] cannot describe. Then our Lord spake unto her in a sweet and gentle voice, saying, "O My mother, I "am about to make thee to depart unto Paradise, "until I come at the last day, wherein I shall dis-"solve the heavens, and shall make the earth to pass "away, and wherein I shall bestow good things upon

My chosen ones, and inflict punishment upon the wicked. On that day will I make thee to ascend into Me in My kingdom."

And it came to pass that when Mary heard these things from her Son, she said unto him, "O my beloved Lord, stretch out Thine hand and lay it upon my eyes;" and He stretched out His right hand and laid it upon her eyes. And she began to make entreaty and to say unto Him, "O my Son, make Thou the memorial of Thine handmaiden[1] to be remembered even unto the end of the world. Receive, O my Lord, the prayers and supplications of all who call upon me in faith, and put Thou away from them times of stress, and calamities, and punishments, and famines, and afflictions, and plagues of every kind. And upon all such as shall celebrate the commemoration of me, or who set apart for me an offering, let not the punishment of pestilence fall, and let not sickness have dominion over their bodies. And whenever those who believe in me shall have desire for the house which shall be built in my name, and shall make mention of me in their prayers, put Thou away from them evil hap, and trials, and severe sufferings. And upon the possessions of him that shall set apart and shall give unto me an abundant gift of that which belongeth unto him, let a blessing rest, and let not the locust, and the insect which layeth waste, appear in his fields | at any time, and let not cold injure his vineyard and his crops. And unto every one who, being in affliction, shall call

Page 107

---

[1] Read ܡܕܘܟܪܢܐ.

"upon my name, O Lord Christ, do Thou be unto
"him a helper. And whosoever, having been seized
"with sickness, shall make mention of my name, and
"shall take refuge in me, heal Thou him, O my Lord
"in Thy mercy. And increase Thou the substance o
"the rich men who shall honour me with their riches
"and bless Thou everything which they shall have
"And of the poor who shall take refuge in my prayer
"fill Thou to overflowing the barns with grain, and do
"Thou satisfy their hunger, and make Thou their stores
"of food to be abundant. And let those who set ou
"on their journeys to travel by land, and who call upon
"my name, be delivered from thieves; and let those
"who travel on the sea in ships be saved from storms
"And unto the women who have been long barren, and
"who wish to become the mothers of children, and who
"call upon my name, O my Lord and my Son, grant
"unto them the power to bring forth children and to
"rear sons and daughters. And visit Thou the earth
"with blessings, with fertile vineyards, and with abun-
"dant crops, and with good things; and let peace reign
"in all the inhabited world for ever and for ever!"

And our Lord answered and said unto her, "O
"My mother, whatsoever thou hast asked of Me I
"will do, and I will also fulfill the petitions of any
"one who shall call upon thee and shall take refuge
"in thee, henceforth and for ever." And it came to
pass that when my Lady Mary heard these things
she laid her hands upon her breast, and delivered
her soul unto her Son; and straightway He took it up
with Him to the mansions of light. And the chariots
were lifted up, and there was a great quietness, and

he odour of sweet scents breathed from the upper
hamber in which Mary was lying.

And it came to pass when the Jews saw that many
iighty deeds were wrought on the day of the de-
arture of Mary from the world (now at the very
ioment in which the blessed woman died all those
;ho were in affliction had relief, and those who were
ick were eased from their pains and were healed
traightway), and that they could do no harm unto
ne body of the holy woman, and that works of help-
ilness were flowing from the Cross and from the nails
f our Lord out of the place wherein they were, | they
esired to hide them from the children of men so
hat they might not be benefited by them.[1] Then the
elieving men who were in Jerusalem, and who were
bout fifty in number, went in to the judge of the
ity, and they related unto him concerning the truth
f Jesus and the wicked acts of the Jews. And the
idge sent by night for the chiefs of the Jews, and
e smote them severely with blows, and admonished
iem that no man should do harm unto the Christians.
Jow the judge had an only son who was sick, and
ie physicians of Jerusalem were not able to heal
im; and the judge said unto the believers, "I entreat
you to pray for my sick son." And they said unto
im, "Carry him to Bethlehem to Mary and the Apostles,

Page 108

---

[1] *B* reads, "But when the Jews saw that the name of Jesus
was honoured, and was exalted among all the nations, and that
benefits were flowing from the spot where the crosses were buried,
and the multitudes which believed on our Lord Jesus Christ, they
wished to hide the crosses from the children of men so that they
might not be benefited by them."

"that they may lay their hand[s] upon him, and h
"shall be healed." Then the judge and his son ros
up and they went to Bethlehem to Mary. And th
judge said unto her, "Peace be unto thee, O tho
"who art full of grace! And peace be unto the Frui
"of thy womb! The tongue and the mouth | of flesl
"are too weak to describe the glories of thy belove
"Son." Then the governor turned round and sav
the Apostles sitting before the blessed woman, an
he said unto them, "Peace be unto you, O ye Apostle
"of the Blessed One, and peace be unto your Maste
"Who hath chosen you for His preaching!" And th
Apostles said unto the governor, "And peace be unt
"thee, and our Lord be with thee! We have hear
"of all that thou hast done unto the Jews. And be
"hold, for five years have we been preaching th
"Gospel of Jesus among all nations, and they hav
"turned from [their] error; but the nation of unbe
"lieving Jews hath not turned from their wickedness
"And this day we are gathered together, as tho
"seest, unto this blessed Mother by the might of th
"Holy Spirit. And there is here one whose countr
"is distant a journey of one year, and there is anothe
"whose country is distant a journey of five months, an
"yet in one night we have been gathered together t
"the Mother of our Redeemer, that we might see he
"and be blessed by her. And behold, she is about t
"depart from the world, and it is meet for us to follov
"in her train and to honour her with psalms of th
"Holy Spirit. It is meet that her holy body | should b
"praised both by the children of men and by angels
"for in it dwelleth the Holy Spirit."

And it came to pass that when the Apostles had said these things unto the governor, he did homage unto them, and he entreated from them the healing of his son; and the Apostles brought his son nigh unto the blessed woman Mary, and she stretched out as it were the similitude of her right hand,[1] and stroked him, and he became as if he had never been ill at any time. And the governor marvelled, and glorified God by reason of all the things which his eyes had seen; and he went back to Jerusalem and narrated unto his companions every thing which he had seen. And a few days later he went up to Rome to Caesar the Emperor, and he related to the Emperor and to his nobles concerning the wickedness of the Jews, and concerning the mighty deeds which the blessed Lady Mary, the Mother of Christ, had wrought, and concerning the coming of the Apostles unto her. And the believers who were in Rome wrote down these triumphs and sent them into the four quarters of the world.

Now our Lady Mary departed | from this temporary life in the three hundred and forty-second year of Alexander.[2] She was fourteen[3] years old when she was frightened by the appearance of the angel, and she was with Christ for thirty[4] and three years, and

Page 111

---

[1] *B* reads, "And she stretched out her right hand, and laid it "upon him and said, 'Our Lord Jesus Christ shall heal thee' (read "ܡܐܣܐ); and as she laid her hand upon him the boy was made "whole, and he became as one who had never been sick."

[2] *I. e.*, A. D. 30. *B* reads, "three hundred and ninety-fourth "year of Alexander".

[3] *B*, "she was thirty years old", etc. In note 3 for ܒܗ read ܕܗܝ.

[4] The word ܡܕܡ is omitted from *B*.

she lived five[1] years after the crucifixion; which years are in all fifty-two.'

And it came to pass that the Apostles came through the Holy Spirit (now they had been made wise by the Spirit), and they said unto one another, "Come, "let us make a distinction between the burial of those "who believe, and of those who do not believe, and "between those who have received the sign of bap- "tism and the heathen and the Magians [and the "Jews],[3] and let us stablish canons of distinction; "and let us make a beginning with this holy body "of Mary, the fountain of life." Then they wrapped in linen the body of Mary for burial, and laid her upon a bier, and they began to sing the service of hymns of the Holy Spirit, even as the Spirit taught them; and the sound of their voices was like unto the voices of the angels[4] who were teaching them. And they took Mary to carry her and to bury her in the cave of the Mount of Olives, | and a multitude of women from Bethlehem and from Jerusalem were following in her train, and were wishing to see where they were going to lay her, so that they might go and pray there.

Now when the Jews saw the service, and the great procession, the like of which had never before been seen, they were ashamed, and they became mad with

---

[1] In *B*, "fifty-five years".

[2] In *B*, "one hundred and twenty-one years", *i. e.*, 30+33+58 years.

[3] The words in brackets are from *B*.

[4] *B*, "and the voices of angels were heard among those of the "holy Apostles".

envy. And they went unto the governor of the city, and said unto him, "My Lord, we know that these "Christian people have gone after error, but to-day "their mother who bore for them the Error hath died, "and behold, they are accompanying her to the grave "with great honour; but now, take thou whatever is "convenient, and rid us of them." Then the governor, having taken the bribe, took no further concern for the Christians. And the governor had a certain soldier of huge size and strength, and the Jews gave him a bribe to go with them, so that when the Christians saw him they might say that they had come from the governor, and that no man might say a word against them.[1] Now the shameful Jews had made a crafty and secret plot concerning the body of Mary, which they wished to burn with fire, and they wished to make an attack upon the bier of Mary. And they said unto Yôphanâ,[2] the soldier whom they had brought with them from the governor, "Do thou lay "hold upon the bier of Mary, whilst we carry off | "her body." Page 113

And it came to pass that, when the Apostles saw that Yôphanâ had come with them, they perceived the craft of the Jews. And the Jews said unto Yôphanâ, "Draw nigh,[3] and breathe only upon Mary, and she

---

[1] *I. e.*, the Jews bribed the chief soldier of the governor of the city to go with them, so that the Christians and other folk might imagine that the Jews had the sanction of the governor for anything they might do.

[2] In the Greek he is described as Εβραῖος τις ὀνόματι Ἰεφωνίας γενναῖος τῷ σώματι (Tischendorf, *Liber de Dormitione Mariae*, p. 110).

[3] For ܒܩܪܒ read ܩܪܒ.

"shall fall from her bier, for, behold, the disciple
"of that Deceiver think that they have conquered
"Jerusalem." Then Yôphanâ drew nigh, and threw
out his two arms upon the two poles of the bier
and he hung his weight upon them, so that the bie
might be broken, and the body of Mary might fal
therefrom, and the Jews might seize it and carry i
away and burn it with fire. Then John the Less turn
ed, and he made the sign of the cross over Yôphanâ
and the angel of the Lord smote him, and his limb;
became weak and powerless. And he shrieked witl
pain, and cried out and said, "O Christ, the Son o
"God, have mercy upon me! For the Jews who cru
"cified Thee have made me to err, and so I came
"to make an attack upon her who bore Thee. Bu
"give Thou me strength in my members, so that I may
"slay the Jews." Then Simon Peter turned, and made
over him the sign of the cross, and his strength re
turned unto him. And he leaped up, and stood upor
his feet, and drew his sword upon the Jews, and they
were not able to stand against the power of his might
and they fled before him. And they entered into the
city, and came unto the governor, and said unto him
"My Lord, | Yôphanâ hath gone over to the Christ
"ians, for he hath left us, and hath holpen the Christ
"ians¹ against us." Then the governor called Yôpha
nâ, and said unto him, "Yôphanâ, what is this tha
"thou hast done?" And Yôphanâ related unto the
governor the cause of what had happened, and he
revealed unto him concerning the affair. And it came

---

¹ B, "Yôphanâ whom thou didst send with us against the
"Christians".

to pass that when the governor heard [these things] he laughed at the Jews, for on account of the great strength of Yôphanâ he was afraid of him. Thus were the Jews put to shame.

And the Apostles bore along the body of Mary with great pomp, and the multitude of people who had come with them from Jerusalem accompanied it, and paid great honour unto it. And they went down to the valley which there is on this side of the Mount of Olives, where there are three very large caves; now one of them was double. And the innermost division of the double cave was new, and up to that time no one had been laid therein; and a stone had been placed against the mouth of it. In this place did they lay the body of Mary, and they placed[1] a stone against the door of the cave. And Simon Peter stood up and spake unto the multitude that was there, | and entreated the believers to set watchmen over the grave of Mary, so that the Jews might not come and carry off the body and treat it with insults and contempt, and burn it with fire. Now the Apostles had received a revelation from God concerning what Christ was about to do with the body of Mary. And Simon stood up and said unto the believing men, "Know ye not what Christ is about to do with the "body of His Church? For Christ knoweth what will "benefit His Church more than anything for which "we can ask. For as the body of the Son of Mary is "divided among all the churches in which the Apostles "have preached, and is given for the propitiation of

---

[1] Read ܐܣܝܡܘ.

"those who receive it in faith, even so is it granted tha "churches shall be built in her name throughout th "whole world, in remembrance of the blessed woman "His mother, and the people there shall be made happ "by the memorial of her. And the place here in whic "her body hath been laid will our Lord hide from a "the children of men, just as the body of our Lor "was hidden when it had been laid in the grave wit

Page 116 "watchmen to watch it. | For He rose and went fort "from among the dead, and put to shame those wh "crucified Him, and made His disciples to rejoice "Even so He will not allow the body of her who gav "Him birth to fall into the hands of the Jews. Depar "ye then in peace to your homes, and pray ye eac "for the other." These things did Simon say unto th assembly of believers who were gathered togethe there.

And it came to pass that after these things th Jews, who were sorcerers, meditated on the matter and gave counsel to the people how to do harm unt the body of the holy woman, and how, in time, the might prevent men and women from going to her grave and from being helped by the benefits which flowe from that spot; now they could not cut off the believer from going there. Then the Jews took counsel to gether, and they dragged the bodies of the dead t the tomb of Mary, and filled the outer cave therewith so that the people might not be able to draw nig unto the place by reason of the foetid smell of cor ruption which was there; but the power of Christ wa not restrained even by this. And the Jews said amon themselves, "Let us burn her body with fire, and the "we shall have rest from it." Then they collected and piled up together round about the cave faggots of wood, and they filled even the cave with wood, and they drew nigh to set light to the fire, but before they could fan the wood into a blaze, the wood of its own accord burst into a blazing, fiery flame, and the fire enveloped them all, and the heads of their chief men were set on fire, and the flames burnt the edges of all their beards.

And it came to pass that, when the Apostles saw that these things | were being done by the Jews, Simon Peter said, "Come, O my brethren, let us pray before "our Lord that He will do what is good for the body "of His mother;" so they prayed and put incense [on the fire]. And suddenly mighty chariots, and chariots of fire and of the Spirit drew up in order round about the cave, and straightway the chariots of the Prophets, and the assemblies of the Patriarchs, and the companies of the Watchers, and myriads of angels, gathered themselves together, and they were all ready to do honour unto the holy body. And the Apostles having been informed thereof entered into the cave, and brought out the honourable body of our Lady Mary; and they laid it upon a bier, and carried it along. And behold, in a moment, a garment of light was woven, and the Apostles wrapped the body in a cloak of light, and they fastened the side thereof with that which resembled the lightning. And behold, above them all, and above the bier of Mary, there was spread out a white garment of light, and the chariots of the men and of the women who were virgins, and innumerable thousands and tens of thousands of angels appeared, and the horns of the spirit beings sounded, and the earth was moved, and mighty earthquake took place. Then the Apostles ra and carried away the bier of the mother of th Lord, and straightway a chariot of light was prepare and in it they laid the blessed woman. And at th moment a cloud shining with splendour appeared, a it took up the chariots, and the Prophets, and t Apostles, and the Patriarchs, and the venerable wome and they began to move along. And, behold, befo the chariot of our Lady Mary went the chariot the Patriarchs Adam, and Seth, and Enos, and Noa and Abraham, and Isaac, and Jacob, and of all t men who were just and righteous. And then car the chariot of the Prophets Isaiah, and Jeremiah, a Ezekiel, and Daniel, and David, and all the oth Prophets. And then came the chariot of the pries Aaron, and Eleazar, and Samuel, and all the priest and all these were paying glory and honour unto t body of the holy woman. And after these there car thousands and tens of thousands of angels who su rounded the chariot in which they were carrying t bier whereon was laid the holy woman. And some them | were carrying the chariot, and some of the were sounding horns, and some of them were blowii trumpets, and some of them were crying out with the voices; but all of them were ascribing praise unto t holy woman with their words and speech. And am all this pomp and glory the holy woman went forwa in a chariot of light. And after the chariot of Ma there came the chariot of the Apostles, Simon Pete and John, and Paul, and of all the Apostles in a bod

And after the chariot of the Apostles there came the chariot of the venerable women Hannah, the mother of our Lady Mary, and Elizabeth, and Hannah, the prophetess, and all the just and righteous women. And her Son carried her, by the might of His Spirit, to Paradise, and He set her in a glorious place therein.

And it came to pass that when the Apostles saw what had happened they bowed the knee and did homage before the body of the holy woman, and then a cloud carried the Apostles from Paradise and set them in the upper chamber in Jerusalem. And they wrote down the triumphs of the Virgin in books among themselves, and sent them into the four quarters of the earth, and they ordered that the believers should celebrate the commemoration of the blessed woman three times in the year. The first was to take place in the month Khânûn, on the eve of the Sabbath which came after the Nativity, for the day of her departure from this world was the day of the birth of our Lord; on the day on which she gave Him birth did she depart from this world. And the doctors of the Church have ordered that the first commemoration of the Virgin should take place after the festival of the birth of our Lord.[1] And this commemoration is celebrated for the sake of the first-fruits of the crops, so that rain may come upon the early and the later crops, and that they may increase at the will of their owners. And the second commemoration they were to celebrate in the month of Îyâr, in the middle of the month, on the fifteenth day,[2] and this commemor-

---

[1] See Wright, *Cat. Syr. MSS.*, p. 284, col. 1 (Add. 14,507, fol. 28 a).
[2] See Wright, *op. cit.*, p. 280, col. 2 (Add. 14,504, fol. 58 a).

ation was placed at this time for the sake of t filling out of the ears of corn, so that they mig come to perfection and might be reaped in peac And the third commemoration they were to celebra in the month of Âb,[1] and this also was to take pla in the middle of the month, on the fifteenth day therec and this commemoration was arranged on behalf the vines and the vineyards, and all the lands whi had to be irrigated.

And it came to pass that when the Apostles had r ceived this book, | they said among themselves, "Com "let us pray that we may see what our Lord will ("with us." And when they had prayed, and had giv the salutation of peace unto each other, immediate a cloud seized upon them and carried each one them into his own country, and into his own city, a into his own district, and into the place wherefrom I had brought him. Those who were alive did the Ho Spirit take back into their places, and they preache and taught with all their might; and those who we dead did the Spirit take back unto their own place and they returned again into their own graves. A just as they were changed on the day whereon the went forth from their graves from the state of death in one of life, even so on the day whereon they return to enter into their graves were they changed from state of life into one of death; and they rested quiet and in peace until the day of vivification.

Come, O my brethren, and hearken unto a thi of wonder. Come, O my beloved, and listen unto

---

[1] See Wright, *Cat. Syr. MSS.*, p. 283, col. 1 (Add. 14,505, fol. 172

most marvellous story. Come, O my friends, and give praise unto our Lord. Come, O ye who love God, and glorify our Redeemer. Come, O ye believing ones, and extol Him. Come, O ye Christians, and bring honour unto Him. Come, O ye who are followers of Christ, and ascribe glory unto Him. Come, O ye who have been baptized, and confess Him. Come, O ye who are members of the household of God, and let us do homage unto Him, Whose great and mighty works created things are not able to describe. But the deeds which He hath done, and doth still do, throughout all the generations of the world are very difficult and very hard to describe; and the man who would dare to attempt to write down the various kinds of His works of understanding must possess an unenlightened mind. But what shall I say? For by the unchanging union and cleaving of the Divine Nature unto the human nature, all rational natures have been enlightened through that Holy Nature. And as concerning the fulfilling of the words which Christ spake unto His disciples, saying, "When the Holy Spirit, "the Paraclete, hath come, He shall make known unto "you¹ [the things which are about to take place]," it was John the Less, the chosen disciple, the man of purity, the man unto whose sanctity his Lord testified, and unto whom was revealed in a revelation of the Spirit that which our Lord Christ did unto her who gave Him birth, it was he, I say, who wrote the following things. | He said, "When my Lady Mary had been "made to rest in Paradise, our Lord Christ left the

---

¹ See St. John XIV. 26.

"heavens, and descended into the Paradise of Ede
"And He cried unto her with His glorious and sublir
"voice, saying, 'Mary!' And suddenly she becar
"alive, and stood up at the sound of His sweet worc
"and she bowed the knee and did homage unto Hi
"And with her there worshipped Elijah the proph(
"and Enoch the just man, and Moses, the chief of t
"prophets, and Simon Peter, the chief of the Apostle
"and John the Baptist; together with the blessed wom;
"did they all worship Him Who giveth us life. A1
"our Lord took the blessed woman with Him, and I
"made her to ascend with Him in a chariot into heave
"and He made to go up with her so that they mig
"pay her honour, the righteous Patriarchs, and t
"Prophets, and the Apostles. And our Lord Hims
"heartened her, and said unto her, 'Come, Moth(
"'come and see the things of glory. Come and see t
"'things, the good things, which are beyond speec
"'Come and enter into the Jerusalem which is in heave
"'the city of God'."

"And it came to pass that when the chariot
"light and the cloud of radiant splendour arrive
"and they began to come to the gates of the firmame
"suddenly there was breathed forth therefrom the sm
"of perfumes, and the odours of sweet-smelling thin;
"And at the first gate the clouds, and the lightnin;
"and the thunders bowed down in worship before Ma:
"And she entered into the heaven which was benea
"and she saw there the treasure-houses of the Lo:
"that is to say, the habitation of ice, and snow, a
"frost, and the habitation of the rain, and the de
"and the heat, and the winds, and the whirlwin

and the storms, and the lightnings, and the thick
darkness; and they all came and worshipped the
mother of their Lord. And again she ascended into
the heaven of heavens, and she saw the angels of
God; and they all ran and came to salute her, and
they bowed down in worship before her. And when
she had gone in through that heaven, and she had
arrived at the Jerusalem which is above, she saw
that it was ornamented with all manner of beautiful decorations. And she saw that twelve walls went
round about it, and that these walls were built of
fine gold; and the stones thereof were of pearls, and
they all shot forth rays of light. And the city had
twelve gates which were decorated with all kinds of
precious ornaments, and upon them were figures
of every kind; and by the side of each of the gates
there sat one | of the Apostles, and above each Page 121
gate the name of the Apostle who sat thereby was
written, and by the side of each Apostle there stood
a multitude of angels. And Mary entered in through
the outer gate, and she saw that beings of the
Spirit and the Prophets stood there, and that they
were playing music on trumpets; and they all ran
and bowed down in worship before her. And when
she entered in through the second gate, the company of the Cherubim bowed down in worship before her. And when she set her foot upon the thresh-
old of the third gate, the company of the Seraphim ran to meet her. And when she arrived at the
wall of the fourth gate, and entered in through the
fourth gate, the Powers made haste to salute her;
and they fell upon their faces before her. And when

"she walked through the fifth gate, the thunders
"the lightnings bowed themselves before her.
"when she passed through the sixth gate, she h(
"from all sides the sound of beings crying, 'H(
"And she saw there the fortress (or palace) w
"cannot be touched by man. And when she ent(
"in through the seventh gate, the fire and the fl
"bowed down in worship before her. And when
"arrived at the eighth gate, the rain and the (
"bowed the knee before her. And when she ent(
"in through the ninth gate, all the winds toge
"bowed down in worship before her. And when
"walked through the tenth gate, the sun and
"moon bowed down in worship before her. /
"when she entered in through the eleventh gate,
"twelve Apostles bowed down in worship before]
"And then our Lord made her who gave Him b
"to pass through the gate through which none
"as yet passed, and He shewed her there the ki
"dom of heaven, and the things which are hid(
"and the things which are secret, and the thi
"which are not revealed, and the pleasures wh
"are hidden in the kingdom, which can neither
"spoken by the mouth nor pronounced by the tong
"And she saw the mansions of splendour, and
"chambers which were decorated, the delight wh(
"of hath never entered into the heart of man
"imagine. And she saw there that which the eye
"man cannot look upon, and that which man is
"able either to describe the like thereof, or to m
"it manifest. And our Lord revealed and shewed
"all the delights which come after the Resurrecti

And she said unto Him, 'My Lord, what are these
'things? And who shall be worthy to enter in hither? Page 122
'And for whom are they laid up?' And our Lord
said unto her, 'This is the country concerning which
'I spake unto those who believed on Me and in My
'name, saying, 'I go to make ready a place for you.'[1]
'And these delights, and these mansions, and these
'chambers are kept for the saints, and for those who
'do My will, and for every one who hath not wrought
'iniquity. And here do all the righteous take their
'delight after the vivification.' And she looked and
saw another country, the aspect of which was hard
and forbidding, and the whole of it was filled with
blackness, and thick darkness, and smoke; and before the terrible sight of that torture flowed the river
of fire, which went forth from that place. And our
Lady Mary said, 'And what is this, O my Lord?'
And our Lord said unto her, 'This is the Gehennâ
'of fire which is laid up for the sinful and the wick-
'ed.' And she said unto Him, '. . . Not[2] from this
'place, and not from one who seeth it.'"

"And after these things it came to pass that our
Lord took His mother and brought her back unto
the Paradise of Eden, and He made her to die again
until the day of the vivification. And sweet-smelling scents and odours breathed forth from that place,
and she was left there until the day wherein He
will make her to ascend into the kingdom which He
had already shewn her."

---

[1] See St. John XIV. 2.
[2] Some words seem to have dropped out here.

"And it came to pass that when our Lord had made "an end of all these things, and when all these things "had taken place, the Apostles returned unto their "places, and Mary remained there, and the believers "took their rest."

Now when the Jews, the enemies of the truth, saw that the Name of Jesus was becoming magnified, and that the triumphs of the holy woman Mary had become noised abroad everywhere (now they were thinking that her body was still lying in that cave), they said, "We have not injured her by the fire; "let us, now, weave another plot." And it came to pass that when it was night, about three hundred mighty men gathered themselves together, and they went with swords, and with lanterns, and they went into the cave to make a mock of that venerable and holy body. And they went and entered into the cave, and they moved away the stone from | the mouth of the cave;[1] and they saw that the cave was filled with light like that of the sun, and with a smell like unto that of sweet scent. And they saw the garments in which our Lady Mary had been swathed lying in the midst of the cave, but there was no body in them; and when they saw this they were astonished, and they marvelled, and they gave glory unto God involuntarily. And many of them said, "In very truth

---

[1] B reads, "Now when the shameful Jews saw what had happen-"ed, and that although they had given a bribe they were in no-"wise benefited, when the night had come, about three hundred "men gathered themselves together, and went to the cave with "swords, and staves, and lanterns; and they set out to make a "mock of the venerable body of Mary therein. And they went "and entered into the outer cave", etc.

"this Jesus, the Son of Mary, is the Christ for Whom "creation waiteth. He knoweth that which we did "meditate in our minds, and what we were wishing "to do unto the body of her who gave Him birth; "but He hath not left it for us to make a mockery "of, and hath delivered it out of our hands. To Him "belongeth victory for ever, and to us belongeth "shame of face for all generations." Now many of them believed upon Jesus Christ, but some of them were wishing to burn the garments of Mary in the fire, and there was division and contention among them; but the company of those who believed was stronger than that of those who did not believe, so those who believed took the garments and carried them into Jerusalem, and multitudes of sick folk were healed thereby.

And the unbelieving Jews who have at all times resisted God gathered themselves together, and made a cunning plot amongst themselves, saying, "It is not "meet for us to cease to visit this cave wherein is "laid the body of Mary, lest the Christians go and "build buildings there, and the sick obtain healing "from that place, and our festivals and our sabbaths "become abrogated." And they went and hired soldiers, and they dragged along the bodies of dead creatures of every kind, and cast them into the cave. And it came to pass that when the believing men who were in Jerusalem heard of this, they went and made it known unto the governor; and the governor sent Yôphanâ,[1] who seized upon and carried off every-

---

[1] Or Yôphanyâ, according to *B*.

thing which belonged unto those who had done this thing. And many believed upon our Lord by reason of the death of Mary, and through the mighty deeds which were wrought by means of her holy body. And our Lord made her a name after her death which was greater than that which she had when she was alive; and every man who made mention of her name, and who took refuge in her prayers, received everything for which he asked.

| And here will I write down [the account of] the miracles which the people of Bethlehem saw were wrought in the upper chamber wherein the blessed woman was lying; and here beginneth the first of them.[1]

Now when the Apostles had come, and they were performing the service therein, and when the hosts of our Lord had descended from heaven, and they were singing psalms and hymns above the upper chamber, the people of Bethlehem saw the clouds coming and sprinkling sweet-smelling dew over all the house, and the stars which descended, and did homage before the upper chamber. And the people of Bethlehem looked through the window of the upper chamber, and they saw Gabriel standing by the pillow of the holy woman, and Michael standing at her feet; and they were holding sceptres of gold in their hands. And the people of Bethlehem saw the Apostles standing round about in fear, and they were offering adoration unto her with their hands spread out to heaven. And the people of Bethlehem saw as it

---

[1] Literally, "The first vision which the children of Bethlehem "saw".

were [the appearance of] the waves of the sea when they break upon the shore, for even thus were the waves of sweet smells and odours which came forth from the upper chamber. And like the rushing water which a full and overflowing spring poureth out in torrents, even so did the odour of sweet scents go forth from the foundations of the upper chamber. And the people of Bethlehem saw the companies of angels, which were without number, and the assemblies of the angelic hosts, which could not be counted, and the Watchers who were saying with their voices, "Hail to thee, O thou that didst give birth to the "Christ! Blessed art thou, and blessed is the Fruit "which was born from thee, the glorious Son of God!" With these words did the angels cry out and ascribe glory unto Mary, and the Watchers were singing psalms and hymns, and the spiritual beings were singing hymns of praise before her. And the people of Bethlehem saw the deaf, and the dumb, and the blind, and the lepers, and those who were afflicted, and those who had been smitten with disease, and the sick people, coming unto the blessed woman; and every sickness, whatsoever it might be | from which they were suffering was healed. And there came besides these all those who were sick, and they used to carry away some of the dust of the upper chamber wherein the holy woman was lying, and rub it small and smear it over their bodies; and straightway they were made whole. And the blessed woman wrought a multitude of signs and marvels of every kind, which the children of men were not able to recount. And the children of men saw all these signs and wonders, and they ascribed glory to God, even against their will. And the people were coming from cities and countries which were afar off, and from Byzantium, and from Alexandria, and from Egypt, and from the Thebaïd, and from Athens. And the sons of the kings, and the sons of the princes of the nations, and the daughters of noblemen and of governors, were wont to come and do homage unto the blessed woman; and they used to bear and bring unto her costly gifts. And they believed in our Lord Jesus, Who was born of her, and they used to enquire of her, saying, "How "was the Christ born of thee without union with man?" And she used to teach them everything which they wished to learn from her. And she used to heal those who were sick, and when the women who had come unto her from remote countries were about to depart, she used to prepare small books which they might carry away with them to their kinsfolk, so that they also might believe in our Lord Jesus Christ. And from year to year the daughters of kings and the daughters of princes were used to come unto her, and they used to celebrate the commemoration of the Passion of our Lord Jesus Christ with her.

And a certain woman came unto her from the city of Beyrût, and she was possessed of a devil which was strangling her continually; and the blessed woman prayed over her, and she was made whole.

And there came unto her also Nûbkar, the daughter of the governor, from Alexandria; now she was covered all over with a running leprosy, but when she had done homage before the Lady Mary she was cleansed straightway.

And there came unto her also Abîgêl, the Egyptian woman, the daughter of Gershôn, who was the beloved friend of the king of Egypt. Now she suffered from giddiness, but having entreated | the Lady Mary, she prayed over her, and straightway she was made whole.

And there came unto her also the lady Palônâ from Thessalonica, whose right eye Satan had destroyed; and the blessed woman made the sign of the cross over her, and straightway she was healed.

And there came unto her also Malcô, the daughter of Sabinus the governor, who was possessed of two devils; the one came upon her in the day-time, and the other used to inflict tortures upon her in the night-time. And our Lady Mary laid her hand upon her head, and she prayed and said these words, "O Thou "mighty one Whom I have in heaven,[1] I pray on be- "half of this soul, that it may be healed." Then straightway there went forth from her those two devils. And they uttered shrieks and cries, and said, "What have "we to do with thee, O thou who didst give birth "unto Christ? Thou, and the Child Who was born "of thee have made Legion to tremble and his hosts "also." And the holy woman cursed those devils, and they were swallowed up in the abyss.

And there came unto her a certain youth from Egypt, who was of the family of Sûfrân, the king of Egypt. Now he had elephantiasis in his head, and he wept before our Lady Mary; and she stretched out her hand over him, and signed him with the sign of the cross, and straightway he was healed.

---

[1] Literally, "Sufficient for me is He Whom I have in heaven".

And there was a festival in Jerusalem, and very many people were gathered together in the city, and those who had come to Jerusalem brought along with them those who were sick and those who were afflicted for the sake of our Lady Mary; and the people told them that she was living in Bethlehem. Then innumerable crowds of people set out and went to Bethlehem; and they knocked at the door of the upper chamber of the blessed woman, but the Apostles opened it not. And it came to pass that when the Apostles did not desire that the door should be opened, the people who were sick cried out from the outside, saying, "Have mercy upon us, O thou Lady "Mary who didst give birth unto Christ." And the blessed woman hearkened unto the words of the people who were crying unto her, and she prayed and said, "He Whom I have in heaven is sufficient for me. "Hearken Thou unto the voice of the souls who make "supplication unto Thee." Then straightway | the power of help went forth from the blessed woman unto the sick, and they were healed. Now there were there two thousand and eight hundred souls, men, and women, and children; and a mighty praising took place on that day wherein all those sick folk were made whole.

Then [the priests] went to the praetorium, and they repeated before the governor that which our Lady Mary had done. And the Jews were afraid, and the Sadducees trembled, and said, "A troublous matter "hath happened in Jerusalem." And the priests cried unto the men who had departed from Bethlehem, and said unto them, "Go ye, and bring out that woman "from thence." And it came to pass that when the Bethlehemites had departed, and they had made a secret plot among themselves to go and to make a fight with the Apostles, on the night the end of which brought in the first day of the week in the latter Khânûn, on the twenty-first day of the month, when the world was asleep, the great glory of God appeared before our Lady Mary as she lay upon her couch in the upper chamber. And whilst the Bethlehemites were standing and watching to go in against the Apostles, suddenly the gates of heaven were opened, and a mighty light streamed forth; and there went out therefrom the odour of sweet-smelling scents, and a very sweet scent pervaded the whole city of Bethlehem. And as men[1] of fire were coming down from heaven shrouded in mantles of flame, John went forth and opened the door of the upper chamber, and he looked up to heaven, and he saw the company of the Cherubim and the company of the Watchers flying about in circles and descending from heaven. And John went in and said unto Simon, "Behold, "the assemblies of the heavenly beings are coming "unto us." Then the Apostles went forth to meet the angels who were coming from heaven, and received them; and a great service of the angels and of the Apostles was held above the upper chamber for three days and three nights. And the Bethlehemites saw this, and they feared with a great fear.

Then the priests stirred up the governor, and said unto him, "O Lord governor, give orders concerning

---

[1] Read ܐܢܫܐ.

"this woman. Let her not remain in Bethlehem, neither "| let her stay anywhere in the whole district of Jeru- "salem." And the governor said unto them, "I have "no power to drive any man out from his house." And the priests said unto him, "And we ourselves "cannot do what we wish. Send now men with swords "that they may go and bring the disciples of that "Seducer, and let the disciples bring Mary hither in "great disgrace." And having made a great outcry and much tumult, they said unto the governor, "By "the life of the Emperor Tiberius, if thou dost not "perform our desire, we will lay information against "thee before him." Then was the governor afraid of the Jews, and he commanded the captain of a thousand men to go to Bethlehem with thirty men, to bring back the disciples, both them and our Lady Mary. And it came to pass that when the men set out to depart the Holy Spirit said unto the Apostles, "Be- "hold, men are coming against you from Jerusalem. "Rise up, and go forth, and fear not, for I will carry "you into the air of heaven, and ye shall pass over "the heads of the men who are coming against you, "and they shall not see you, for the might of the "Highest, Who is to be adored,[1] is with you." Then the Apostles rose up and went forth from the upper chamber. And Peter bore one [side] of the bier of our Lady Mary, and John another, and Paul another, and the rest of the Apostles and angels were giving praise and were going before her. And as the Apostles were bearing along the bier, the Holy Spirit was

---

[1] Read ܣܓܝܕ.

accompanying them, and was praising them, and the Holy Spirit made them to pass over the heads of the men who had come against them, and they saw them not. And as the men were coming on their way from Jerusalem, they heard the sound of a great tumult above[1] their heads, and they stood up and gazed about, and said unto each other, "What is "this tumult?" For they heard the sound of the wings of the Seraphim as they rustled, and the sound of the cohorts of the angels, and the sound of the movements among the spiritual beings, and the sound of the praise to which the beings of fire were giving utterance. And wonder fell | upon them, and they said unto each other, "What, then, is this thing?"

And it came to pass that when the Apostles arrived in Bethlehem (now they remained there in order that the Jews might not think within themselves that they were afraid of them, and that they had fled before them), they went into the house of our Lady Mary; and they performed over her a service which lasted for five whole days and five whole nights. And when the men [sent by the governor] had come to Bethlehem, they searched on their hands and knees how they might open the door; and when they had opened the door of the upper chamber they went inside, but they found nothing. Then the men laid hold upon the Bethlehemites, and said unto them, "It was ye who went in to the governor and to the "priests, and told them that the disciples of Jesus "were coming unto Mary. Come now, and go into

---

[1] Read ܠܥܠ.

"Jerusalem along with us, and tell the governor and "the priests that we have found nothing, so that they "may not think that we have taken a bribe from the "disciples, and have let them escape from us." So the Bethlehemites went into Jerusalem, and the other men with them, and they came to the governor, and said unto him, "We have found nothing." And the priests said unto them, "The disciples of that Seducer "have worked spells and have made blind your eyes "and ye did not see them." And the governor said unto them, "If ye hear any news of them in any "place whatsoever, seize them, and bring them to me."

And it came to pass that after five days the angels of the Lord appeared, and they were going in and coming out from the house of the blessed woman in Jerusalem. And again, on another night, the angels appeared bearing horns and lights, and they were coming from heaven; and the people of Jerusalem were afraid with a great fear. And in the morning the priests were gathered together, and they said, "Go ye and enquire who it is that liveth in the neigh-"bourhood of that woman." And when they had enquired of the people who lived in the neighbourhood, they said unto them, "Our Lady Mary hath come to "her house, and these | glorious things have taken "place before her; and the angels descended and "did homage unto her." And those who had been sent went and told the priests. And the priests rose up and went to the governor, and said unto him, "O Lord governor, there will be a war in Jerusalem "on account of this woman." And the governor said unto them, "What shall I do for you?" And they

said unto him, "Let us go and burn down the habitation wherein she is." And the governor said unto
them, "Whatsoever ye wish to do, that go and do."
Then the people of Jerusalem gathered themselves
together, and they took fire, and wood, and went to
burn down the habitation¹ of Mary. Now the doors
thereof were shut, and they put forth their hands to
set them on fire; and straightway the angel of the
Lord dashed his wings in their faces, and the fire
blazed away from the door. And the flames burned
up strongly without any man touching the fire, and
the faces and beards of the men were burned, and
not a few of them died. And there was great fear
in that place. Now when the governor saw this sight,
and that the fire was blazing away without any man
throwing fuel thereon, he drew nigh unto the door,
and he saw that it was not injured in any way whatsoever. Then the governor stretched out his hands
to heaven, and he cried out with a loud voice and
said, "In very truth this sight which I have seen must
"belong to the Son of God, Who was born of Mary."

And it came to pass that on the following day
the governor sent and gathered together all the Jews
who were living in Jerusalem, that is to say, the
priests, and the holy men, and the Sadducees, and
said unto them, "O nation of crucifiers, who have
"crucified the Christ Who came unto you, ye are a
"people bitter of soul, and stiff of neck, and ye are
"workers of your own will. I myself give thanks unto
"God that I do not belong to your country. It was

---

¹ *I. e*, the courtyard of her house.

"the emperor Tiberius who made me your governor "and who sent me unto you. Ye are indeed a stiff "necked nation, and it was for this reason that the "edict came forth from the Emperor that one of your "own countrymen | should not be appointed governor "over you. Indeed ye are evil men."

Then the governor commanded that all the people of Jerusalem should be gathered together, and when they were assembled they came and stood before his house. And he made them to take an oath by the God of Israel, and by the Holy Books which Moses wrote, that every man who believed in Mary, and in Him Who was born of her, would separate himself, and set himself by himself, and that he who did not believe should make it clear that he did not believe. Now, the cursed nation of the Jews was afraid of taking oaths, and there were not many among them who would tell a lie if they were made to take an oath by the God of Israel. Then were the people divided into two parts, and those who believed separated themselves and stood on one side. And the governor said unto those who believed on Christ, "Do ye believe in the Child Who was born "of Mary?" And they said unto him, "We believe "that the Christ Who was born of Mary is the Son "of the Living God." And the governor said unto them, "I believe you rather than the Gentiles, for ye "were born and reared in Jerusalem. But, behold, "there are found among you some who adore Christ, "and some who deny Him. Here there hath been no "power exercised by anyone on behalf of the Em- "peror to force you [to speak thus], but of your own

'freewill ye have said that Christ is the Son of the
'Living God." Then the unbelievers said unto him,
'We know from our Scriptures that the Christ hath not
'yet come." And the governor said unto them, "Then
'what think ye of this Man?" And the unbelievers
;aid, "We think that He is a seducer, and that He is
'not to be compared even unto one of our righteous
'men." Then the governor said unto those who be-
ieved in Christ, "I would that the secret things of
'your wills might be revealed. Until this day ye have
'reckoned me among the unbelievers who crucified
'our Lord; but from this day forth it is meet that
'[ye should reckon me among you] who are called
'the people who have confessed the Son of God.
'May you and I have a portion set apart with Him |
'at the last day when He shall come with His holy   Page 133
'angels upon the clouds of heaven. And now reveal
'ye unto me concerning the signs and wonders which
'He wrought in Jerusalem, and in the country round
'about."

And the unbelievers said unto him, "May we speak
'first?" And the governor said, "Say on." Then the
ınbelievers said, "It is written in our Scriptures that
'the Christ shall come, but as yet He hath not come.
'This Man of whom ye speak Who hath called Him-
'self the Son of God is the Son of Mary." And the
overs of Christ said unto the unbelievers, "Declare
'ye the signs and wonders which the men of olden
'time, and the men of a later time, and the men of
'these last days, have wrought, and we will shew
'that the signs and wonders which Christ hath wrought
'are greater and more in number than those wrought

10

"by all other men." Then the unbelievers said "Whence can ye shew us that the Son of Mary i "the Christ?" And the lovers of Christ said, "W "will shew you." And the governor said unto them "Speak ye your words neither noisily, nor with wrath "ful pain, but argue ye with one another from you "Scriptures in a gentle voice, for I myself wish t "see and to understand the force of your words. And the lovers of Christ said, "Our father Adam "when he was dying, commanded his son Seth, say "ing, 'O my son Seth, behold offerings of gold, an "'myrrh, and frankincense have been placed by m "'in the Cave of Treasures, for the Christ is abou "'to come into the world. And He shall be seize "'by evil men, and He shall die, and he shall b "'His death work the vivification of all my posterity "'And He shall rise on the third day from the grave "'and He shall make my body to ascend with Hi "'into heaven, and he shall make it to sit upon "'chariot on His right hand. And, behold, Magian "'shall come from Persia, and they shall take thes "'offerings which I have placed [there], and th "'Testament which I have made, and they shall carr "'them to the Son of God Who shall be born of "'virgin in Bethlehem of Judea.' And thus hath "come to pass. For the Magians came, and the "brought offerings, and they brought with them th "'Testament of Adam'.[1] It is owing to this thin

---

[1] See Wright, *Contributions to the Apocryphal Literature of the Ne Testament*, 1865, p. 61; Renan, *Journal Asiat.*, 1853, p. 427; Wrigh *Syriac Literature*, p. 25; Wright, *Cat. Syr. MSS.*, p. 782; and a *Book of the Bee*, p. 85.

"that the [Jewish nation] knoweth that Adam made 'a Testament. And thus was it written unto Seth by Adam, and from | Seth was it written to all 'families; and hereby knew the Jewish nation that 'Christ was coming, and that He was to be born in 'Bethlehem of Judea. Now as for us, we are not 'ashamed of that which we say, but what have ye 'to say?" Then the unbelieving Jews said, "In what 'thing is Christ better than Jacob? For he saw a 'vision the like of which man had never seen. He 'went up and slept in the mountain of Gilead, and 'God opened his eyes, and He spake with him, and 'he was shewn a ladder which reached from earth 'even unto the heavens, and the angels came down to salute him."

And the lovers of Christ said, "Jacob, and the angels, and the ladder shewed forth the coming of Christ, and declared His death." Then the unbelieving Jews said unto the lovers of Christ, "The ascent of Elijah is, then, held in contempt by you, although everything which he spake in the heavens hath been heard." And the lovers of Christ said, "Elijah ascended in a whirlwind into the heaven wherein the sun and the moon are fixed, but no man hath worshipped him except his disciple Elisha. Now Christ ascended into heaven, and not into one heaven only, but He ascended into all the heavens, and went up above them all. And, behold, He sitteth on the right hand of His Father, and all the created things which are above, and all those which are below, have bowed their heads and have worshipped Him. For no one hath gone up into the heaven which is

"above all the other heavens except Him Who ca
"down therefrom, that is to say, the Son of M
"Who was in heaven." And the unbelievers sa
"Let Moses, and the signs and wonders wherew
"he smote the Egyptians, whereby he delivered Isra
"be considered. And because Pharaoh sought to ke
"them back from coming unto the sea, Moses to
"a dry rod¹ in his hand, and smote the waves of t
"sea so that they became piled up in heaps."

Then the lovers of Christ said, "Jesus, Who w
"born of Mary, also rebuked the devils, and th
"were scattered from before Him. And when the s
"wished to swallow up Simon Peter, He stretch
"out His hand, and took him up, and it did not dra
"him down. And unless Jesus had been Lord ov
"the sea, and Lord over the dry land, and Lord ov
"all created things of every kind | how would the
"have been obedient unto Him?" And the unbelieve
said unto the lovers of Christ, "We are not able t
"contend with you in words, because ye have taste
"and learned error from the doctrine of the Son ‹
"Mary; if ye were to contend in words with Sata
"himself ye would overcome him." Then the lover
of Christ said unto the unbelievers, "Not one wor
"of that which ye have spoken hath any truth therei

---

¹ This rod was cut from the tree of good and evil, that is tł
fig-tree, by Adam before he left Paradise. It passed from him t
Seth, Noah, Isaac, Jacob, Jethro, Moses, Joshua, the son of Nu
Phineas, who hid it in the dust at the gate of Jerusalem, Josepl
the husband of Mary, to whom it was shewn by the Divine Will, an
Jacob the brother of our Lord. It was stolen from Jacob by Judɛ
Iscariot, who gave it to the Jews who crucified our Lord, whe
they lacked wood for His arms. See my *Book of the Bee*, pp. 50, 5

"and ye have not gained the victory; depart ye then "from this praetorium." And the unbelievers said unto the lovers of Christ, "Is not David, the Psalmist "of the Spirit, or Elisha, the son of Shaphat, who "made to live the dead man by the side of whom "he was laid in the grave, or Enoch, whom God re- "moved from the earth, and no creature knew what "had become of him, as excellent as Christ, Who "was born of Mary, and was called the 'son of the "'carpenter'?" Then the lovers of Christ said unto the unbelievers, "Neither in heaven nor upon earth "is there any who is like unto the Son Who was "born of Mary the Virgin, except His Father Who "sent Him unto us. And thus do we confess. And 'those who are dead from their graves will testify 'at this moment that He Who was born of the Vir- 'gin is the same Being Who shall come [again]; 'for Him all created things wait, that He may make 'the light to rise upon them. And from the time 'that He was born of Mary He hath made the power 'of Satan to be of none effect. And no mouth can 'declare, and no tongue can explain, nor any celest- 'ial being, nor any terrestrial being, and no one can 'declare sufficiently the mighty deeds, or the deeds 'of power, or the marvellous acts, or the signs and 'wonders which He hath wrought in the world."

Then the governor commanded that certain men of the unbelievers should be beaten, each with four severe beatings. And after they had been beaten, the unbelievers said unto the lovers of Christ,[1] "Since

---

[1] We must surely read, ܐܢܫܐ ܕܠܐ ܗܝܡܢܘ ܠܪ̈ܚܡܝ.

"ye imagine that ye have vanquished us we will, "ye wish, shew you what we have done unto yo "and we will reveal all the lying things which ha\ "taken place in Jerusalem before this excellent gove "nor; for God hath sent him to require from us[1] "the disgrace which hath been put upon Him." The the governor said unto the lovers of Christ, "Say y "whatsoever ye wish to say concerning Christ, an "fear not." And the lovers of Christ spake forthwitl saying, "Where hath the tree upon which our Lor "Jesus was crucified been hidden? And where aɪ "the nails which were driven through His hands an "His feet? And where hath the sponge in which yɛ "offered Him vinegar been placed? And where is th "spear wherewith one smote Him? And where "the crown of thorns which ye[2] put upon His head "And where are the garments of mockery wherewit "ye[2] clothed Him? Declare ye where they are hidden. And the governor said unto them, "Speak ye an "reveal ye everything which they have said unto you. And the unbelievers said, "They also know what w "know." Now when the governor saw this, he ros up upon his throne, and he took an oath to thos men who believed in Christ, and said unto then "By Christ, Who was born of the holy Virgin Marʝ "and in Whom ye have believed, as also have I, rɛ "veal and declare ye unto me everything which y "know concerning Christ." Then all those who love

---

[1] Literally, "from you". The speeches of the Jews and tʰ Christians have here become mixed.

[2] Literally, "we".

Christ¹ cried out with one voice, saying, "O wise "judge, woe be unto us by reason of the judgment "of Christ! Woe be unto us, for how have we treat- "ed Him with great contumely! And not Him only "have we so treated, but His Father also, Who hath "sent Him." Then the governor said unto them, "Re- "veal ye unto me where the wood on which He was "crucified hath been put, and the crown of thorns, "and the spear wherewith He was smitten, and the "garments of mockery in which they dressed Him." And they said, "When we had obtained them they "came into the hands of one of us, and we took "them, and they were placed with His cross. And "we dug a hole in the ground, about thirty cubits "deep, and we wrote upon His cross, which, however, "we separated somewhat from those of the thieves "who had been crucified with Him; then we gather- "ed together stones and earth and heaped them up "over the crosses, and thus we buried them thoroughly. "And in front of the head of the cross of our Lord "we made a narrow opening in the earth, through which "| the hand of a man could reach unto the cross of "our Lord; and when any affliction came upon one "of our people he used to go, and stretch out his "hand through the hole to the cross, and straight- "way he used to receive help, and be made whole. "And we swear unto thee, O lord governor, and we "lie not, that the cross of Christ hath, by thy life, healed "ten thousand, five hundred souls, of men, and women, "and children, more or less, whose names we have

---

¹ Read "unbelievers"?

"written down by us. And from whomsoever wa
"healed, they used to take money, and they gav
"orders among us, saying, 'Whosoever shall revea
"'this secret shall be slain, both he and his wife'
"And one said among us, 'If any man shall ask us
"'What is there in that place?' let us say, 'The po
"'of manna, and the rod of Aaron which budded
"'and it is these things which give help unto all thos(
"'who come thither.' And now, O lord governor
"bring Jônâdhâbh, and beat him, because of the on(
"nail which is in his house, for it belongeth unt(
"those which were fixed in the hands of our Lord
"and it hath redeemed five hundred and fifty soul
"from death. He hath become enriched [thereby], bu
"he knoweth not what he possesseth." And the go
vernor said, "Now that ye are in a rage, each witl
"the other, ye reveal that which is hidden among
"you; but if the Emperor heareth of it he will tak(
"off the heads of you all. Go ye, then, and shev
"me where the nails and the crosses have been hidden
"and the place where the opening hath been mad(
"by you." And they went and shewed him. Thei
the governor said unto them, "What shall I do fo:
"you?" And they said unto him, "O lord, do thou
"give the command, and let us take up the cros:
"whereon our Lord was crucified, and let it be place(
"in the Temple of Jerusalem, and let it be adore(
"by all created beings." And the governor said unt(
them, "I have no orders from the Emperor to d(
"this thing; but I will make you to be shameful thing:
"before all created beings. For I myself will no
"draw nigh unto the cross of Christ, but Christ Wh(

"was crucified thereon will bring it up out of the
"earth in which it is buried; and from all the ends
"of creation peoples and tongues shall come, and
"they shall do homage unto the cross of Christ, and
"He shall give life unto every creature that believ-
"eth in Him." And the governor commanded, and
they brought great stones and heaped them up upon
that place to the height of twenty times the length
of the fore-arm; and they wrote down these words
which they had heard from the governor. Then, afterwards, the disciples of the Apostles wrote unto mount
Sinai, and unto Egypt, and the Thebaïd, and Asia,
and Pontus, saying, "Great is the glory in which the
"blessed woman hath gone forth from this world."
And the disciples of the Apostles wrote for themselves the Book of her Departure, that is to say,
how she went forth from this world, and they took
it with them to Byzantium. For all countries are full
of the praises of the blessed woman, and a multitude
of people innumerable, both of men and of women,
believed upon her after that he who had been made
governor had gone up (died?).

And here [the book] relateth how she was a helper
of those men and women who called upon her, and
from the time when men in this city of Byzantium
believed she hath appeared several times unto all
those who put their trust in her prayers. For she
appeared here on the sea when it was greatly disturbed, and when it had risen and was about to destroy the ships which were sailing upon it; and the
sailors called upon the name of the blessed woman,
and she rose upon them like the sun, and delivered

Page 138

the ships, which were ninety-five in number, and saved them from destruction.¹

And again, she appeared in a certain mountain wherein thieves had fallen upon some men and wished to slay them; and the men cried² out, | and said "O Lady Mary, have mercy upon us." And straight way she appeared unto them like a flash of light ning, and blinded the eyes of the thieves, and they could not see the men who escaped from their hands

And again, she appeared unto a certain woman who was a widow, whose son had gone to look into a well of water and had fallen therein; and there was no man to bring him up out of it. And the woman cried out and said, "My Lady Mary, have "mercy upon me;" and the Virgin drew up the child and there was no injury upon him.

And again, a certain man was sick with a very grievous sickness, and the physicians were not able to do him any good. And after twenty years, where in he had been nearer unto death than life, he re membered the Lady Mary; and he put incense on the fire, and he was made whole immediately on tha' very day.

And again, a certain ship was dashed to pieces by the sea, and all those who were therein had fallen

---

¹ *B* reads, "And again there were ships on the sea (read "ܟܣܦܐ ܟܠܐ), and the billows were greatly moved and the "waves of the sea rose and stood upright; and the dwellers in "the ships took refuge in the prayers of the blessed woman, the "Lady Mary, and they remembered her, and they put incense on "the fire, and straightway the sea became calm, and the wave "went down, and the sailors glorified God."

² Read ܐܟܠܘ.

into the water. And suddenly the Lady Mary appeared | running upon the waves¹ of the sea, and she was carrying the souls of the men, and taking them to the dry land so that they might not be drowned.

Now there was a certain merchant in that ship which was dashed to pieces, and he also fell into the sea; and he was confiding greatly in the prayers of the Lady Mary. And it came to pass that as the sailors were journeying over the sea, they lost their way, and the ship fell among the rocks, and was dashed to pieces; but the merchant escaped upon a plank of wood. And the merchant made ready another ship, and he loaded it with all kinds of rich merchandise, and then he began to put out to sea; and that ship also was dashed to pieces, but he himself escaped, a second time, upon a plank of wood. And he made ready yet another ship, and it also was dashed to pieces; but he himself escaped upon a plank of wood. And the sea cast him up upon an island, which man had never entered, and there were date trees and fig trees in the island, and one aged anchorite who was worthy to be blessed. And when the merchant had gone up into that island, he began to walk about in it, and he found there the anchorite; and he rejoiced in him with an exceedingly great joy, and he was comforted for his afflictions, and he related unto the old man all his affairs. And the old man said unto the merchant, "Behold, three times "hath our Lord saved thee from drowning through

Page 140

---

¹ Read ܓܠܠܐ.

Page 141 "the prayers of the Lady | Mary; rise up now, and "take mud from this island, and knead it well, and "make therefrom three great bricks, each as large as "ever thou canst carry in thy hands. And when the "night cometh, go up, and sit down by the tree which "is in the middle of the island; and, behold, there "shall come forth a certain mighty wild beast, in the "mouth of which there will be a pearl, and it will "lay the pearl under the tree. Do thou then cast "upon the beast one of the mud bricks." And the merchant did according to what the anchorite had said unto him.

And it came to pass that when it was dark, a most fearsome wild beast went forth, and it set down upon the ground a pearl out of its mouth under that tree; and the pearl lit up with light the whole island. And the merchant cast one mud brick over the pearl, and buried it, and the wild beast fled and entered into the water. And when midnight had come, the beast put forth another pearl; and the merchant did the same thing in the matter of it. And at the end of
Page 142 the night, the beast put forth yet another | pearl, and laid it under the tree. And the merchant did the same thing in the matter of this pearl also; and the beast did not appear again.

And it came to pass that when the day had dawned, the merchant went down and took the three pearls, and he went to the old man the anchorite, and shewed them unto him. And the old man said unto the merchant, "Knowest thou aught of "pearls?" And the merchant said, "A little." And the old man said unto the merchant, "See, O my

"son, Christ hath made ready two-fold for thee
"everything which hath left thee many times; for ob-
"serve, these pearls are beyond all price. Rise up,
"and walk through the island, and thou shalt find
"wood of aloes, wherefrom thou shalt make a box
"which shall be as large as thy two hands can em-
"brace." And the merchant said unto the old man,
"Who shall bring me forth out of this place?" And
the old man said unto him, "My son, to God no-
"thing is difficult." So the merchant did according as
the old man had said unto him; and he tarried with
him until the month of Nîsân, and the clouds began
to gather over the sea. And the old man spake
unto the angel that governed the clouds, saying, Page 143
"Whither are these clouds driving?" And the angel
said unto the old man, "Unto such and such a city."
And the old man said unto him, "Take this man,
"and carry him unto his house." Then the old man
said unto the merchant, "Embrace tightly with thine
"arm this box of aloe wood, and go to sleep, and
"rest thyself. And look in every place in the earth
"whereon thou standest, and look on thy right side, and
"lay the foundation of the building of the house in the
"name of the Lady Mary, on account of which our Lord
"hath given thee these three pearls, two for thyself,
"and one for the building of the house in the name
"of the blessed woman, the Lady Mary." And the
angel took the merchant and set him down upon the
land of the East, which was nigh unto his own house;
and immediately he had descended upon the earth, he
looked on his right hand, and set out the marks for
the house. Then the merchant went to his own

house giving thanks, and glorifying God, Who had delivered him from the sea through the prayers of the Lady Mary. And it came to pass that the merchant waxed exceedingly rich, and he built the building of the house in that place, and he set out the marks for the house in the name of the blessed woman, the Lady | Mary. Now it was the merchant himself who related these things.

And again it came to pass that two women were journeying by themselves along the road to Egypt, when there came against them a mighty serpent to swallow them up. And as they took to flight before him with shrieks, and cries, and tears, they made mention of the name of the Lady Mary. And when the serpent drew nigh to swallow them up, the Angel of the Lord smote him, and he was rent in two parts, from his head even unto his tail; and he fell apart into two pieces. And the women related these things throughout all Egypt, and all those who saw the serpent glorified God.

And again the Lady Mary appeared unto a certain merchant who had set out on a journey with one thousand dînârs wherewith to traffic, but he dropped them on the road; now, the purse which held them dropped from him on the journey and was lost. And it came to pass that when he had travelled some distance through the mountains, he sat down to eat, and he sought for the purse, but could not find it; and he wept and cried out loudly. And as he came along the road he prayed, saying, "O Lady Mary, "have mercy upon me." Then the blessed woman had mercy upon him, and she took him, and made him to stand over the purse, and he took that which belonged unto him, and glorified God. Now, whilst the Lady Mary wrought these mighty deeds, and many others besides them, the Apostles in Rome, and in all the other countries were with her. By her prayers may the Churches of Christ be preserved from the Evil One, and from his hosts! Amen. By her prayers may priests and kings be reconciled! Amen. By her prayers may those who believe be preserved from the wickedness of the unbelieving Jews! Amen. Whosoever cometh unto her festival, and rejoiceth in her commemoration, let him be aided by her prayers! Amen. And may all those who give alms from their houses on that day to the poor be rewarded an hundredfold; and may they have happiness, and rejoice, and be glad, and may all troubles and afflictions be cast away from them! Amen. May the grayheaded be strengthened, and the young men be made sound in the fear of God! May the young children be reared, and may the women be preserved without blemish! [Amen.] May the sick be healed, and may atonement be made for the sinful! [Amen.] May those who are afar off be brought back to their homes in safety, and may those who are near be preserved! [Amen.] May those women who are barren conceive like Sarah and Hannah, and may those who are virgins be kept in a state of chastity! [Amen.] By the prayers of the Lady Mary may all sorts and conditions of men be provided | henceforth with the provisions of the commemoration! Amen. And may every one who shall celebrate her commemoration, and shall set apart some portion of his house for the church which shall be built in her name, be blessed in his house through her prayers! Amen. And may her prayer be with the writer of this book, and with the reader thereof, and with those who hearken thereunto! [Amen.] And unto the people of the Christians may there be rest and peace! Amen.

Glory be to God! And upon us and upon every one who shall read and expound this book, be His mercy and graciousness! Yea and Amen.

And again, by the hand of God I write down the account of the wonderful thing which the blessed woman, the Lady Mary, wrought; may her prayer be a rock wall unto us!

Know ye, O my beloved brethren, that the Fathers and Doctors of the Holy Church have related unto us concerning the miracles and wonderful deeds which the pure Virgin, the Lady Mary, wrought after our Lord Jesus Christ ascended into heaven. | And the Fathers have said that there was in the city of Apamea a certain man who was a true believer, and that he believed in the Lady Mary, the Mother of Christ, with a great belief. And from year to year he was wont to make a great memorial feast, and to gather together a mighty multitude of people from every city, and from every village, and from every country. And it came to pass that one year he made his memorial feast according to his wont, and he invited thereto the Bishops, and the Metropolitans, and the monks who were solitaries, and the priests and the deacons, and a very large number of people who were believers; and thousands, and tens of thousands of people came (now they were without number), and they were glad and rejoiced in the commemoration of the chariot of the Lady Mary, the mother of Christ. Now the name of the man who made the memorial feast was Andronicus, and the name of his son was Andrew, besides whom he had no other son. And it came to pass that his father sent him down to the sea-shore, to those who caught fish, to bring some fish which they might prepare for the feast of the Bishops and the monks. And when the boy had gone out, and had departed and arrived at the sea, at the place where the fishermen were, he bought some fish from them, and sent them home to his father's house with his servants. Now he himself did not return with the servants, but he remained on the shore with the fishermen. And he began to play in a boat which was there on the sea-shore, and he went up on it and embarked therein. Then, straightway, the boat became loose of its own accord, and got away from among the ships, and drifted out to sea, without the knowledge of any of the sailors. And when the boat had floated out to sea a little way, the waves and billows rose up against the little ship, and the boy fell out of it, and went down to the bottom of the sea.

And when the servants who had with them the fish arrived at their master's house, he enquired of them concerning his son. And the servants made answer, and said unto him, "Lord, he would neither "hearken unto us, nor would he be persuaded to "come with us; and we did not like to thwart his will,

Page 148 "for he besought us | to let him play there for about "the space of an hour, and then he would come back." And his father rejoiced when he heard thus, and he occupied himself with the company that were in his house.

And when the time of evening had drawn nigh and had arrived, and the boy did not come back, his father went quickly to the fishermen and enquired of them concerning his son, and what had become of him. And the fishermen said unto him, "Mayest "thou live for ever! Thy son hath this day been "drowned in the sea. Immediately after thy servants "had gone back, leaving the boy with us, he went "and began to play in one of the boats which be- "came unfastened whilst he was inside it, and then "drifted out to sea; and the billows dashed against "the boat, and thy son fell out of it and sank into "the sea. Now we were far away from the boat, and "were not able to render him help; but it was here "that he was drowned and sank into the sea. Now "therefore, thou knowest." And the father of the boy made answer to the fishermen, and said unto them, "I bid you swear by the Great Name of God "that ye will tell unto no man this mystery until the "blessed festival of the Lady Mary, the mother of our "Redeemer, be ended, so that our gladness may not "be changed into sorrow and mourning, and our joy "into anguish and sadness." Then Andronicus, having made them to take the oath and admonished them, returned to his house.

And when he had returned, his wife saw him, and said unto him, "Where is thy son Andrew? And why "hast thou not brought him with thee?" Her husband answered and said unto her, "I left him to "play there." Now he did not wish to reveal unto her the news of the drowning of her son until the festival was ended. And the wife waited a little longer, and again said unto her husband, "Where is "the boy?" And Andronicus said unto her, "What "could I do? For the boy wanted to play with the "other children, and I was unwilling to thwart his "will." And he did not reveal unto her that the boy was drowned, lest the progress of the festival should be interfered with and stopped, and joy should be turned to anguish and weeping.

And it came to pass that when the morning had come his wife said again unto him, "Where is the "boy, | our son?" And he rebuked her, and said unto her, "I am unwilling to trouble him, for behold, "he is playing with the boys his companions, and is "rejoicing with them. Speak thou no further on the "matter." And he did not reveal the matter unto her until the people had partaken of the sanctification of the Holy Mysteries of the Body and Blood of Christ. Then the multitudes began to eat and to drink, and the festival was duly celebrated with everything which was right and proper, and all the people wished to depart to their homes. And it came to pass that, when the crowds had departed to set out on their journey, the mother of the boy said unto her husband, "Where is thy son? Peradventure he is lost." Then her husband said unto her, "Woman, thy son "was drowned in the sea yesterday. Immediately our "servants had brought away the fish, our son Andrew "embarked in a little boat, and began to play there-"in, that is to say, on the deck (?)¹ of the boat; and he "fell out of the boat into the sea and was drowned. "And now, whatsoever thou wishest to do, that do." And when the mother of the boy heard the amazing news that her son was drowned, she began to cry out, and to weep, and to utter loud shrieks; and she pulled loose her plaited hair, and scattered dust upon her head, and smote herself upon her cheeks. Now when all the multitudes heard the sound of the shrieks and the crying, they turned back from their ways, and came to see what had happened. And when they had entered into the city of Apamea, they began to ask, "What is this noise, and this outcry, and this "commotion?" And the people said unto them, "An-"drew, the son of Andronicus who made the memor-"ial feast in the name of the Lady Mary, was drowned "in the sea yesterday." And the priests and a great multitude of believing folk gathered themselves together, and came to the parents of the boy, and they saw that they were sorrowing and weeping because of the drowning of the boy; now all the people who had come to the feast had returned. And all the people went forth in a body from the city along with the father and mother of the boy, and they came with them to the sea, and they began to ask the catchers of fish about the place where Andrew sank and was drowned.

Then the Bishops, and the monks, and the elders,

---

¹ ܐܠܦܘܢܐ is a boat with a portion of it covered over to serve as a deck; ܐܠܦܐ may be this deck.

and the deacons, and all the people, and the assemblies of believing men, stood up and began to pray, and to make entreaty unto God. And they cried out with the sound of weeping, and they made supplication unto the Lady Mary, and said, "O Mother "of our Redeemer, save the child through thy prayers." Then swimmers dived down into the sea, and went round about therein, and they came to the place where the boy had sunk; and they saw him still alive, and they brought him forth out of the sea. And all the people rejoiced in him, and were glad, and great fear fell upon them; and they remained wondering and marvelling at what they had seen, and they lifted up praise unto God. And they drew nigh unto the boy and asked him, saying, "O boy, tell us, "and make us to know what happened unto thee." Then the boy Andrew began to speak, and he said unto them in a loud voice, "Hear, O all ye people, "what I have to say, and I will tell you what hath "happened unto me. O my brethren, yesterday I "came hither, with the servants whom my father had "sent, to buy fish for the meal which we were mak- "ing for the Bishops and monks. And we bought "fish from those who catch them, and the servants "took them and went [home]; and I stayed here by "myself under the deck (?) in a boat. And I got up on "it, and put out to sea a little way, and then the "waves rose up and beat upon the boat, and I fell "out of it into the sea. And when I began to sink "and to drown, I saw there a woman who was shin- "ing with light like unto the sun. And she was wrap- "ped about with glory and splendour, and she was

"dressed in apparel of light; and she was crowned
"with glory, and she was clothed with garments both
"purple and violet-coloured.¹ And she lifted me on
"to her knees, and she clasped me unto herself and
"embraced me; and she put one arm round about
"my neck, and the other she laid upon my mouth,
"so that the water might not enter therein." And she
"said unto me, "Fear not, O my son." And I saw
"also two men who were glorious and splendid, and
"they were burning like unto fire, and they had also
"wings of fire; and they were standing round about
"that woman to pay her honour. And whenever any
"of the large fish which are in the waters drew nigh
"unto me to swallow me up, those two men blew
"upon him that came and he was consumed.² And
"that woman held me upon her knees thus from yester-
"day until now. And it came to pass that when the
"swimmers descended after me, the woman saw them,
"and when they were near me, she said unto me,
"'Rise, O my son, and go up with these swimmers
"'who have come down into the sea for thee'; and
"she kissed my face, and delivered me over unto
"them, and I came up with them. And behold, I
"stand among you now as ye see."

And every one who heard this wonderful thing
marvelled, and gave glory unto God, and exalted
our Lady, the Lady Mary, and paid honour unto her
who gave birth unto Christ, our Redeemer. And every
man of all those who were there set out to depart

---

¹ *I. e.*, ܒܢܦܫܝ.
² Read ܘܣܦ.

again unto his own country in joy and gladness, and they glorified God; and they gave thanks unto, and paid honour unto, and magnified the holy Virgin, the Lady Mary, because of everything which they had seen and heard. And Andronicus, the father of the boy, made a most solemn vow that the festival and commemoration of the Lady Mary should never fail to be kept in his house; and behold, to this day the people thereof celebrate, in the city of Apamea, on the day on which this great and marvellous thing was wrought, the festival and commemoration of the Lady Mary. And every one who heard these words glorified God, to Whom glory and honour are meet, now and at all times, and for ever and for ever. Amen.

And now, O my beloved brethren, know that we beseech and entreat Christ, Who was born of her, and Who rose from the womb of the pure, and holy, and blessed Virgin, that in His mercy and graciousness He will bless whosoever shall celebrate the festival of the Lady Mary, | and shall honour and magnify the festivals and commemorations with praisings and hymns of the Holy Spirit. And we also beseech Christ to let His rest and peace abide in every country wherein they honour the festivals of the Virgin, the Lady Mary, and to let His good things be multiplied therein; and unto all the inhabitants thereof let there be help and deliverance from the fire of Gehenna! Yea, and Amen.

Here endeth the History of the blessed woman, the Lady Mary, the Mother of Christ our Lord. And

unto God be glory, and honour, and exaltation, and
worship, for ever and for ever! Amen.¹

---

¹ The colophon of the MS. states that the copy of the work published in this book was made by one 'Îsâ, the son of Isaiah, the son of Cyriacus the deacon, who belonged to the village of Ekrôr, in the country of the Sendâyê, at Al-ḳôsh. It was finished on the 11th day of the Latter Kânôn, A. D. 1889, "in the days "of Mâr Êliyâ XIII, the Catholicus Patriarch of Babel of the East." At the end it is said that I paid for the copying of the work.

THE HISTORY OF THE LIKENESS OF CHRIST,
AND OF HOW THE ACCURSED JEWS IN THE
CITY OF TIBERIAS MADE A MOCK THEREOF
IN THE DAYS OF THE GOD-LOVING EMPEROR
ZENO.

THE HISTORY OF THE LIKENESS OF CHRIST, AND OF HOW
THE ACCURSED JEWS IN THE CITY OF TIBERIAS MADE A
MOCK THEREOF IN THE DAYS OF THE GOD-LOVING EMPEROR
ZENO.[1] O LORD, HELP ME IN THY MERCY! AMEN.

From Philotheus, the Deacon of the Country of
he East, to the spiritual Fathers, who are in every
country, and in every province, in Jesus Christ our
Lord and God; peace be multiplied!
I would have you to know, O my brethren, that
was exceedingly anxious in the love of our Lord
o go up to Jerusalem, the City of the Great King,
ind to see the exalted regions wherein Christ walk-
:d, and the holy Places wherein He wrought mighty
leeds and miracles. For I had desire to go to Beth-
ehem, and to enter into the Cave and to see the
)lace where[2] He, Who fashioneth babes in the wombs
)f those Who are with child, was wrapped in swad-
lling-bands and laid in a manger. And from thence
would go to the Jordan that I might understand
1ow the river could bear Him Who created it, Him

---

[1] Emperor of the East A. D. 474—491.
[2] Here and elsewhere for ܪ̈ܚܡܐ we should probably read
ܐܬܪ.

Who holdeth the waters of the sea in the hollow
His Hand, and Who hath set the sand as an ii
passable boundary therefor. And I would go up al
to Cana and see the place where He, Who coi
manded the earth to produce trees of every kii
which should bear fruit each having the taste aft
its kind, sat at meat, having been invited to the fea;
and changed the water into wine. And I would alig
at and pass through the Porch of Solomon, and s
the place where lay the paralytic, whose sickness h;
cleaved unto him and vexed him throughout eig

Page 158 and thirty years, to whom He | spake one wor
and raised him up from his bed; for to God ever
thing is easy.² And I would see the well of t
Samaritan woman, and how he who had been blii
from his mother's womb was healed. And I wou
pass by the grave of Lazarus, and I would go ι
from thence to Golgotha, and I would see whe
was fixed the Cross of Him Who stretched out t
ladder from the heavens to the earth in the mou
tain of Gilead for the sake of Jacob His belove
And I would go into the grave and see where t
Lion's Whelp, concerning Whom the prophets wrc
in their mysteries, crouched in the habitation of She
for three days and three nights. And afterwards
would go up to the Mount of Olives, where He li
ed up His holy hands and blessed the Apostles a
ascended unto his glorious Father. And I would al
enter into the upper chamber where He, Who we
forth from the womb and did not destroy the sig

---

¹ See p. 171, note 2.
² Read, according to Add. 14,645 ܐܗܝ ܦܫܝܩ ܠܗ ܟܠܡܕܡ.

of virginity of her who gave Him birth, went in to His disciples, the doors being shut. This, then, was the earnest desire which possessed me. And I set my face, and drew nigh unto my Bishop, and I persuaded him to permit me to go to perform my journey. And he received my entreaty and sent me away, and blessed me, saying, "Go, and may the Lord God, Who hath kindled in thee the desire to journey in His path in the belief of the truth, go with thee. May He make straight thy way before thee so that thou mayest go in peace and come in peace; and may He make marvellous things to flourish at thy hands, and mayest thou come and tell us concerning the glorious things which thine eyes have seen. Mayest thou be a builder up of the belief of the truth, and an overthrower of the Jews whose wickedness thou shalt see, and concerning whose shame thou shalt make proclamation! And do thou pray on our behalf in the holy temples into which thou shalt enter, and do thou have me in remembrance before the Grave of our Lord." With these words of blessing, then, was I provided for my journey by my Bishop, and he spake unto me as it were a prophecy, for every thing which he spake unto me came to pass.[1]

And it came to pass afterwards that I rose up and went forth from the house of my fathers, and having committed my soul to the living God I crossed over the river, the great Euphrates; and I journeyed through provinces, and I meditated in my heart,

---

[1] For ܗܘ, read ܗܘܐ.

Page 159 and I understood matters. And I passed through Pa[l]stine and through the country of Tiberias; I s[aw] cities which had become heaps and mounds, palac[es] which had been overthrown, villages which had be[en] destroyed, and homesteads which had been ma[de] desolate and had become graves for the lords there[of.] I saw dead bodies which had been scattered abo[ut] and bones which had been stripped of their flesh, a[nd] human limbs which had been thrown down broadca[st] and I thought within myself that this country m[ust] have been Sodom whereupon God made to fall fire a[nd] brimstone. And as I was marvelling if it were so [or] no, not knowing whom I could ask to inform me, [I] bowed the knee, and prayed and said, "O Go[d] "Who in Thy love wast pleased to descend from t[he] "heavens to the earth to redeem the children of m[en] "from error, do Thou make to meet me a man w[ho] "feareth Thy holy name that he may show me wh[at] "mean these things which mine eyes have seen, a[nd] "what cause hath called this destruction [upon t[his] "country]." And it came to pass that whilst I w[as] praying a certain man rose up before me, gre[y] haired but goodly of form and desirable in his a[p]pearance, and his words were gracious; and I loo[k]ed upon him and knew that God had sent him. A[s] I drew nigh unto him and saluted him, and I rece[iv]ed a blessing from him, and I made entreaty un[to] him, saying, "I beseech thee, O master, to tell [me] "and to show me what is the cause of the overthr[ow] "of all these cities and villages over which I ha[ve] "passed and which have been turned into a wild[er]"ness, and when they received this judgment." Th[e]

ıe holy one opened his mouth and spake softly nto me, and said unto me, "Rise up, O my son, hearken, and I will show thee. It was thus from the beginning. When God saw that Adam had been brought low and had been cast into Sheol, and that his posterity had been led captive by Satan, and had been brought into servitude under the yoke of sin, He sent His Son Who came down and put on Adam through the Virgin Mary; and He was born and rose upon the world with unspeakable wonder, even as He desired and as was good in His sight. And the Magi came, bearing offerings, and the angels came down, singing praises with their voices, and the Seraphim, rustling their wings, and | they cried Page 160
out at the door of the cave in which He was born, saying, 'Holy, Holy, Holy is the Son of God Who 'hath come down from the heavens to the earth'. And He became like the children of men, and He attained to perfect stature like all [men] born of women. He hungered and thirsted like the children of men; He slept like the children of flesh; He wrought mighty deeds; He made manifest marvellous works like God; He cleansed the lepers, and cast out devils; He drove away demons; He made whole the sick; He healed those that were diseased; He gave life unto the dead; He made straight those that were crooked with disease; He opened the eyes of the blind; He made the deaf to hear; He commanded the water, and it became wine; and He blessed five barley-loaves, and five thousand men ate thereof and were satisfied. By His coming He made to be at peace the heavens and the earth

"which had been moved to wrath; in the wildernε
"there was abundance; in the tilled land there wε
"wonders; in the height there was glorifying; and
"the depth there was praise.

"But the people of the Jews had envy of Him, a
"they laid hands upon Him, and seized Him, and rev
"ed Him, and despised Him, and uttered blasphem
"concerning Him; and they delivered Him to the juc
"ment of death, and they smote Him and they buffet
"Him. They set up a Cross and hung Him thereς
"He cried out from the top of the wood, and the s
"became darkened in the firmament. The veil of t
"door of the Temple heard His voice and was re
"in twain; the rocks perceived it and split asundι
"the graves were opened and the dead went fo
"therefrom. He delivered His soul into the har
"of His Father; and they took Him down from t
"Cross, and laid Him in the grave. He entered iı
"the abode of the dead, and did not see corruptiι
"The angels came down and rolled away the stc
"from the door of the grave; He rose from the to
"on the third day, and raised up many with H
"He appeared unto His disciples after [His] Res
"rection from the dead, and He blessed them, a
"ascended into heaven unto His Father, Who ┝
"sent Him into the world, and He raised up w
"Him the body of Adam. And, behold, He sitteth
"the right hand of Him Who sent Him."

"Now this destruction which thou hast seen, t
"is to say, the cities and villages which have bι
"overturned upon their inhabitants, hath taken pl
"because they despised His commandments and wo

not receive Him, and because they contemned His
goodness and because they did not | believe that Page 161
He was the true God Who came forth from the true
God. Now the reason for this judgment is this:
When Christ was dwelling in Jerusalem His disciples
drew nigh unto Him and showed Him the building
of the Temple of Jerusalem; and they said unto Him,
'Behold, see how beautiful is the building of this
'Temple, and how great, and glorious, and lofty,
'and splendid it is!' And Jesus answered and said
unto them, 'Verily, I say unto you, Because the
'Father is not served therein with holiness, and the
'Son is not adored therein with praise, and the
'Spirit is not cherished therein with devotion, one
'stone shall not be left upon another which shall not
'be overthrown; and the beauty thereof shall be de-
'stroyed, and the Temple shall fall to the ground.'
And thus it came to pass, for it was overthrown even
to its foundations. And the Jews rose up afterwards
to set it up again and to build it as it was aforetime, and to make the holy words of Christ to be
a lie. And the anger of the Lord went up and
He waxed wroth against them, He looked upon the
earth and made it to tremble, He commanded it
and it reeled, and its spirit descended and it turned itself over upon its inhabitants. And, had it not
been that the mercy of Christ sustained creation,
destruction,[1] absolute and entire, must have come
unto it. This is the cause of the desolation which
thou hast seen. But do thou, wheresoever thou goest,

---

[1] Read ܚܒܠܐ.

"proclaim and teach and speak (and thou shalt
"be afraid), that this Jesus, Who was born of M
"the Virgin, is God Who came forth from the I
"ing God, and that He was with His Father fr
"everlasting. May every soul, and every domini
"and all powers worship and glorify Him, to Wh
"praise and adoration are due for ever and for ev
"Amen."

And it came to pass that, when I had stood
and had listened to the words of the man of G
and had laid [them] in my heart, he was hidden fr
me, and I knew not whither he had gone. So I
gan to journey forwards on my way, and I w
and entered into Tiberias,[1] and as I was going rou
about I saw therein horrible signs and fearful sigl
that is to say, confusion which was without orde
among the enemies of Christ and those who ha
God. There were children who were without fa
and fathers who had no truth in them; they enter
in scoffing, and they came forth mocking; they w
forth blaspheming, and they came back sinning. A
I rose up, and marvelled, and pains laid hold up
me like a woman who is about to bring forth; I r
ditated anxiously, and my spirit was troubled. I lo
ed on the right hand, and I saw that there was nc
who knew me; I longed greatly to hear the sw
voice of the cry which proclaimed concerning 1

---

[1] *I. e.*, the strongly fortified capital of Galilaea which was situ
ed on the south-west coast of the sea of Tiberias; it was b
by the tetrarch Antipas in honour of the Emperor Tiberius,
lay at a distance of about 84 miles from Jerusalem.

ith of our Lord Jesus Christ, and there was none.
nd moreover, whilst I was[1] pondering this thought,
What is this heathenism, and where is the root
thereof that it hath not as yet dried up?" and whilst
was marvelling concerning everything which mine
yes had seen I left [that place] and went forth out-
de the city. And I went away therefrom about the
istance of one mile, and I set the knee, and prayed,
nd said, "O Lord God, Who art merciful, and pro-
tecting, and long-suffering, and abundant in goodness and truth, Who desirest that the children of men
may live, Who lovest rest and peace, let there be
found for me a man Who feareth Thy holy name
that he may show and declare unto me what is the
cause of this sin, and what is the promise of this
wickedness."

And it came to pass that as I was making sup-
lication and praying unto God I found that man,
ho had appeared unto me aforetime, standing be-
re me; but his appearance was changed, for he
as clothed with wrath, his speech was hot with in-
ignation, and he was like unto a man who had es-
ped from a band of thieves. And he cried unto
e and said, "What seekest thou, O man? What
ause hath called thee to this country? Whither is
hy face set to go?" And I drew nigh unto him,
d I saluted him, and I received a blessing from
m, and I made entreaty unto him concerning that
hich he had spoken unto me. And I asked him,
ying, "I entreat thee, O my lord, tell me what is

---

[1] Read ,ᎴᏒ.

"thy name, and whence comest thou, and why th
"appearest to me like a man driven onwards
"violence, and like a man who hath escaped from
"band of thieves, and like a hostile man who is ar
"ed for war? For although thy appearance be f

Page 163 "and thy speech straight, yet thy wrath | is cruel, a
"I am afraid to look upon thee." Then he open
his mouth and spake unto me, saying, "I am t
"captain of the hosts of the Lord, and I minis
"unto the majesty of the Son of God. I prayed ur
"Him, and He hath sent me to show thee that wh
"thou hast asked and to inform thee concerning t
"desire; and behold, He hath sent me unto thee twi
"For when pure prayer is offered unto Him, straig
"way He commandeth, and the prayer entereth
"before Him and receiveth that which it hath ask
"and goeth forth; for God is the merciful One, a
"He heareth likewise the prayers of all those w
"believe. And, behold, we have received the cc
"mand from Him, and we are wont to bring in [l
"fore Him] the prayers of all those who are penit
"through the gate of the glory of the exalted maj
"ty; and we do not dare to look at Him Who
"ceiveth them.¹ And because thy prayer hath enter
"in before Him, behold, I have been sent unto tl
"twice that I might make known unto thee that wh
"thou hast asked in thy prayer from God. And
"concerning that which thou hast said, that thou d
"look upon me as upon one armed for battle, I sta
"ready so that if it was permitted unto me I wo

---

¹ The better reading is that of Add. 14,645 which has ܡܩܒܠܢܐ

straightway destroy all those who crucified [Christ]. And I would cast down the dead bodies of the Jews, and would make an end[1] of the nation that provoketh to wrath, and would blot out from the face of the earth all the sons of Jacob who have dared to revile, and to buffet, and to crucify, and to slay Him upon the outermost edge of the abiding-place of Whose Majesty we do not dare to look. It is for this reason that my wrath hath mounted up. But hearken, and I will show thee an iniquity which the wrath-provoking sons of contumacious fathers have wrought, which is greater than all else in this city which was stirred up thereby. And I prayed to God that He would show thee, for the ears of the children of men are not able to hear this iniquitous thing, nor is their tongue able to speak concerning this wickedness, for it is great beyond measure, and abundant beyond counting, and vast beyond bounds. Atonement cannot be made for it, and offerings cannot be offered up therefor, for its retribution is Gehenna, the wages thereof are the worms, and the punishment | therefor is darkness, and the inheritance thereof is woe and gnashing of teeth. Hearken now, and I will show thee, O believing man, and receive my words, and ascribe glory unto God Who hath been so long-suffering towards this contumacious people. For when they were in Egypt, and the Egyptians were making them serve with the service of mud and of bricks, and were embittering their lives with cruel labour, they cried out unto God and He heard

---

[1] Read, with Add. 14,645, ܚܪܬܐ.

"their groaning, and He remembered His covenɛ
"and had mercy upon them. And He sent Mos
"and Aaron unto Pharaoh the king of Egypt, tɧ
"He might deliver them out of the hand of those w
"were afflicting them. He wrought miracles and wondɛ
"ful deeds among them by the cruel plagues with whi
"He smote the Egyptians, and He brought the peoɿ
"out from thence. He divided the Sea of Reeds ƃ
"fore them, and He heaped up the waters, as it wɛ
"in skin-bottles, and the waters stood up straig
"on their right hand and on their left, and becaɪ
"unto them like a wall, and the people passed throu;
"the sea on dry land. And Pharaoh the king
"Egypt followed after them, and Moses brought ƃ
"hand back over the sea, and it returned upon Ph
"raoh and upon all his host; and the Egyptians pɛ
"ished, and were drowned among the waves. A:
"the Hebrews went up with praise and exultatic
"and God led them into the desert. He made thɛ
"to march in the day time in a pillar of cloud,
"that they should not be afraid of the hand of tho
"who might afflict them in the noonday, and by nig
"in the radiance of fire, so that they might not stumƃ
"in the darkness. He fed them with all manner
"good things, and He satisfied them with all mann
"of glorious foods; they ate the bread of angels, ƴ
"they asked for onions and garlic. The nations wɛ
"laid waste and cast down before them, yet th
"desired anxiously to be buried in Egypt; and th
"said unto Moses, 'Why didst thou not leave us
"'die in Egypt?' They became fat like stalled beaː
"with the good things of the sea and of the lar

'yet their mouth was filled with blasphemy and com-
'plaint. He cleft the rock in the wilderness, and brought
'out running waters from the stone, and they com-
'plained against God, | and said, 'Since He hath Page 165
"smitten the stony rock, and waters have flowed
"down and He hath made springs to gush out, per-
"adventure He is also able to give us bread or to
"make ready meat for His people.' And the Lord
heard, and was wroth, but because of His covenant
with Abraham He turned back His anger that He
might not destroy them. And the Lord cried unto
Moses, and said unto him, 'Speak unto the children
'of Israel, that they sanctify themselves and be holy;
'and do thou come up unto me into the mountain,
'and I will give thee the Law and the Commandment
'which thou shalt hand down to them.' And Moses
did as the Lord said unto him, and while he was
coming down from the mountain the people stood
up against Aaron, and said unto him, 'Make unto
'us gods that they may go before us.' O foolish
nation, O stubborn nation, O contumacious nation,
could ye not perform His commandments? And con-
sider the strength of God Who worked on your behalf, Who turned the waters into blood, and Who
on your account punished the Egyptians severely
with lice, and with blains, and with fire, and with
hail, and with the death of the first-born, and with
afflictions of every kind? And yet ye would require
a God! And they made themselves a calf, and
they bowed down before him, and they changed
their glory into the similitude of an ox that eateth
hay. And because of this thing my wrath went up.

"But hearken, and I will shew thee iniquity which
"greater than all these things. And I prayed un{
"God, and I entreated Him to shew thee the iniquit
"which the wrath-provoking sons of rebellious fathe
"have wrought in this city, whereby it hath becon
"perturbed. Hearken then, and receive my words, ar
"ascribe glory unto God, Who hath been so lon;
"suffering with this contumacious people."

"Now those who crucified the Son of God wrote
"their covenants to their sons, and to their sons' son
"saying, 'We seized Christ, the Son of Mary, becau:
"'He called Himself the Son of God; and we deliver(
"'Him over to the judgment of death, and we cr
"'cified Him, and we slew Him. And He did n
"'rise of His own accord, but by favour He was bui
"'ed by the children of His people. And after H
"'death we seized His disciples, and we persecut(
"'them, and we slew them, and we drove them fort:
"'from the congregation; and they went round abo
"'begging. And ye also, O children of fathers wl
"'wrought these things, make no mistake. If the
"'should be any man who would make you to e
"'[by following] after the doctrine of that seduc(
"'or if ye should find any man confessing Him,
"'we have done even so do ye.' But the fooli
"nation did not know that these things had be
"inscribed for their shame, and that they had be
"written down for their reproach. And all their ch
"dren who were in this city gathered themselves 1
"gether, and they also meditated within themselv
"how much disgrace they were able to heap up
"the honourable Name of Christ; and they took cot

sel, one with another, how to make a picture of the
Likeness of Christ upon a panel of wood, and how
to make a mock of Him and how to insult Him.
And the nobles took counsel together, and they
sent and called a certain painter and said unto him
craftily, 'We know that our fathers who crucified
'Christ acted very wickedly, and we do not consent
'to the wickedness which they wrought. But we
'entreat thee to take as much gold as ever thou
'wishest, and to paint for us a likeness of Christ.'
And these mad people did not know that they were
weaving a crown for their shame! And the painter
said unto them, 'I cannot paint a likeness of Christ
'for the nation that crucified Him upon the wood,
'lest the governors hear thereof, and take off my
'head as being a man who participated in the secrets
'of the Jews.' And the chief priests said unto him,
'We ourselves believe in Christ, and every one who
'heareth that thou hast given unto us a likeness of
'Christ that we may worship Him (for we believe
'in Him with our whole heart), will multiply the
'praise of thee.' And the painter said unto the Jews,
'How would ye have me to portray Him? And in
'what manner would ye have me to depict Him?'
And the priests said unto him, 'Paint Him for us
'upon a large panel of wood, hanging upon the
'cross, and clothed in purple apparel, and having
'the crown of thorns upon His head.'"

"And the painter took a panel of wood, and painted
a likeness of Christ upon it even as they had told
him. And the Jews took it and set it up in an
nner chamber that they might insult | it and work

Page 167

"their will upon it. And they knelt down upon th(
"knees, and they paid homage unto it, and th
"said, 'This is the Christ Whom our fathers crucifie
"'and we also give our consent to what they did
"'the matter. And we would follow in their footste｢
"'and we would emulate their acts; and had we be
"'living in their days we would have performed t
"'deed much better than they did.' Then one
"them ran, and took a spear, and grasping it in l
"hand said, 'I myself also do even as my fathe
"'did'; and he drave the spear into the side of t
"likeness of Christ, and made a mock of it the whi
"Then straightway blood and water came forth ther
"from. And the people who would crucify saw tl
"and marvelled, and some of them confessed, sayin
"'Verily He Whom our fathers crucified in Jerusale
"'is the Son of God, and He is the true God; a〉
"'this wonderful thing is indeed great.' And th〈
"began to try and hide the matter as if nothing h;
"taken place. And it came to pass that, whilst th〈
"stood whispering, and were seeking to hide tl
"matter so that it might not be heard of, a certa
"blind man who was standing there heard them wh
"pering. And he answered and said unto them,
"'entreat you to bring me nigh unto the likeness
"'that I may insult Him Who, being a man, ma〉
"'Himself to be the Son of God.' And the Je〉
"thought that he was [speaking] the truth, and th〈
"took the blind man and brought him nigh unto
"and the blind man stretched out his hand, a〉
"clasped the likeness. And, as all the people we
"looking on, he took some of the water and blo〈

and smeared it upon his eyes, and he cried out
with a loud voice, saying, 'O Christ, the Son of
God, as Bar-Ṭîmî (Bartimaeus) cried unto Thee,
and Thou didst lay Thine hand upon his eyes and
he saw the light, even so open Thou mine eyes
for me in this hour, and I will confess Thy goodness, and Thy holy Name shall be glorified.' And
immediately that the water and the blood touched
him, his eyes were opened, and he saw the light,
and he became as one whom hurt had never touch-
ed; and he gave thanks and glorified God | for the Page 168
act of grace which He had wrought for him. Then
the Jews took counsel among themselves, and said,
'Come, let us kill this blind man so that he may
not go forth and proclaim in the world that which
hath happened unto him. If we do not do this our
priesthood will come to an end, and our laws will
be abrogated, and our nation will perish, and our
synagogue will be destroyed, and we shall die.'"
"And it came to pass that when those who believed in Christ heard these things, they planned means
whereby they might rescue him from out of their
hands. And they said unto them, 'Nay, not so, it
is not good that we should kill him, lest the report
thereof go forth the more into the world, and it
lead every man astray after Christ, and the people
say, They rose up and killed that blind man because Christ opened his eyes. But let us give him
such a bribe as is necessary, and when he has
accepted it let us teach him to say that we laid
upon him the ark which is filled with our Holy Scriptures, and the Tables of the Law which Moses

"'wrote, and the Rod of Aaron, and the Coffer of
"'Manna, and he saw the light.' Then the priests
"called the blind man, and said unto him, 'What
"'sayest thou, O man? Choose thee one of two
"'things. Either accept gold, as much as thou know-
"'est [how to ask], and conceal this matter, or get
"'thee forth out of this city, and go whithersoever
"'thou wishest to go. In the latter case we shall
"'drive out along with thee all thy kinsfolk, and we
"'shall not allow any of thy people to remain here.
"'And besides all these things, if thou wilt not be
"'persuaded [so to do], thou and all those who are
"'acquaintances of thine shall receive the judgment
"'of death.' And the blind man answered and said
"unto them, 'Even though I were to die for the
"'Name of Christ it would be gain unto me. How
"'can ye tell me to deny Him upon Whom I cried,
"'Who in one moment gave unto me the light
"'which I had not seen having been vexed, even by
"'day, by the darkness for these forty years past?
"'And behold, this act of grace hath been given
"'unto me at your hands, and I have seen the light
"'which is much to be desired.' And when the Jews
"heard the words, 'This gift hath been given unto
"'me at your hands, | and I have seen the light,' they
"rejoiced greatly and they imagined that they would
"be what he would say before all people. So they
"let him go forth free from the chamber wherein the
"likeness stood, and he had in his hand also some
"of that gracious gift which went forth from the like-
"ness, and which he had smeared upon his eyes and
"so gained his sight."

THE PARALYTIC AT THE SYNAGOGUE. 189

"And it came to pass that by the door of that
"synagogue, on the right hand side, there was plac-
"ed a bench whereupon lay a certain paralytic, who
"had been sorely vexed by his affliction for a very
"long time. Now God had preserved that gracious
"gift [of the water and blood] for the shame of the
"Jews. And the paralytic saw the blind man as he
"was coming out, and he perceived with his under-
"standing, and he said within himself, 'This man who
"'hath now come out is he who was blind, and who
"'used to go in and come out of the synagogue; he
"'went in this day being blind, and, behold, he hath
"'now come out with his eyes open. What is this
"'wonderful thing? Who, then, can have opened his
"'eyes for him? Can it be that the Ark of the priest[s]
"'hath given him light? Behold, he was wont to go
"'in and to come out with them every day, and yet
"'no man ever helped him before. Or am I to think
"'that the Law of Moses hath opened the pupils of
"'his eyes for him? Yet he was hearing the Scrip-
"'tures always! Peradventure he is not the same
"'man as the one I knew who was born blind, but
"'some one who is very much like unto him.' And
"whilst he was thus thinking he cried out unto that
"blind man, and said unto him, 'Tell me, O man,
"'what is thy name? By the God of Israel hide it
"'not from me, and by Êl-Shaddai, the great and
"'true God, tell me what is thy name, and whence
"'comest thou.' Then the blind man said unto him,
"'Inasmuch as thou hast conjured me by Him, I will
"'tell thee; but if thou hadst not conjured me by
"'Him I would never have told thee. My name is

"'Judah, and I belong to this city; and I dwell by
"'the side of the courtyard of the house of Ezra, the
"'chief of the congregation.' And the paralytic said
"unto him, 'Art thou not he | who was blind, and
"of whom people related that thou wast born blind?'
"And the blind man said unto him, 'I, even I, am
"'he who was blind, and whom each day thou didst
"'see going¹ in and coming out from the synagogue;
"'but I never saw thee.' And the paralytic said unto
"him, 'Tell me how thine eyes were opened, for,
"'behold, I have been lying here in this place for
"'twenty and one years, and I never saw or heard
"'that the eyes of any blind man had ever been
"'opened except thine.' And the blind man said unto
"him, 'Hast thou ever heard of the Name of Jesus
"'Christ, the Son of God, Who, they say, came into
"'the world, and wrought mighty deeds, and worked
"'miracles, and made manifest marvellous things? And
"'the Jews laid hands upon Him, and they scourged
"'Him, and insulted Him, and crucified Him, and de-
"'livered Him over to death.' And the paralytic said
"unto him, 'I have heard of Him of Whom thou
"'speakest, that He rose from the dead on the third
"'day, and ascended into heaven.' And the blind
"man said unto him, 'It was He who opened my
"'eyes for me, and through Him I saw the light
"'which I had never before seen.' And the paralytic
"said unto him, 'Tell me how He opened thine eyes
"'for thee, and how thou didst believe in Him.' And
"the blind man said unto him, 'I believed in Him,

---

¹ Read ܢܪܚܫ.

"'and I still believe in Him; and I am ready to die
"'rather than to deny Him.' And the paralytic said
"'unto him, 'By Christ, the Son of God, in Whom
"'thou hast believed, tell me how He opened thine
"'eyes for thee. Didst thou call upon Him? And
"'did He send an angel unto thee? Tell me how He
"'opened thine eyes for thee, and how thou didst see
"'the light.' And the blind man said unto him, 'Hear-
"'ken and I will tell thee, and do thou thyself be-
"'lieve; and if thou dost believe, thou shalt at once
"'receive healing, and thou shalt be made strong,
"'even as He also gave me power and I saw the
"'light.' And the paralytic said unto him, 'Speak,
"'and I will listen, and will believe.' And the blind
"man said unto him, 'The chief priests, and the
"'Pharisees considered among themselves, and they
"'made a great likeness, | and set it up in an inner
"'chamber which they had in the refectory wherein no
"'man except the priests entered. And in order that
"'God might make manifest His wonderful acts, and
"'that He might testify concerning His Son, Who came
"'from Him, and Whom He had sent into the world,
"'and that there might also come to me an act of
"'grace, God caused it to happen that I should be
"'among them when the matter which I am about to
"'narrate to you took place. Now the Jews made a
"'likeness of Jesus, and as soon as they had brought it
"'into the chamber, they began to make a mock of it,
"'even as their fathers had done of Christ. And some
"'of them knelt down upon their knees, and did homage
"'unto it, and some of them smote it with a reed,
"'and some of them spat on its face, and as they

Page 171

"'were making a mock of it one of them took a
"'spear and smote it in the side, and straightway
"'blood and water came forth from the likeness. And
"'they saw it and marvelled, and astonishment laid
"'hold upon them; and some of them believed in
"'Christ, and said, 'Verily, He Whom the Jews cru
"'cified in Jerusalem was the Son of God, and He
"'it was Whom creation awaited.' And I was stand
"ing among them listening, and I also feigned to be
"like one who sought to make a mock of it. And
"I spake unto one of them, and I conjured him, say
"ing, 'By the Great Name, take me nigh unto the
"'likeness so that I may make a mock thereof, and
"'that I also, whom God hath caused to be among
"'you, may have participation with you.' And the
"man led me, and brought me nigh unto the likeness
"'and I stretched out my right hand, and took some
"'of the water and blood, and smeared it upon my
"'eyes, and I prayed, and cried out upon the Name
"'of Christ; and straightway He appeared unto me
"'And it came to pass that when mine eyes had
"'been opened, the Jews beat upon their faces with
"'their hands, and they wanted to kill me; but God
"'delivered me from them.' And the paralytic said
"unto him, 'By Christ, upon Whom thou didst call
"'Who gave thee healing and thou didst see th
"'light, and Whom thou dost confess, as this act o
"'grace hath happened unto thee, and thou has
"'gotten | the light which thou hadst not before, per
"'form for me also an act of grace that I also ma
"'receive healing, and may be relieved from thi
"'affliction which hath vexed me for so many years

THE CURE OF THE PARALYTIC.

"Go in, and bring me some of that water and blood, "and anoint for me my limbs, and I have confidence "in Him that He will give me also healing; and this "act of grace shall come to me at thy hands.' And 'the blind man said unto him, 'With the greatest "difficulty only did I escape from those who wanted "to kill me, and wouldst thou send me unto them "again?' And the paralytic said unto him, 'But what "can I do? I cannot stand up, and if I tell one of "them¹ concerning this thing, they will stone me, "and grief the more will be added unto me, because "I am nigh unto the water and the blood, and there "is no man to bring it unto me. Would that some "such wonderful thing as this would happen—that "He would descend, and would walk, and would "come unto me, and would heal me of this affliction!' 'Now the paralytic did not know that some of the gracious gift was in the hand of the blind man."

"And the blind man answered and said unto the paralytic, 'If thou knowest that thou dost believe "in Christ, and dost confess that He is the Son of "God, even as I myself have confessed Him, I will "bring thee some of the water and the blood; and "immediately it shall touch thy body thou shalt be "healed, and thou shalt become like unto one who "hath never at any time been attacked by any dis-"ease whatsoever.' And when the paralytic heard these words from the blind man, he said unto him, 'By the Son of God, Who came down from heaven 'unto the earth, and Who gave thee [power] and

---

¹ *I. e.*, the priests.

"'thou didst see the light, in Whom thou dost b
"'lieve, withhold not from me this gracious gift. F
"'I believe in Him, and in His Father, and that I
"'is God Who cometh from the true God; and i!
"'have any doubt whatever concerning Him, then]
"'some affliction which shall be more grievous th
"'that which I now have come upon me.' And wh
"the blind man heard the confession of the paralyt
"and was confident in his own mind that he w
"confirmed in the faith, he drew forth his hand fro
"beneath his garment, and brought it nigh unto t
"body of the paralytic, and rubbing him | with t
"water and the blood said unto him, 'In the nar
"'of Christ, upon Whom I have believed, upon Who
"'I called, Who answered me and gave unto me tl
"'true Light, rise up from where thou art.' And
"came to pass that when the water and the blo(
"touched him, he was healed straightway, and ro
"up; and the paralytic gave thanks, and glorifi(
"God, Who had given him healing."

"And when the chief priests and the scribes sa
"him who had been made whole and who stood u
"they sought means whereby they might also hi(
"this wonderful thing, so that the name of Christ mig
"not in any way be magnified; but the more the
"wished to hide it, the more was it proclaimed. A1
"they called the paralytic, and said unto him, 'T(
"'us how thou wast made whole, and how thou wa
"'freed from [thy] affliction.' And the paralytic a
"swered and said unto the priests, 'It was Christ, t!
"'Son of God, Who was crucified in Jerusalem, Wl
"'sent unto me healing of the affliction in which

"'lay.' And the priests said unto him, 'How could
"'He, Who could not help Himself when the Jews
"'seized Him, and crucified Him, and slew Him (and
"'He died, and was buried, and even His disciples
"'forsook Him, and fled, and were scattered), send
"'healing unto thee? And who was it that was sent
"'from Him that came and gave thee healing? If such
"'a being was in truth seen by thee, then will we
"'believe that He sent him.' And the paralytic said
"unto them, 'Ye are not worthy to see him [that
"'brought healing to me from Him], for if ye believe
"'not in Him, how will ye receive His ambassador?'
"And the priests said unto him, 'Be not deceived,
"'for no one hath given thee healing except God
"'and the Law which He hath sent by the hands of
"'Moses, and which is read in this country; and be-
"'cause thou hast been lying helpless at His gate for
"'a very long time past, He hath had compassion
"'upon thee, and hath given thee healing.' And the
"paralytic answered and said unto them, 'Against
"'your wills ye speak the truth, for indeed it is not
"'man who hath given me healing, but God only;
"'for[1] He unto Whom I cried, and on Whom I have
"'believed, is God, and He hath given healing unto
"'me. He | is the true God, and He it is Who gave   Page 174
"'the Law unto Moses out of the mountain, and He
"'it is Who came into the world of His own will.
"'And your fathers laid hands upon Him, and they
"'buffeted Him, and He bore from them insult and
"'ignominy that He might redeem the posterity of

---

[1] Read ܠܗܘ.

"'Adam. And as for you, your minds are blind li
"'those of your fathers, and ye do not believe
"'Him.'"
"And it came to pass that when the priests hea
"these things from the paralytic they were filled wi
"great wrath, and they became like unto a flame
"fire; and what to do they knew not. Then th
"answered and said unto him, 'If thou wilt heark
"'unto us we will advise thee on a certain matt
"'which shall benefit thee, and we will put away tl
"'insult which we have heard from thee. Now v
"'have no anger against any man unto whom G
"'hath given healing, but go thou into the refector
"'and worship, and confess the God Who hath hea
"'ed thee, and hearken unto the laws of Moses. A
"'we will entreat God on thy behalf, so that l
"'may put away from thee thy folly wherewith the
"'hast wronged His goodness.' Now the paralyt
"desired greatly to see the likeness of Christ, ar
"he accepted the words of the priests, and he we
"in and cast himself down before the ark, as clos
"ly as he could so that he might be near the chamb
"wherein was the likeness; and he inclined his ea
"and he hearkened unto the service and the lav
"like unto one who, in very truth, accepted the
"words. And it came to pass that when the tin
"for all the people to go forth from the refector
"had arrived, the paralytic drew nigh and deceive
"the priests, and he bowed his head like every othe
"man and was blessed by them."

"And when all the people had gone forth, h
"stretched out his hands towards heaven, and sai

"'O God the Father, Who didst send forth Thy Son,
"'our Lord Jesus Christ, Who of Thine own free
"'will didst send unto us a Redeemer and Deliverer
"'Thy beloved Son, the Light of Thy glory, and the
"'splendour of Thy Majesty, since Thou, in Thy grace,
"'hast made me to be worthy of Thy grace and I
"'have gotten healing through Judah, the blind man,
"'who hath believed in Thee, and since I also be-
"'lieve | in Thee, hearken, O Lord, unto my voice *Page 175*
"'at this moment wherein I cry unto thee, and make
"'me worthy to see thy glorious Likeness and Thy
"'beautiful Form.' And after he had ceased his prayer,
'he drew nigh unto him that kept the door of the
'refectory, and he entreated him, and said unto him,
"'By the awful Name which is preached in this country,
"'shew me where the likeness of Christ is placed.'
'And the doorkeeper said unto him, 'Since thou hast
"conjured me by the awful Name, I will shew thee
"the chamber, but it is not possible for thee to enter
"therein, because it is sealed with the priest's seal,
"and no man can enter it unless the seals be broken.'
'And the paralytic answered and said unto him, 'Let
"it be according unto thy word. Shew me the chamber
"from the outside, for I do not wish either to go
"therein or that the seals should be broken.' Then
'the doorkeeper led the paralytic into the inner court-
'yard, and he shewed him, saying, 'Behold, the like-
"ness of Christ standeth on the right hand side of
"that chamber which looketh towards the north.'
'And when the paralytic saw the chamber, he look-
'ed straight towards the East, and he prayed, say-
'ing, 'O Christ, the Son of God, deprive me not of

"'the sight of Thy glorious appearance, but, in Th[y]
"'grace, open unto me the door at which I knock
"'and I will worship and give thanks unto Thy glo[-]
"'rious Name.' And immediately the doors stoo[d]
"open upon their hinges, and the paralytic went i[n]
"and cast himself down before the likeness, an[d]
"prayed, saying, 'O Christ, the Son of God, mak[e]
"'Thou me also¹ worthy to go forth and to preac[h]
"'Thy Gospel in the world, and grant me [power]
"'to stand against the threatening[s] of the Jew[s]
"'and deliver me from their wickedness.'

"Now when the doorkeeper saw what had happen[-]
"ed, he also ran and fell down before the likenes[s]
"and he made entreaty thereto, saying, 'O Lord, re[-]
"'ceive me also, and number me among the lamb[s]
"'of Thy fold. And forgive me the sinful blasphe[-]
"'mies of thy Name which I uttered ignorantly.' An[d]
"when the paralytic saw that the doorkeeper als[o]
"confessed the Christ, he answered and said unt[o]
"him, 'Bring me | a new horn that we may take som[e]
"'of this gift of grace; and thou shalt see a grea[t]
"'and a marvellous thing, the like of which hat[h]
"'never taken place in the world.' Then the doo[r]
"'keeper went, and brought a new horn, and wipe[d]
"'some of the water and blood from off the likenes[s]
"'and filled the horn full therewith.' And the par[a]
"lytic said unto the doorkeeper, 'If the chief pries[t]
"'hear that this wonderful thing hath taken plac[e]
"'and that the doors have been opened—no ma[n]
"'having opened them—and that we have gone i[n]

---

¹ Read ܐܦ.

"'and have paid homage to this likeness of Christ,
"'and that we have believed on Him, both thou and
"'I, straightway they will burn us with fire. But come,
"'let us cast ourselves down before this likeness,
"'and let us entreat God that He will make it to be
"'removed from here unto such place as He willeth.'
'And the doorkeeper said unto him, 'In thy hands
"'is the knowledge of Christ, Whom thou hast con-
"'fessed; whatsoever thou shalt say unto me that will
"'I do, and I will never leave thee until I die.'"

"Then the two of them sat down before the like-
'ness, and they cast ashes upon their heads, and
'prayed, saying, 'O God, Whose dwelling-place is
"'in the highest heights of heaven, and Whose eyes
"'look into the lowest depths of the earth, Who
"'triest the heart and the reins of the children of
"'men, hear Thou our voice at this time, and remove
"'from this country Thy holy Form. Lord, let not
"'this baleful people insult it, for they will say, 'We
"'were worthy to insult Him, and we have blasphem-
"'ed His likeness which He hath not redeemed out
"'of our hands.' Lord, cast not away from before
'Thee our petition, but¹ let the likeness be taken
'away from here, and given unto a holy nation;
'and let these doors be shut fast again, and let the
'seals be found sealed in their proper places. And
'let Thine enemies see it and be put to shame, and
'Thou shalt be praised, and Thy servants shall
'rejoice.'"

"And it came to pass that, as they made an end

---

¹ Read ܪܕܟ.

"of their prayer, the doors were shut fast as afore-
"time, and the seals stood in their places. And they
"heard a voice which said unto them, 'Depart in
"'peace, O blessed men, and confirm yourselves | in
"'your faith, and fear not; everything that ye shall
"'ask shall be [given] unto you, and I will be with
"'you, and many people shall believe on Me through
"'you.' And it came to pass that, whilst they were
"standing and marvelling concerning the voice which
"was heard by them, suddenly the Angel of the Lord
"came down from heaven, and went into the place
"where the likeness was; and a great earthquake
"took place. And the Angel took the likeness from
"where it was standing, and he removed it, and no
"man hath ever seen it since. And we wrote upon
"the door of that chamber, 'Enter in, O priests, and
"'people of the Jews, and look upon your shame;
"'for the likeness which ye placed here to make a
"'mock of hath been lifted up into heaven, notwith-
"'standing that the doors were shut fast, and that the
"'seals remained in their places. For ye do not be-
"'lieve in Christ, even as your fathers did not be-
"'lieve in Him, when He rose from the grave and
"'the seals stood unbroken upon it. And now, open
"'ye, and come, and enter in, and see that He hath
"'not allowed you to work your will upon His glor-
"'ious Form.'"

"Then the blind man and the paralytic went forth
"together from the refectory, and they had with them
"the horn which was filled with the gracious gift of
"the water and blood. And the doorkeeper took the
"paralytic and they went into his house wherein was

"a brother of his whose left hand was withered, and
"whose arm was bent double, and he was not able
"to stretch it out straight. Now he had been injured
"in this manner from the time when he was a child,
"for when his mother was carrying him, Satan smote
"him at the noon of the day, and made his arm to
"dry up; and he suffered greatly by reason of his
"left side. And the doorkeeper said unto the para-
"lytic, 'Rub some of this gift of grace upon this poor
"'man, for he is my brother, and it is a long time
"'indeed since he hath stretched out his hand straight.'
"And the paralytic said unto him, 'It is not possible
"'for this gift of grace to be brought nigh unto him
"'unless he confess Him, Who hath given it unto us,
"'and unless he believe on Him, and confess Him,
"'even as I have believed on Him, and have been
"'made whole, and behold, | I was grievously vexed   Page 178
"'with sickness a long time. Thou thyself knowest
"'how long I lay by the side of the door of the re-
"'fectory, and that no man helped me, until I was
"'helped by this gift of grace. And Judah the blind
"'man also cried upon Him, and confessed Him with
"'his whole heart, and straightway He gave him the
"'light which he had never before seen. And so,
"'likewise, shall it be with thy brother; if this gift of
"'grace come nigh to him, and he believe on Christ,
"'he shall be healed straightway.'"

"Then the man [with a withered hand] answered
"and said unto them, 'Whether I be made whole or
"'not, I have seen a paralytic who hath been made
"'whole, and a blind man who hath been made to
"'see the light; and I believe that He [Who hath

"'done these things] is indeed the Redeemer of the
"'world. And whosoever doth not confess Him with
"'all his soul, and with all his heart, and with all
"'his strength, and with all his mind, and whosoever
"'hath any doubt whatsoever concerning Him, or that
"'He came down from heaven, and is God of very
"'God, and that in His love He put on a body of
"'the Virgin Mary, and was crucified by the Jews,
"'and blood and water flowed from Him for the atone-
"'ment of the children of men, and He died, and
"'was buried, and came to life [again], and rose, and
"'ascended into heaven, and behold, He sitteth on
"'the right hand of the His Father, and the angels
"'in heaven and the children of men upon earth adore
"'Him, let his life come to an end upon earth.' Then
"the paralytic, on hearing the praises of the afflicted
"man, drew nigh unto him, and cried unto him, and
"said unto him, 'Draw nigh, and rest thy head upon
"'this horn, and cry out upon Christ that He may
"'have mercy upon thee.' Then the afflicted one drew
"nigh, and bowed his head before the horn, and
"prayed, saying, 'Hearken, O God, unto the petition
"'of Thy servant, and answer thou me at this time.
"'And if Thy Godhead shall know of the existence
"'of any doubt in my mind, let no help follow me from
"'Thy gift of grace; but if not, then deprive me not
"'from being made whole, for I believe on Thee, and
"'on Thy Father, and on the Holy Spirit.' And the
"paralytic poured some of the gift of grace into his
"hand, and he rubbed the afflicted one therewith,
"and said, 'In the Name of our Lord | Jesus Christ,
"'Who gave me healing, on Whom I believed and

"'was made whole, stretch out thy right hand, and "'get healing, and confess His graciousness.' And it "came to pass that as soon as the gift of grace touched "his arm, he was straightway healed; and he became "like one who had never at any time had any injury "whatsoever."

"Now that day was the first day of the week, and "on the day following the priests went to the refectory, "but they did not find the doors open, as they were "accustomed to find them and everything made ready, "neither did they find there the doorkeeper. And the "priests went into the chamber where the likeness "was [to see] if the seals were unbroken, and they "saw that they were unbroken and that the doors "were shut fast. And they found written upon the "door an inscription which read thus, 'Enter in, O "'priests and people of the Jews, and look upon your "'shame with your own eyes; for the likeness of Christ "'which ye set inside these doors under seals, and at "'which ye were wanting to make a mock, hath been "'taken up into heaven, and the seals have not been "'destroyed.' And it came to pass that as they stood "there reading the inscription a mighty tumult took "place, and the people rushed in and read the in-"scription against the will of the priests; and the "priests were greatly afraid. And they said, 'Perchance "'this thing hath been done in a mystery. If the "'doors are thrown open, and all the people go inside, "'and the likeness be not found therein, we shall "'become a laughing-stock. And all the people will "'believe on Christ, and this thing will be worse than "'everything else which our Lord hath made manifest.

"'But let us be patient, and when the sun hath set,
"'and the people have departed and gone hence,
"'we will open the door, and go in and see if that
"'which is written upon the door be true.'"
"And it came to pass that whilst they were meditat-
"ing these things all the people rose up against the
"priests, and they cried out with one voice, saying,
"'We will not depart from this place unless the doors
"'be opened before us, and we see if that likeness
"'be therein or not. If it is therein, we will burn it
"'with fire; and if | it is not, then will we believe on
"'Christ, by reason of this wonderful thing which hath
"'taken place.' And the priests said unto all the
"people, 'We are not permitted to break the Sabbath
"'and to transgress the Law; and we cannot put away
"'the Scriptures of God and take heed unto others.'
"Now the priests said these things that they might
"make the disturbance among the people to cease.
"But all the people cried out and said, '[We swear]
"'by the God of Abraham, and of Isaac, and of Jacob,
"'that we will not depart from this place until the
"'doors have been opened, and we have learned the
"'truth.' Then the priests removed the seals, and they
"opened the doors and went in, and they found nothing.
"And all the people lifted up their voices, and cried
"out, and said, 'Verily, He Whom our fathers crucified
"'in Jerusalem was Christ, the Son of God, and it is
"'He Who hath wrought this wonderful thing.'"

"And one of those who believed in Christ stood
"up in the midst, and said unto them, 'Although we
"'are now persuaded that we believe on the Son of
"'God, and that He is God of very God—even as we

"'have received in our Scriptures—yet we did not
"'believe that He rose from the grave, the door thereof
"'being shut fast, and the seals being unbroken; but
"'this last thing which hath happened maketh certain
"'the former thing. Now, since His likeness was placed
"'under seals so that it might not be insulted, and
"'He hath removed it and hath not permitted it to
"'be treated with contumely, how can we have any
"'doubt concerning His Body, which rose on the third
"'day and did not see corruption. Which does it
"'appear to be to you, truth or falsehood?'"

"And it came to pass that when the chief priests
"heard these things, they answered and said unto him,
"'When didst thou begin to teach the Law? Or per-
"'adventure thou hast taken a bribe from the disciples
"'of that Deceiver, and they have taught thee to
"'say these things.' Then straightway a great uproar
"took place, and every man was divided against
"his fellow; and report thereof reached the governor
"of the city. And the priests sent a bribe unto him,
"and said unto him, 'O lord, we would make supplica-
"'tion unto thy greatness. When we are in the refectory
"'according to our wont we read the holy laws. But
"'certain men have been found, that is to say, sorcerers,
"'who have shut the eyes of the people, and they
"'say that we heal the paralytics, and the blind, and
"'the sick. And when we wished to lay hands upon
"'them so that they might be questioned before thine
"'integrity, that thou mightest know the truth of the
"'matter concerning them, they took the opportunity
"'and escaped, and where they are we know not. And
"'behold, the people have fallen each man upon his

"'fellow, and many murders will take place unless
"'thy greatness doth stand up.' Now the priests, as
"they imagined, confounded the story so that the
"wonderful deed might not become revealed."

"And it came to pass that when the governor had
"received the bribe from the chief priests, he sent
"the Greek officer and his forces with staves, and
"swords, and ropes, and chains, and he commanded
"them, saying, 'Go ye, and say unto the chief priests,
"'and unto the elders, and unto all the people of the
"'Jews, Whosoever maketh trouble in this city, so
"'that murders take place by reason of his speech, and
"'I hear of it, I will take off his head, and I will cast
"'him into the sea. Let every man abide in peace
"'lest he receive the punishment of the sword. As
"'for these man, concerning whom ye have spoken
"'unto me, should ye hear of the report of them in
"'any place, come and tell me, and I will send and
"'seize them, and I will cast them into prison until
"'I learn the truth concerning their actions.'"

"Now when the paralytic heard what the Jews had
"done, he said unto the doorkeeper of the refectory,
"who was in the house of him whose hand had been
"withered, 'Whether we wish it to be so or not, the
"'Name of Christ will be preached throughout all
"'creation. Let us not, then, have doubt concerning
"'His goodness unto us, but rise up, and let us go
"'and seek for our brother Judah until we find him;
"'and let us cleave unto one another, and let us go
"'forth and preach and teach the Gospel of our Lord
"'throughout all the world. And should it happen
"'that we be seized by judges or by governors let

"'us not be afraid, for | Christ is with us even as Page 182
"'He promised us.' And the two of them rose up
"straightway, and they went forth, and they made
"the sign of the cross upon their foreheads, and they
"prayed to God, and said, 'O God, Who desirest the
"'lives of the children of men, and Who art merciful,
"'and compassionate, and long-suffering, and abundant
"'in grace and truth, hearken unto our prayer, and
"'make straight our way; and grant that we may
"'find our brother Judah and may not be separated
"'from his love.' And it came to pass that having
"gone round about in the city they arrived at the
"gate thereof, and when they had gone outside the
"wall of the city and had departed from it for about
"the distance of one mile, they found Judah standing
"in a certain hidden place praying. And the two of
"them drew nigh unto him, and saluted him, and they
"said unto him, 'Brother Judah, hast thou heard what
"'hath happened in this city?' And Judah said unto
"them, 'What hath happened?' Then the paralytic
"said unto him, 'After thou hadst left me, the gift
"'of grace having come [upon me] from thy hands,
"'the priests seized me, and brought me into the
"'refectory, so that by reason of me this our brother
"'might find deliverance for his life; and they tormented
"'me to deny Christ Who had given healing unto me.
"'Now, because I desired greatly to see the beautiful
"'Form of Christ, I made myself to be like unto one
"'who accepted their counsel, until I had the opportu-
"'nity of drawing nigh unto that chamber wherefrom
"'I had gotten help. And the time having passed,
"'and all the people having gone forth from the

"'refectory, and the priests having departed unto
"'their habitations, I drew nigh unto this our brother
"'who, as thou knowest, kept the door; and I prayed
"'and entreated him to shew me the likeness. And
"'he said unto me, 'The doors are shut fast, and
"'seals have been put upon them; and thou canst
"'not go in to see it.' And I said unto him, 'Let it
"'be according to thy word; only shew me the
"'chamber, for I do not wish to enter therein, and
"'shew me the chamber from the outside.' Then I
"'drew nigh and stood before it, and I cried upon
"'the Name of Christ, and I asked Him | in prayer
"'to shew me the path of His glory. And immediately,
"'in the twinkling of an eye, the doors were opened
"'and stood upon their hinges, and I went into the
"'chamber and cast myself down before the likeness.
"'And I prayed unto Him, and I gave thanks unto
"'Him for the healing which He had given unto me
"'at thy hands. And the goodness of God called
"'this our brother also, and mingled him with us, so
"'that he might be wholly one with us in the mystery
"'of the Trinity. And again we made supplication
"'and prayer, and entreated Him Who receiveth the
"'prayers of all the children of men that He would
"'remove the likeness from that chamber, and that
"'the doors thereof should be shut fast, and that the
"'seals should be found as they were aforetime. And
"'it happened even so. And we wrote upon the
"'doors, saying, 'Enter in, O priests, and look upon
"'your shame, and see that your intentions have not
"'been accomplished; for the glorious likeness o
"'Christ, notwithstanding that the doors were sealed

"'hath been taken up into heaven.' And a voice was
"heard by us which said, 'Depart in peace, O blessed
"'men, and fear not, for I am with you, and I will
"'never forsake you.'"
"And it came to pass that when Judah heard all
"these things he gave thanks and glorified God. And
"he answered and said, 'God's will be done!' And
"whilst they were standing in the place wherein they
"had found Judah, who was standing [there] and
"praying, they began straightway to perform a service,
"and they raised a Psalm, and said, 'O come, let
"'us give glory unto the Lord, and let us sing psalms
"'unto God our Redeemer; let us come before His
"'face with thanksgiving, and in hymns let us glorify
"'Him.'[1] And so on with the whole of the section [of
"the service]. And after they had ended the service,
"they said, 'Glory be to the Father, and to the Son,
"'and to the Holy Ghost, for ever and ever, Amen.'
"Thus they brought the prayer to an end."

"And Judah answered and said unto his companions,
"'My brethren, if our Lord please and if it be good
"'in His sight, let Him order our way, and let that
"'which is necessary therefor, that is to say, the
"'sign of baptism, be given unto us, and let Him
"'reckon us among the number of His lambs, and
"'let Him mix us with the assemblies of those who
"'give praise unto Him. And, behold, our joy shall
"'be made complete.' Then the companions of Judah
"said unto him, 'Whatsoever thou orderest shall be
"'[observed] by us, for the Divine grace first of all

---

[1] Psalm XCV. 1 ff.

"'called thee, and thou art the counsellor that dot
"'benefit us.' And Judah answered and said unt
"his companions, 'I counsel you to do this thing, the
"'is to say, let us commit the matter unto God, s
"'that He alone may fulfil our petitions. For it i
"'not meet that we should forget the words whic
"'we have learned, 'Cast thy care upon the Lor(
"'and He shall sustain thee; and He will never l(
"'His righteous ones be moved.'¹ Now this accurse
"'nation of the Jews hath made ready to persecut
"'and to slay every one that loveth our Lord Jest
"'Christ. But God, in His righteousness, is about t
"'do away their dominion, and to scatter them abroa(
"'and to make them despised and rejected amon
"'all nations. For although God hath been longsufferin
"'with them because of His covenant with Abrahan
"'and the oaths which He sware unto Isaac, and H
"'testimony unto Jacob that their seed should nev(
"'pass away, yet their loftiness shall be brought lov
"'and their dominion shall pass away, and the
"'honourable estate shall be abated, and they sha
"'become of no account whatsoever. And us ourselv(
"'they will seek after that they may do us harn
"'Then there came a voice unto them, saying, 'I wi
"'never forsake you.'"

"And it came to pass that when Judah had sai
"these things, the time had arrived for them to sa
"the service for the ninth hour. And they bega
"the Psalm, and said, 'Be not envious of th
"'wicked, neither be thou jealous of the workers (

---

¹ Psalm LV. 22.

"'iniquity',[1] and so on. And when they had finished "'the service they prayed, and said, 'O Lord, the "'God of the spirits of all flesh, Thou hidden Being, "'Whose honourable Majesty abideth in the heaven of "'heavens, Thou God, Who of thine own freewill hast "'adorned the earth with the colours of flowers of "'every kind which are much to be desired, receive "'our entreaty, and hearken unto our supplication, "'and purge away and remove utterly from us the "'spots of our sins; and make answer unto our "'petitions, for we put our hope in Thee. And give "'us, O Lord, the sign of baptism whereby our sins "'may be purged away, and propitiation made for "'our iniquities, and let us become unto Thee chosen "'vessels and good servants who do the will of their "'Lord.'"

"And after these things they stood up straight, "and they lifted up their eyes and saw a certain "place which was like unto a vessel for baptism; "and it was full of soft and limpid water, which was "sparkling in its appearance and the smell of which "was sweeter than that of perfumes; and the light "which came from it was greater than the sun and the "radiance thereof. And, behold, a certain man, very "aged and of glorious countenance, who was clothed "in a white garment, and was holding a garment in "his right hand, was standing there and sanctifying "the water; and when we saw him we were afraid. "And we inclined our ears to hear what he was "saying, and he opened his mouth and said, 'I seal

---

[1] Psalm XXXVII. 1.

"'this water in the name of the Father, and the Son, "'and the Holy Ghost.' And he was making entreaty "and supplication, saying, 'Come, come, O Holy Spirit, "'descend and abide upon this water, and sanctify "'Thou it that it may serve for the atonement of "'iniquities and for the forgiveness of sins. And may "'it give Thy grace and Thy mercy unto them; yea, "'O Father, and Son, and Holy Spirit, for ever and "'for ever. Amen.' And it came to pass that, as we "were standing and were afraid to draw nigh unto him, "he opened his mouth and cried unto us, and said, "'Unto you I speak, O brethren, draw nigh unto "'me.' And we drew nigh unto him and we received "a blessing from him. Then he spake unto us, say-"ing, 'Your prayer and entreaty have entered in be-"'fore the Lord, and He hath sent me to give you the "'sign of baptism, and to teach you what it is meet "'that ye should do; and I will baptise you in the "'Name of the Father, and the Son, and the Holy "'Ghost.' And after they had received from him the "sign of life, he said unto them, 'Take ye the horn "'which ye have, and which is filled with the gift "'of grace, and go ye and enter into this city, and "'do ye therein mighty deeds and miracles, so that "'the Jews may see and may be put to shame. And "'proclaim ye concerning our Lord Jesus Christ, that "'He is the Son of God, and fear ye not, neither be "'ye troubled. For in whatsoever place ye shall call "'upon Christ He shall come to your aid, | and He "'will put into your mouths the words wherewith ye "'shall overcome your enemies; go ye in peace, and "'our Lord shall be with you.' And Judah answered

"and said unto him, 'Lord, pray Thou on our behalf
"'for confidence in our Lord; and whatsoever Thou
"'shalt say unto us that will we do.'"
"And they went and entered into the city, having
"in their hands the horn that was filled with the gift
"of grace, and they arrived at the gate of the city.
"And, behold, men were carrying a certain young
"man upon a bier, and they were going to bury him,
"and his aged father was going on before him; and
"he was plucking out his white hairs and casting them
"upon the ground, for he had no other son, and he
"was smiting his face until his eyes became dark.
"And the blessed men saw him, and they were very
"sorry for him. And Judah answered and said unto his
"companions, 'My brethren, let us draw nigh unto the
"'bier of this dead man, and let us anoint him with
"'some of this gift of grace; and let us entreat Christ
"'on his behalf, and let us make mention of the Name
"'of God over him, and straightway he shall come to
"'life. And when he doth live and stand up the Name
"'of Christ shall be greatly exalted, and His faith shall
"'be proclaimed abroad.' And the three of them went
"and stood before the bier, and they said unto the
"men who were bearing it, 'Put down this bier from
"'off yourselves, and set it upon the ground, and ye
"'shall see the glory of God;' and much people were
"thronging to that place. And it came to pass that,
"when they had put the bier upon the ground, Judah
"brought out the horn from under his garment, and
"he turned himself towards the East, and prayed,
"and he made the sign of the cross between the
"eyes of that dead man, and he poured out some

"of that gift of grace upon his nostrils and upon his
"cheek. And he answered and said, 'Come, O spirit
"'of this young man from whatsoever place thou art in
"'in the Name of our Lord Jesus Christ, and enter
"'in, and be at rest, and abide in the body which
"'is thine; and let this young man rise up from
"'his bier!' And immediately that he mentioned the
"Name of Christ over him, he came to life, and
"stood up; and all who saw him gave glory unto
"God; and in that hour there believed | about three
"thousand people, both men and women. And the father
"of the young man drew nigh, and cast himself down
"before the blessed men, and said unto them, 'I do
"'homage unto you, O my lords, because ye have
"'had compassion upon my gray hairs, and because ye
"'have given back to me this my only son that he may
"'be the staff of my old age; blessed are ye before
"'God, and blessed be Christ, the Son of God, Who
"'hath hearkened unto you and hath brought back my
"'son to life. Henceforth, even unto my death, I will
"'never separate myself from the love of Christ your
"'Lord, and I will give thanks and will worship His
"'gracious Name. And if my whole body were mouths
"'and tongues which could speak they would not suffice
"'to give glory unto the Son of God, Who sent you
"'to work for me this act of grace.' And the blessed
"men dismissed him, and said unto him, 'Go in peace
"'O man, and be thou ever mindful of Jesus Christ
"'Who had compassion upon thy gray hairs, and gave
"'thee thy son back alive.' So the old man went away
"from thence, and the blessed men departed unto a
"place in the midst of the city."

"And, behold, a certain man had a devil which
"troubled him, and suddenly, when he had seen them,
"he lifted up his voice and said, 'Fie upon you, O
"'generation of crucifiers, why have ye come against
"'me? By the skin of my teeth only did I escape from
"'Christ when He was upon the earth and walking
"'about therein; why have ye taken and made a likeness
"'of Him that it may be a goad to vex me? The gift
"'of grace which flowed from Him it is that persecuted
"'me. Fie upon you, O unbelievers! Was it not He
"'Who persuaded the Legion of devils to go into the
"'sea?[1] Why have ye brought upon me this temptation?
"'And, behold, I burn with fire at the sight of you.'
"And Judah answered and said unto that devil, 'Shut
"'thy mouth, O thou enemy of man, thou most feeble
"'of all things that exist, and go forth from this
"'young man.' And straightway the devil cast the
"man upon the ground, and he was much bruised
"and became sick; and people not a few gathered
"round about him at once. Then Judah brought out
"from under his garment the horn which was full of
"the gift of grace, and anointed him; and he lifted
"up his eyes unto heaven, and prayed, and said,
"'O Lord God, the Father of our Lord Jesus Christ,
"'Thou Who didst send Him forth, by Whose power
"'and by Whose command Satan was cast out and
"'thrown down, together with all those who served
"'him, so that they were scattered and drowned in
"'the sea, by Whose power the sick bodies of the
"'children of men which had been wounded by the

---

[1] St. Mark. V. 9.

"'blows of Legion were made whole, do thou, O Lord,
"'now also in Thy mercy command this helpless one
"'to rise up healed from the place wherein he is.
"'And let the devil that dwelleth in him be swept
"'into the sea, and let him no longer have power
"'to do harm unto the generation of men.' And
"having made his prayer, Judah gave him some of
"that gift of grace which he had upon him, and
"straightway the man stood up upon his feet; and
"the devil that was in him cried out before all the
"people, and left him, and fled. And every one who
"was near, and who saw and heard what had hap-
"pened, gave glory unto God."

"Now, a certain woman was standing there, and
"she was weeping bitterly; and this woman was a
"widow. And she was crying in great pain, for she
"had a daughter who had overcome many by her
"beauty, but never had any man seen her or known
"her; many men had entreated her, but she had never
"submitted unto them. And it came to pass once at
"midnight that the young woman went out from the
"door of the house wherein she lived, and, behold,
"a devil in the form of a beautiful young man came
"unto her swiftly and seized her. And he said unto
"her, 'Come with me, and I will make thee my wife;'
"now she imagined that in very truth he was a man.
"And she said unto him, 'I will never be the wife
"'of any man.' And it came to pass that whilst he
"was contending with her she lifted up her hands
"against him, but she was not able to reach him,
"and then she knew that he was a disciple of Satan.
"And as she was wishing to lift up her eyes to heaven,

"and to cry out to God to come to her aid, the
"devil threw her down upon the ground outside the Page 189
"door; and she was beaten and bruised until she
"was [well nigh] dead. And having remained outside
"for a long time, and not having gone in again
"according to her wont, her mother rose up and went
"out after her, and she found her cast upon the
"ground sick and bruised. Then her mother drew
"nigh unto her and lifted her up, but she was like
"a dead body; and her mother called unto her, but
"she did not answer her. Then her mother lifted up
"her voice and wailed bitterly, and her neighbours
"who were nigh unto her came thronging about her
"from every side; and her mother rent the garment
"which she had upon her, and she cast ashes upon
"her head. And the neighbours took the young
"woman and brought her into the house, and laid
"her upon a bed; and her mother sat before her the
"whole night beating her face. And at day-break
"the soul of the young woman entered into her, and
"she cried out unto her mother; and her mother
"answered and said unto her, 'What aileth thee, O my
"'daughter, and what hath happened unto thee?'
"And the young woman related unto her the whole
"matter concerning herself, even as it had happened.
"And from that day Satan persecuted her constantly,
"and frequently he made her go out to the grave-
"yard, and her mother used to go out after her, and
"take hold of her to bring her back into her house;
"but she was not able to overcome the strength of
"the devil that was dwelling in her. And many times
"she used to open the door of the grave-yard, and

"go inside, and shut it in her face; and her mother,
"and other people along with her, used to go in and
"bring her out. Now when this poor mother had
"heard concerning the blessed men, she rose up
"straightway and went to them. And when she saw
"what they were doing, how they were giving healing
"unto all those who drew nigh unto them, she also
"came near and said unto them, 'O men, what is your
"'report? And who hath sent you to do these mighty
"'deeds and miracles? And by what might do ye do
"'these things and are not afraid?' And when the
"blessed men heard the words of the woman, they
"meditated among themselves, saying, 'It seemeth to
"'us that one | of two things moveth this woman:
"'either she speaketh without understanding, or the
"'priests have put words into her mouth and have
"'sent her unto us as a woman who would make
"'enquiries, so that she may learn from us in the
"'sight of all men that which they have commanded
"'her [to learn]. But let us put our trust in our
"'Lord, for the Gospel of Christ shall not be pro-
"'claimed in secret.'"

"And having meditated in this wise the blessed
"men answered and said unto her, 'We are the
"'disciples of Christ, the Son of God, and by His
"'power we do these things, for our own origin is
"'of no account and humble. And as concerning that
"'which thou hast said unto us, Ye fear not and ye
"'tremble not, we are not afraid, because the might of
"'His grace hath clothed us round about and because
"'through Him we overcome our enemies.' And when
"the woman heard the certainty of their faith, she

"'lifted up her voice with a sob, and said unto them,
"'By the might wherewith your Lord hath clothed
"'you from on high, and whereby He hath made
"'Satan and all his hosts to be subject unto you,
"'I entreat you to have mercy upon my old age.
"'Have compassion upon my gray hairs, and have
"'compassion upon me, because there remaineth not
"'upon my feet even one nail by reason of the
"'multitude of the stumblingblocks in my path. By
"'Christ, the Son of God, Who hath chosen you to
"'be His preachers, send me not away from you,
"'for my lot is bitter. That ye should visit the sick
"'your Lord hath sent you, let therefore the de-
"'liverance which ye have dawn upon me.'"

"Then the blessed men made her to be quiet, and
"they said unto her, 'Be thou silent, O woman, and
"'tell us what is the cause of thy outcry, and so far
"'as the power in us lies we will toil on thy behalf.
"'And inasmuch as thou hast conjured us by Christ,
"'the Son of God, we will devote ourselves to the
"'death unto thee. But tell us only what it is that
"'causeth thee pain.' Then the woman said unto
"them, 'I have an only daughter, and, behold, for
"'seven years past Satan hath led her captive and
"'taken her outside the city. And among the tombs
"'he beateth her each day, and very little life re-
"'maineth in her; she is well nigh dead, and except
"'for bones stripped of flesh she hath nothing in her.'
"And the blessed men said unto her, | 'Where is thy
"'daughter now?' And the woman answered and said
"unto them, 'Behold, I have shut her up in the house,
"'and I placed fastenings upon it and came to inform

"'you.' And the blessed men said unto her, 'Wilt
"'thou promise us that we may betroth her to the
"'heavenly Bridegroom?' Now the woman thought that
"'they were speaking to her about a man, and she
"'answered and said unto them, 'My lords, I entreat
"'you to let her be a virgin and a free woman all her
"'life.' And the blessed men said unto her, 'The Bride-
"'groom unto Whom we would betroth her wisheth
"'her to live in a state of virginity and holiness;'
"and then the woman understood their words as
"referring to Christ, when they told her that they
"wanted to betroth her daughter to a bridegroom.
"And she said unto them, 'She and I deliver our-
"'selves unto Him that we may be His handmaidens,
"'and we will serve that Bridegroom of Whom ye
"'spake.' And when the blessed men heard the words
"of the woman they rose up and went with her to
"her house. And when they had gone into the
"courtyard they found the fastenings broken in pieces,
"and the doors wide open, and her daughter had
"gone forth; and they sought her, but they found
"her not. And her mother said unto them, 'My lords,
"'I entreat you; She is to be found among the tombs;
"'come ye with me, and let it not be a trouble unto
"'you.' So they departed again and went forth after
"her, and much people clave unto them."

"And it came to pass when they had arrived at
"the gate of the city that the people thereof saw
"them and the multitude of folk that were coming
"with them; and they also joined themselves to them,
"and they went along with them. Now the good God
"had so appointed that they should see the wonderful

"works which were to be wrought in the Name of
"Christ, and how He answereth every one that calleth
"upon Him in true faith. And it came to pass that
"when they had gone forth outside the city two
"stadia, the mother and also the blessed men who
"were with her lifted up their eyes, and they saw the
"young woman wandering round about among the
"tombs and beating her head. And the young woman
"also saw them, and she looked at them, and the
"devil | lifted up his voice and said unto them, Page 192
"'Whither come ye against me? Am I not near
"'enough unto you? Cursed (?) be ye! I entreat you
"'to depart from me. I am unable to resist your power,
"'and I cannot wage war against you, for the might
"'with which ye are clothed round about is invisible.
"'The sword which is girt upon you is dipped in
"'flame, and your arrows have been poisoned with
"'blood and water; depart ye from me, for ye have
"'taken away my dominion.' These were the words
"which the devil spake as they were following him.
"And it came to pass that when the devil saw that
"he was overcome, he began to lead away the young
"woman along a path which went to the sea, so that
"she might fall into the sea and be drowned; and
"the young woman began to depart with swift steps
"like a man who fleeth before some evil beast. And
"Judah lifted up his voice from afar off, and said,
"'I say unto thee, O thou foul devil, thou enemy of
"'the children of men, in the Name of Christ, the
"'Son of God, thou shalt not lead the young woman
"'away from this place.' And when the devil heard
"the Name of Christ, he straightway threw the young

"woman down headlong in that place, and he beat
"her so that her soul might go forth from her. And
"whilst Judah and her companions were coming up
"to her, the man who had been a paralytic said unto
"Judah, 'My lord, quicken thy step a little, for if thou
"'dost not do so we shall not find any life left in
"'her;' then straightway they ran quickly and came
"up to her, and Judah brought forth the horn im-
"mediately and anointed her with the gift of grace.
"And he answered and said, 'Tarry in thy body, O
"'soul, in the Name of our Lord Jesus Christ.' And
"Judah prayed and said, 'O God, Who didst create
"'Adam in Thine image, and didst give him dominion
"'over everything that Thou hadst made in Thy good
"'pleasure, and didst give him every thing that was
"'in the earth, and on his account didst send Thy
"'beloved Son Jesus Christ, and He came into the
"'world and endured sufferings on his behalf, O Lord,
"'Thou knowest that we do not do this thing by
"'way of boasting, or for our own vain glorifying,
"'or that we may receive anything from any man,
"'but in order that Thy Holy Name may be glorified,
"'| and that Thine adorable Godhead may be exalted,
"'and that all men may know and believe that Thou
"'art He Who giveth help unto those who call upon
"'Thee with a pure heart.' And when Judah had
"said these words, he turned to the young woman
"and said unto her, 'I say unto thee, O foul devil,
"'thou feeblest of all natures, in the Name of the
"'Trinity, go forth from this young woman, and draw
"'not again nigh unto the race of the children of
"'men.' And when the devil heard these words, he

"straightway went forth out of the young woman,
"and he uttered a roaring sound, and departed and
"fled. And all those who heard and saw [this] lifted
"up their voices and glorified God, saying, 'Glory
"'be to Thee, O Christ, the Son of God, Who hast
"'sent Thy servants for the deliverance of creation;
"'henceforth we will confess and believe in Jesus
"'Christ, and He is the Redeemer of the world,
"'and Him will we worship, and Him will we glorify
"'for ever and for ever. Amen.' And Judah drew
"nigh, and taking the hand of the young woman
"gave her to her mother. And he said unto her,
"'Take thy daughter and depart. But remember
"'that which thou hast promised to us, that thy
"'daughter shall lead a life of wariness and holiness;
"'and thou shalt worship and confess Him who de-
"'livered her from the captivity in which she had
"'been led captive.' Then the mother of the young
"woman took her daughter, and went away giving
"thanks and glorifying God, Who had guarded her
"and restored her unto her."

"And it came to pass that whilst the blessed men
"were working these glorious miracles in Tiberias,
"by the grace of Christ which accompanied them,
"their report went forth into all the country, and into
"all the land which was round about the city; and
"people not a few were gathered together and came
"unto them. And multitudes of people who were
"sick with divers kinds of diseases, and who went
"unto the blessed men in true faith, were healed
"straightway of their sicknesses. And those who saw
"the blessed men in the city of Tiberias said concerning

"them, 'We saw men who were strangers from a "'remote country, and they had with them a certain "'medicine, the like of which we have | never seen "'or heard of in the world; it cureth every kind of "'sickness and disease, and no pain can stand against "'it, and every person whom it toucheth is immediately "'made whole. For this medicine doth not permit "'pain to tarry with any person whom it hath once "'touched. And we think that this medicine which "'they have hath been given unto them from the "'highest heights of heaven, because, whenever any "'sick person is brought unto them, these men look "'up with their eyes towards heaven, though no man "'knoweth that which they say. But it is well known "'that they call upon God Who gave them this cure, "'and that when they have looked up into heaven "'they bring the medicine nigh unto the person who "'is sick or afflicted, and he is made whole. And "'what is more wonderful than all else is that they "'take nothing from any man. And on account of "'this [great] benefit multitudes come unto them from "'remote countries, bringing with them people who "'are very sick and ill, and they are all made whole "'and they go to their homes, rejoicing and giving "'thanks unto God Who hath given succour unto the "'children of men.'"

"Now there was in the country which belonged to "that city a certain village wherein dwelt Samaritans; "and these people were not wont to mix with the "inhabitants of the city, and their religion was different "from theirs; for the religion of the Jews is not the "same as that of the Samaritans. Now the man who

"had been made the governor of the whole village
"was, as far as the things of the world are concerned,
"a wise man; and he had had a brother who died and
"left behind him a young maiden who was exceedingly
"beautiful. And from the time that she was three
"years old she was betrothed to the son of that
"governor. And it came to pass that when she was
"full grown and her betrothed was about to take
"her to wife, as she was walking under a portico
"Satan threw her down headlong, even as a man
"whom something hath smitten, and she fell down in
"the courtyard, and all her bones were broken. And
"she became grievously sick, and many physicians
"bound up her wounds, but they did not in any
"way benefit | her; nay, for every time that she
"came unto them her pain was increased. And the
"governor heard of the report of the blessed men,
"and that they were mighty physicians who cured
"sicknesses of every kind, and he prepared a bed
"for the damsel, and laid soft bedding thereupon,
"and he harnessed to it a gentle and quiet animal,
"and he took the damsel who was like a dead creature,
"and laid her upon the bed. Now she was crying
"out and uttering loud groans by reason of her
"great and frequent pain, and every one who heard
"her suffered very much more than her own kinsfolk,
"because they perceived that she was praying for
"her own death. And when they arrived at the gate
"of the city, the governor with tears enquired for
"the blessed men, saying, 'Where dwell the physicians
"'who are in this city?' And the people of the city
"said unto him, 'What is thy business, O man? And

"'whom seekest thou?' And the governor said unto
"them, 'I have an only daughter who is nigh unto
"'death and is in grievous pain. And I have heard
"'concerning these men that they have a certain
"'medicine which cureth all sicknesses.' Then the
"people of the city said unto him, 'Weep not, O man,
"'neither be thou distressed, for as thou hast heard
"'concerning these men, even so it is.' And the
"people of the city also went nigh unto the damsel
"and looked upon her, and they wept; and they
"accompanied the governor and his following, and
"went to the blessed men."

"And when the governor saw the blessed men,
"he went and knelt down and fell at their feet; and
"the people wept, and entreated them to draw nigh
"and to visit the maiden, and to anoint her with the
"gift of grace which they had. And the blessed men
"said unto the governor, 'Whence art thou, O man?
"'And of what religion art thou?' And the gover-
"nor said unto them, 'I am from the village of Na'mî
"'of the Samaritans, and I am a Samaritan.' And
"the blessed men said unto him, 'We shut the door
"'in the face of no man, so that every man may
"'turn unto God. The medicine which we have is
"'beyond price, | and not every man is able to buy
"'it.' And the governor said unto them, 'I entreat
"'you, O my lords, to have compassion upon me;
"'give me some of it, and I will give you whatsoever
"price ye ask for it.' And the blessed men said unto
"him, 'The price of the medicine is that a man should
"'believe upon Him Who gave it unto us.' And the
"governor said unto them, 'And who is he that gave

"'it unto you, in whom ye wish me to believe?' And "the blessed men said unto him, 'Have ye never "'heard of the report of Jesus Christ, the Son of "'God, Who came down from the heavens to the "'earth for the redemption of the children of men?' "And the governor said unto them, 'I have heard of "'the report of Him, but I know Him not.' And the "blessed men said unto him, 'He it is Who hath "'given us this medicine of life; whatsoever sickness "'that hath the man who believeth upon Him is cured, "'and every pain and every disease.' And the gov- "ernor said unto them, 'Behold, the people of the "'Jews do not receive Him, neither did our fathers "'believe in Him. Nay, according to what history "'relateth concerning Him, they even laid hands upon "'Him, and treated Him with contempt, and made "'Him to endure many evil things. And now, how "'can ye say unto me that it is He Who hath given "'unto you the medicine of life? For the history which "'concerneth Him is very ancient, whilst ye, who "'bear His gift and who heal every man of his "'sickness therewith, have only appeared in the world "'to-day.' And the blessed men said unto him, 'The "'Lord hath had pleasure in us, and He hath chosen "'us to be members of His household, and this gift "'of grace which thou seest with us hath been given "'unto us by Him for the help of the children of "'men, and for His praise, and for putting the Jews "'to shame.' And the man said unto them, 'Are ye "'not yourselves of the children of Israel? How then "'is it now that ye proclaim concerning their shame "'and concerning their fall, seeing that ye belong

15*

"'unto them?' And the blessed men answered and "said unto him, 'We have already told | thee, but "'again will we teach thee. Hast thou never heard "'of the report of Jesus Christ, the Son of God, Who "'was born of Mary the Virgin? He hath been unto "'us the true Light, and He hath made straight our "'way unto Him, and for His sake we deny that "'nation which hath cut itself off from the kingdom "'of God. And not unto us only hath grace called, "'but also unto every one that wisheth to inherit life. "'Now Paul the Apostle was one of them, and having "'gone forth to persecute the disciples of Jesus, grace "'called unto him, and made him an apostle. And "'to Zacchaeus also, the collector of money at the "'[city] gate, [did grace cry], for His gate is open "'unto all those that repent. And in His abundant "'mercy He hath also given unto us the hand (i. e., "'opportunity), and hath cried unto us, and we have "'drawn nigh unto Him, and He hath raised us up "'out of the slough of destruction. And we, if thou "'wilt hearken unto us, will shew thee the straight "'way which will take thee up into heaven; and if "'thou wilt believe on Him, whatsoever thou shalt "'ask He will give unto thee.'"

"And it came to pass that when the governor heard "these wonderful things, he answered and said unto "them, 'I confess Christ Who hath shewn us the true "'light, Who hath made straight our way unto you, "'Whom we know through you; far be it from us "'henceforth to leave Him even unto death.' Then "Judah answered and said unto his companions, 'Come, "'let us pray for this maiden, and let us cry out "'unto Christ to send help unto her; and we will "'anoint her with this gift of grace, and she shall "'be made whole and shall stand up.' Then Judah "drew nigh and stood over the maiden and he saw "that she was already [well nigh] dead, and that only "a very little breath remained in her. And he lifted "up his eyes, and prayed, and said, 'O Lord God, "'Thou mighty God, Who art the Father of our Lord "'Jesus Christ, Who didst send Him forth, and didst "'of Thine own free will put on the mortal body of "'Adam, and didst deliver him from the subjection "'of Satan, do Thou now, in Thine abundant mercy, "'send forth healing and help unto this helpless "'maiden, and let her be made whole and stand up. "'And call her, and bring her nigh unto Thyself, "'and let her become unto Thee | a chosen vessel "'wherewith Thy Godhead may be well pleased.' "And immediately Judah had ended his prayer, he "drew nigh unto the maiden and gave her some of "the gift of grace, and straightway she was made "whole, and stood up; and every one who saw this "gave glory unto God Who had done the will of "those who feared Him."

"Now when her betrothed saw what had happened, "he answered and said unto his father, 'In very truth "'the sickness of this maiden hath been of great "'benefit unto us, for by means of it we have found "'deliverance for our souls. For otherwise whence "'could we have learned that Jesus Christ giveth "'healing unto every one that believeth in Him? Or "'how could we have learned that there is to be a "'judgment, and punishment, and a kingdom, and

"'life which passeth not away, in the new world that
"'never cometh to an end? Whence could we have
"'heard all these things? But behold, we have now
"'gained two benefits: we have found life for our
"'souls, and we have gotten healing for this maiden.'
"Then the two of them entreated the blessed men
"and said unto them, 'We beseech you, O our lords,
"'ye servants of our Lord Jesus Christ, to shew us
"'the straight way wherein ye know that it will please
"'your Lord that we should walk, and pray ye on
"'our behalf that Christ will forgive us our offences.'
"Then Judah answered and said unto them, 'Go ye
"'and seek out and look for a village wherein a
"'church hath been built, and be ye baptized and
"'receive the sign of life, and become ye participators
"'in the Body and Blood of our Lord; and believe
"'upon Him with all your soul, and with all your
"'strength, and give thanks unto Him for the goodness
"'which He hath wrought for you.' So these men
"went, and they did as Judah had told them to do,
"and they believed upon our Lord, both they and
"the people of their village."

"Then one of the enemies and haters of God went
"and informed the priests, and told them everything
"which he had seen and heard that the blessed men
"were doing. And when the chief priests had heard
"these things they were all gathered together in their
"synagogue, and they took counsel one with another.
"And they gave a bribe unto the governor, and said
"unto him, 'Lord, we beseech thy mighty | power [to
"'have regard unto] these seducers concerning whom,
"'a short time ago, we brought information to thy

"'greatness. Behold, they are going round about
"'the city, and they are leading astray much people,
"'and they make them blind with the things which
"'they do, and they teach lying things, the which
"'have no foundation; and multitudes become con-
"'vinced by their words, and go astray after their
"'doctrine. We beseech thy greatness concerning
"'them. Command that they be seized, and that they
"'be summoned unto thy royal judgment hall, and be
"'questioned before thee, and that they receive from
"'thee such punishment as is meet for their falsehood.'
"And it came to pass that when the governor of the
"city had taken the bribe, he sent and seized the
"blessed men and cast them into prison, and he gave
"orders concerning them, saying, 'Let them be guard-
"ed carefully until they stand before me.' Now when
"the blessed men had been shut up in prison, they
"prayed and made supplication unto God, and they
"ceased not to teach their doctrine. For they were
"strenuous concerning the doctrine of Christ, and
"the true faith was blazing up in their minds like a
"flame of fire. There was no fear in their hearts,
"and they were not afraid in their minds; for their
"confidence was in Christ, and He hearkened unto
"everything which they asked, and performed their
"will."

"And when it was the time of evening, the three
"men stood up in prayer, and they sang hymns, and
"they said the whole of the Psalm which beginneth,
"'An avenging God[1] is the Lord.' And when they

---

[1] Psalm XCIV.

"had finished the service they prayed and said, 'Look,
"'O God, and see the iniquity and wickedness of
"'this contumacious people, and turn back their own
"'iniquity upon them, and let the wrath of Thine
"'anger overtake them; and grant that we may preach
"'Thy Gospel unto all those who believe. And shew
"'Thou mercy upon the nations that err and that
"'have not received Thy spiritual doctrine, and turn
"'them to the knowledge of Thy truth; and enlighten
"'the eyes of their hearts so that they may know
"'and have understanding of Thy great and terrible
"'Name, for in the blackness of error | they have
"'lost their way.' And when they had ended their
"service, the angel of God appeared unto them and
"said unto them, 'Fear not, neither be ye troubled,
"'O ye servants of God, for your prayer hath been
"'heard before God, and many people are about to
"'believe in Christ through your spiritual doctrine;
"'and your enemies shall not have the power to do
"'evil unto you, for God will be with you at all
"'times, and He will never forsake you.'

"Now many people were shut up in prison, and
"they were taking heed diligently and were observing
"the blessed men as they were performing their
"service; and [the blessed men] were constant in
"fasting and prayer. And these men drew nigh unto
"them and said unto them, 'We beseech you, O our
"'lords, to tell us: What is your doctrine? What is
"'your religion? and whether the God Whom ye wor-
"'ship is stronger than are the gods whom we wor-
"'ship? For, behold, we see that ye are constantly
"'praying to your God, although He is not nigh unto

"'you.' Then the blessed men opened their mouths "and said unto them, 'Our God is near and He is "'to be found by those who call upon Him; and in "'whatsoever place a man shall cry unto Him with "'a perfect heart, there is He. On the sea and on "'the dry land He ruleth with His will; and in the "'height and in the depth His command is fulfilled. "'But now, who are your gods?' And the men who "were bound in prison answered and said unto the "blessed men, 'Our gods are many. Some worship "'Venus Astarte, and some confess Apollo, and some "'worship Sîsînôs,¹ and some of us do honour unto "'the great god Zeus.' And when the blessed men "heard these things they said unto them, 'The gods "'whom ye worship are not gods at all, but dead "'idols, the work of the hands of the children of "'men; they can do neither good nor harm, and they "'cannot stand up to help those who worship them. "'And if | ye do not believe me, call upon them, and "'let them take you out from the prison wherein "'ye are bound.' And the men answered and said "unto the blessed men, 'Why doth not your own "'God come and deliver you, and take you out of "'the prison?' And the blessed men answered and "said unto them, 'Our God liveth, and He will take "'us out from this prison. And not only will He "'answer us, and deliver us from our enemies, but "'you also; for He receiveth and rejoiceth in those "'who turn unto Him, and delivereth them from their "'afflictions.'"

Page 201

---

¹ A corruption of the name 'Dionysos'.

"And there was in that prison a certain man, a
"councillor, who was imprisoned until he could be
"tried; now he had only one eye. And when he
"heard the blessed men talking about the wonderfu:
"things of God, he answered and said unto them,
"'O ye servants of God, entreat Christ, Whom ye
"'preach, on my behalf, that He may receive me
"'among the number of His lambs.' And when the
"blessed men heard the confession of the councillor,
"they answered and said unto him, 'If thou art firm
"'in the faith of Christ, the Son of God, we will
"'shew thee the way of Christ; now the way of Christ
"'leadeth those who love Him unto His Father. For
"'thus hath He taught us in His Gospel, saying, 'No
"'man cometh unto the Father except by Me.'[1] And,
"'He who seeth Me hath seen the Father.'[2] And for us
"'who believe doth He do our will whensoever we ask
"'Him, and whensoever we call upon Him He cometh
"'to our help. And that it may be certain unto thee
"'that these things are thus, if thou dost believe in
"'Christ, we will straightway call upon Him, and we
"'will bring some of this medicine nigh unto thine eye,
"'and immediately it shall be opened, and thou shalt
"'see the light therewith.' And the councillor said unto
"them, 'In very truth I believe upon Him, and that
"'He, the Christ, is the Son of the living God, the
"'Light of the world, and that He in His grace and
"'mercy hath sent you unto us that ye might illumine
"'the eyes of our understanding with your spiritual
"'doctrine.' Then Judah poured some of the gift of

---

[1] St. John XIV. 6.   [2] St. John XIV. 9.

"grace into his hand, and he anointed the eye of
"the councillor, and said, 'May Jesus, the true Light,
"'Who by coming hath made to rejoice the creatures
"'that were in darkness, illumine with the true light
"'this pupil of the eye which is in darkness!' And
"immediately that the gift of grace touched it, it
"became light and as if it had never at all been
"diseased. And when those who were bound in prison
"saw what had happened, they lifted up their voices,
"and said, 'Glory to the true God, Whom Judah and
"his companions serve! We believe that He is the
"'true Light, and that there is no other god besides
"'Him, and that He giveth strength and healing unto
"'those who believe in Him.'"

"And it came to pass that when the keeper of the
"prison heard what had happened, he ran and made
"it known to the governor, and said unto him, 'I
"'entreat thee, O my lord. These men, who by the
"'command of thy lordship have been bound in prison,
"'have been performing great and mighty deeds and
"'miracles therein. And all night long a most glorious
"'light from the chamber wherein they are illumineth
"'the prison; and when those who were imprisoned
"'along with them heard their doctrine and saw what
"'they were performing, they too believed upon them.
"'And further, I believe that if they wished it, the
"'doors of the prison would open themselves before
"'them, and they could depart. And, moreover, the
"'lord councillor himself also hath believed in their
"'doctrine.' Now when the governor of the city heard
"the words of the keeper of the prison, he straight-
"way commanded the clerk of his troops, and ....

"and he said unto them, 'Take ye fifty armed Greeks, "'and go to the prison and bring hither the lord "'councillor and all those who are imprisoned with "'him.' And when those who had been sent [to the "prison] had departed, they saw other soldiers sur-"rounding them, and they heard from them the true "doctrine. | And those who had gone for [the men "in prison] answered and said unto them, 'The judge "'hath sent us for you;' and they rose up with "them and went to the praetorium. And the chief of "the troops went in and said unto the governor of "the city, 'Behold, the men who were bound in prison "'are standing outside.' And the judge answered "and said unto them, 'Let the lord councillor come "'in;' and when he had gone in, and they saw that "both his eyes were opened, they marvelled at him "greatly. And the judge said unto him, 'My lord, "'for what cause hast thou been cast into prison?' "And the nobleman said unto him, 'My companions "'uttered calumnies concerning me before thy great-"'ness, and thou didst give the command concerning "'me, and I fell into prison.' And the governor said "unto him, 'Answer falsely nothing which I am about "'to ask you. Was not thine eye destroyed when "'thou didst fall into prison?' And the nobleman "said unto him, 'From the time when I could distin-"'guish between good and evil I never saw the light "'with it until I was shut up in prison.' Then the "governor said unto him, 'Thy falling into prison "'was, then, an advantage unto thee. But tell me "'how it was that thou camest to see the light with "'it, and who it was that gave thee light in thy blind

"'eye?' And the nobleman said unto him, 'O my lord
"'the governor, thou sayest unto me truly that in
"'being bound in prison I gained great benefit; and
"'I did so both bodily and spiritually; for that light
"'which is inside the pupil of my eye which was
"'dark is stronger than that of all those who are
"'born [with sight]. But now, I will tell thee how it
"'happened. These blessed men, Judah and his com-
"'panions, whom thou hast bound in prison, were
"'praying and making supplication by night and by
"'day, and they never ceased to perform their service.
"'And I heard the voice of the angel which came
"'down to them, and encouraged them, and I saw
"'also the most excellent light with which the chamber
"'wherein they were bound was filled. And one
"'morning I went in to them and saluted them, and
"'when they saw that I had received their doctrine,
"'Judah brought forth the medicine from beneath his
"'garment, and put some of it upon my eye, | and Page 204
"'called upon the Name of Christ; and straightway
"'my eye became sound, and I saw the light.' And
"when the judge heard the words of the nobleman,
"he answered and said unto him, 'Go thou in peace
"'to thy house, and render thanks and gratitude unto
"'Him Who hath given thee this great gift.'"

"Then the governor sent and called the blessed
"men, and said unto them, 'Ye must know that the
"'chief priests and the heads of the synagogue have
"'laid information concerning you before me, and
"'these men have told me that ye are seducers, and
"'that ye shew yourselves to be those who make the
"'eyes [of men] to be in darkness, and that ye lead

"'astray the innocent of heart and the simple-minded
"'folk, and that ye make disturbances in this city,
"'and that many murders are committed among you,
"'because ye are divided the one side against the
"'other. And I as a judge must follow their words,
"'lest I should fall under the condemnation of the
"'Emperors, as being a judge who hath heard of
"'tumult in his city and hath not been able to abate
"'the cause of the strife, but I have been led captive.
"'But since the lord councillor, whose eye I know
"'was destroyed, hath come unto me and he hath
"'apologized for you, saying that ye lead good lives,
"'and he hath shewed us also that his right eye which
"'was destroyed hath been opened, I now believe that
"'they spoke falsehoods against you through envy.
"'And now, I entreat you to deal graciously with me
"'also, even as ye have done for the lord councillor.'
"And the blessed men answered and said unto the
"governor, 'My lord, for this purpose also were we
"'sent by Christ, that unto every man who wisheth to
"'journey in the way of truth, and to turn unto the
"'religion of God and to hate that which abideth not,
"'and to love the happiness that abideth for ever, we
"'should shew the way. For the time of this world
"'is short, and it passeth away, and vanisheth, and
"'is consumed; and the life thereof cometh to an end,
"'and the dominion thereof is dissolved and goeth
"'away quickly, and it passeth like the shadow that
"'turneth, and it abideth not for ever. But those
"'who desire greatly | to see that world shall inherit
"'the happiness that never cometh to an end, and
"'the habitation that goeth not away, and the kingdom

"'which never passeth away, and the joy which is
"'never abated, and the praise which is never destroy-
"'ed, and the Light which maketh happy those who
"'see it for ever and for ever. But woe be unto the
"'sinners and unto the wicked who have not kept the
"'commandments of God when justice is revealed upon
"'them, and when they stand naked before the throne
"'of power, and the books are opened, and words are
"'tried! They shall make entreaty, but there shall be
"'none to answer; and they shall make supplication,
"'but there shall be none to hearken; and they shall
"'be in despair. There justice shall be lifted up, and
"'grace shall shine forth. No man shall make entreaty
"'for his fellow, and no man shall become surety for
"'his companion; offerings shall not be accepted there,
"'and supplication shall not be listened to, for there
"'is a gulf between the righteous and the wicked.
"'And sinners shall cry out, but they shall not be
"'heard; neither shall compassion be shewn unto
"'them, nor refreshing be allowed unto them. No
"'son shall aid his father there, and no father can
"'make entreaty on behalf of his son; there is no
"'accepting of persons in that place, for the judgment
"'of God is just, and every man shall be rewarded
"'according to his deeds. There the bond and the
"'free are as one, and the master and his servant
"'are equal, and the rich and the poor stand together.
"'He who acquired dominion [upon the earth] doth
"'not stand in his greatness, and the beggar doth
"'not return to his former lowly estate. This is the
"'constitution of the world which is to come. Blessed
"'is he whose iniquity hath been forgiven, and whose

"'sins have been covered! Blessed is the man to
"'whom the Lord will not reckon his sin, and in
"'whose heart there is no guile.'"
"And it came to pass that as these holy men
"sowed in the ears of the judge words which were
"full of pain and repentance, suffering and sorrow
"clothed him about. And he turned to God, and he
"received their doctrine like the good and rich ground
"which receiveth seed, and yieldeth fruit thirtyfold,
"and sixtyfold, and a hundredfold; even thus did he
"receive their doctrine. And he confessed Christ,
"and became greatly confirmed in the faith | of our
"Lord."

"Then the governor entreated the blessed men,
"saying, 'Now that the true light of your doctrine
"'hath illumined the eyes of my understanding, and
"'hath shone into my mind, I would make one request
"'of you; withhold it not, for I am confident and
"'certain that it is easy for you to grant it unto me.'
"And the blessed men said unto him, 'Ask whatsoever
"'thou wishest; and if we are able to grant it, good
"'and well, and if not, we will pray unto God and
"'entreat Him to give thee the petition of thy heart.'
"And the governor answered and said unto them,
"'I entreat you, O my lords. I have no son, and
"'my wife is barren. But I have a son of the house,
"'and one day he was occupied in some work of
"'folly, and I became enraged with him, and I took
"'a whip to beat him; and as I smote him, the thong
"'went into his eye, and destroyed it, and he hath
"'one eye [only]. And the grief wherewith I grieved
"'concerning him was greater than that wherewith I

"'grieved because I had no other children. And this "'day, the day whereon our Lord hath shewed His "'glory unto me, and your teaching hath drawn me "'unto life, I entreat you to fulfil your goodness "'towards me. Lay some of the medicine which ye "'have upon the boy, and let his eye be healed, "'and let him see the light; and I will rejoice in "'your coming unto me.' And the blessed men said "unto the governor, 'Every difficult thing is easy unto "'God, and to Him there is no crookedness which He "'cannot make straight; and whosoever believeth upon "'Him receiveth whatsoever he asketh. But tell me: "'What religion hath the boy?' And the governor "said unto them, 'Both he and I worship the gods "'whom the Emperors worship.' And the blessed men "said unto him, 'These gods whom the Emperors "'worship are not [gods] at all. But the King whose "'kingdom standeth for ever and ever is Jesus Christ, "'Whom we serve. His promise is faithful and true, "'and it is He Who giveth light, and life, | and king- Page 207 "'dom, unto those who believe upon Him. It is He "'Who giveth light to the blind, and hearing unto the "'deaf; it is He Who bringeth the dead to life, and "'He is the hope of the living. There is no one who "'can deliver and save like unto Him, but without belief "'in Him no man is able to draw nigh unto God.'"

"And it came to pass that, when the governor "heard these words from the blessed men, he spake "unto them further, and said, 'In very truth your "'doctrine is the true light, and, as we have heard "'concerning you, ye shew the way of life unto the "'children of men that they may serve the living God;

"'and I have seen with mine own eyes the things
"'which have taken place. But I entreat you now to
"'bring some of that medicine which ye have nigh
"'unto the boy, and let his eye which hath been
"'destroyed be made whole.' And the blessed men
"answered and said unto the boy, 'Tell us, O boy;
"'What happened unto thee?' And the boy answered
"and said unto them, 'I entreat you, O my lords.
"'The matter happened unto me thus. My lord was
"'wroth with me because I had offended him, and
"'he took a whip to beat me therewith; and as he
"'was beating me the thong of the whip came into
"'my eye, and blinded it.' And the blessed men said
"unto him, 'If one were to make it whole, what
"'wouldst thou promise him?' And the boy said unto
"them, 'My master hath made me the steward of
"'every thing that he hath, and he hath delivered
"'into my hands every thing that he possesseth,
"'together with his riches, and the goods which he
"'hath laid up, and all his treasury; whatsoever that
"'man should ask of me that would I give him.' And
"the blessed men said unto him, 'We require this of
"'thee: thou must believe upon Him Who shall give
"'thee the light.' And the boy answered and said
"unto them, 'My lords, I believe on Him with all my
"'soul, and with all my mind; He is the true God,
"'and the compassionate Lord. Henceforth I will
"'have no other lord with Him, and I will never again
"'put my neck under the yoke of another service,
"'and I will never again know any other god except
"'the Lord God.' And when the blessed men heard
"'these things from the boy, they answered and said

"'unto him, | Look up to heaven, and cry unto the [Page 208]
"'God Who dwelleth therein, Whose eyes look upon
"'the whole earth.' Then straightway the boy lifted
"up his gaze towards the celestial heights, and he
"prayed and said, 'O Lord God, Thou mighty God,
"'Who makest straight the way for sinners, and
"'Who callest the lost ones into Thy fold, hearken
"'Thou now, O Christ, to my voice, and grant that
"'I may enter into Thy spiritual fold, and let me be
"'one of those who have believed upon Thee. And
"'pardon me my offences in that I erred ignorantly
"'in following after dead idols, and make me to be
"'a participator with those who serve before Thee
"'with purity and holiness; yea, O Father, and Son,
"'and Holy Ghost, for ever! Amen.'"
"And it came to pass that, when the blessed men
"had heard the confession of the boy, they marvelled
"and gave glory unto God. And straightway Judah
"brought forth the horn, and poured out some of
"that gift of grace and laid it upon his eye, saying,
"'In the Name of our Lord Jesus Christ! May He
"'Whose door is open unto all those who believe,
"'Who desireth the life of all those who repent,
"'open thine eyes! and mayest thou see the light.'
"And when Judah had said these words, the eye of
"the boy was opened straightway, and he saw the
"light; and every one who was nigh and had seen
"what had happened, gave thanks and glorified God,
"Who worketh the will of those who fear Him when-
"soever they call upon Him. And the blessed men
"also anointed the wife of the judge and said, 'May
"'the Lord give thee fruit of joy!'"

16*

"And when the chief priests had heard that the
"governor, and all those who were with him, and all
"his troops, had believed on Jesus Christ, they medi-
"tated thereon among themselves. And they chose
"out from their people fifty men who were mighty
"men of valour, and gave them to eat and to drink;
"and when they were merry they said unto them,
"'Take as much gold as ye wish, and rise up this
"'night and arm yourselves, and go by night, without
"'any man knowing about you, and seize these
"'seducers, that is to say, Judah and his companions,
"'and go and cast them into the sea, and let them
"'be drowned.' Now there | was there among those
"who believed on Christ a certain just and righteous
"man, who was a fearer of God, and his name
"was Eutychus. And when he heard what the chief
"priests were wishing to do unto the blessed men,
"he busied himself diligently, and sent messengers
"unto them, saying, 'If ye do not save yourselves
"'by flight this night ye will perish in the sea. For
"'the chief priests have made a plan, and have
"'brought fifty men who are mighty men of valour,
"'and they have given them to eat and to drink,
"'and have distributed money not a little among
"'them, that they may come and seize you this night
"'and cast you into the sea. And no man knoweth
"'of the plan except me who have sent unto you.'
"And when the blessed men heard of the secret
"plan from the believing man, they rose up and
"went forth from the city; and they went down
"and journeyed through all the land of Palestine.
"And they passed on and came unto the country of

"Asia, and unto Galatia, and they preached unto
"every man in that country and taught there. And
"they came unto Phrygia and unto Cilicia, and in
"Cilicia they built a monastery wherein they dwelt
"all the days of their life. And they taught every
"one who went unto them to serve God with all their
"hearts, and they preached concerning Jesus Christ
"that He is the Son of God. And every one who
"was sick or ill of any disease whatsoever, if he
"went unto them believing in the power of God
"which clave unto them, he was healed whatever
"his disease might be. And they dwelt in that mo-
"nastery all the days of their life, and they preached
"the goodness of our Lord Jesus Christ, and they
"healed everyone who went unto them in the faith
"of God and who took refuge in the victorious power
"of the atoning blood of Christ."

These things, and a great many more besides them, which mine eyes have seen and mine ears have heard, have I, Philotheus the deacon, written down and shewn forth, and made known concerning | the most amazing and shameful deed which the crucifiers of Christ who were abominable in everything, committed; for in all that they did shame came upon them, but unto us by reason of what they did came the adoption of sons. Now all ye believers who are in every place, give thanks and glorify Christ, Who for the sake of our life sent His angel unto me, and made known to me these things for the redemption of our souls. Remember ye my feebleness, and the treasure of life for which I have laboured and have laid up for your aid in this history. And let us give thanks together, and let us glorify the Father, and the Son, and the Holy Ghost, now and at all times, and for ever and ever! Amen.

Here endeth the History of the Likeness which the Jews made in the city of Tiberias to make a mock of, and of how they received their punishment. And to God be everlasting glory! Amen.

A COMPLETE LIST OF

BOOKS & PERIODICALS,

PUBLISHED AND SOLD BY

LUZAC and Co.,

Publishers to the India Office, the Asiatic Society of Bengal, the University of Chicago, etc.

(With Index)

1740

LONDON:
LUZAC & Co.
46, GREAT RUSSELL STREET (OPPOSITE THE BRITISH MUSEUM).
1898.

MESSRS. **LUZAC & Co.** having been appointed **OFFICIAL AGENTS FOR THE SALE OF INDIAN GOVERNMENT PUBLICATIONS** and **PUBLISHERS TO THE SECRETARY OF STATE FOR INDIA IN COUNCIL,** are able to supply at the shortest notice all Works published by the **GOVERNMENT OF INDIA.**

They have also been appointed **OFFICIAL ENGLISH AGENTS AND PUBLISHERS** to the **ASIATIC SOCIETY OF BENGAL,** and **THE UNIVERSITY OF CHICAGO,** and keep all Works published by the above Society and University in stock.

ORIENTAL STUDENTS are invited to submit to **Messrs. LUZAC & Co,** their **MANUSCRIPTS** for publication before sending them elsewhere.

Messrs. LUZAC and Co. are able to Supply, at the Shortest Notice and most favourable Terms, **all English, Foreign,** and **Oriental Books** and **Periodicals. Monthly Lists** Issued Regularly and Sent Gratis on Application.

Messrs. LUZAC and Co. have a Large Stock of New and Second-hand Oriental Works, of which they issue regularly Lists and Catalogues, which are to be had on application.

COMPLETE LIST OF
BOOKS AND PERIODICALS,

PUBLISHED AND SOLD BY

LUZAC and Co.

American Journal of Theology. Edited by Members of the Divinity Faculty of the University of Chicago. Vol. I. (Vol. II in progress). Quarterly. Annual Subscription. 14s. 6d.

"The theologians of America are attempting to supply a real need... it aims at a complete presentation of all recent theological work... we give it a hearty welcome, as a scheme likely to prove of real utility to theological students and to the cause of truth." — *Guardian*.

American Journal of Semitic Languages and Literatures (continuing Hebraica). Edited by WILLIAM R. HARPER and the Staff of the Semitic Department of the University of Chicago. Vol. I—XIII. (Vol. XIV in progress). Published quarterly. Annual subscription. 14s.

American Journal of Sociology. Vol. I—III. (Vol. IV in progress). Published quarterly. Annual subscription. 10s. 6d.

Anandás'rama Sanskrit Series. — Edited by Pandits of the Ánandás'rama. Published by Mahádeva Chimnáji Ápte, B.A., LL.B., Pleader High Court, and Fellow of the University of Bombay. Nos. 1 to 35. In 42 Vols. Royal 8vo. Price of the set £ 16. Single Vols. at different prices.

Asiatic Society of Bengal, Journal of. Messrs Luzac and Co are the sole agents for Great Britain and America of the Asiatic Society of Bengal and can supply the continuation of the Journal at 3s. each No., of the Proceedings at 1s. each No. As they keep a large stock of the Journal and Proceedings, they can also supply any single No. at the published price.

Assab'iniyya. — A philosophical Poem in Arabic by Mūsā B. Tūbi. Together with the Hebrew Version and Commentary styled Bāttē Hannefeš by Solomon Immānuēl Dapiera. Edited and translated by HARTWIG HIRSCHFELD. 8vo. pp. 61. 2s. 6d. net.

Assyrian and Babylonian Letters. 4 vols. See: Harper.

Aston (W. G.) — A Grammar of the Japanese Written Language. Second Edition, enlarged and improved. Roy. 8vo. Cloth. pp. 306. (Published 28s.) Reduced-Price, 18s.

Aston (W. G.) — A Short Grammar of the Japanese Spoken Language. Fourth Edition. Crown 8vo. Cloth. pp. 212. (Published 12s.) Reduced-Price, 7s. 6d.

Babylonian and Oriental Record. (The) — A Monthly Magazine of the Antiquities of the East. Edited by Prof. TERRIEN DE LACOUPERIE. Vol. I—VI. (Vol. VII in progress). Published monthly. Single Numbers, 1s. 6d. each.

Babylonian Magic and Sorcery. See: King.

Bāna's Kadambari. Translated, with Occasional Omissions, with a full Abstract of the Continuation of the Romance by the Author's Son Bhushanabhatta, by C. M. RIDDING. 8vo. Cloth. pp. XXIV, 232. 10s.

Bāna's Harsa Carita. An Historical Work, translated from the Sanskrit, by E. B. Cowell and F. W. Thomas. 8vo. Cloth. pp. XIV, 284. 10s.

Bezold (Ch.) — Oriental Diplomacy: being the transliterated Text of the Cuneiform Despatches between the King of Egypt and Western Asia in the XVth. century before Christ, discovered at Tell el Amarna, and now preserved in the British Museum. With full Vocabulary, grammatical Notes, &c., by CHARLES BEZOLD. Post 8vo. Cloth. pp. XLIV, 124. 18s. net.

"For the Assyriologist the book is a servicable and handy supplement to the British Museum volume on the Tell El-Amarna tablets. The author is specially skilled in the art of cataloguing and dictionary making and it is needless to say that he has done his work well". — *The Academy*.

"Die in dem Hauptwerke (The Tell el Amarna Tablets in the British Museum with autotype Facsimiles, etc.) vermisstte Transcription des Keilschrifttextes der Tafeln, sowie ein sehr ausführliches, mituntur die Vollständigkeit einer Concordanz erreichendes Vocabulary bietet die Oriental Diplomacy von C. Bezold, das eben deshalb gewissermassen als Schlüssel zu dem Publicationswerke betrachtet werden kann." — *Liter. Centralblatt*.

„Wichtig und sehr nützlich vor allem wegen der Einleitung und des Wörterverzeichnisses... Transkription und kurze Inhaltsangabe der Briefe sehr zweckmässig.... eine anerkennenswerthe Leistung."
Deutsche Litteraturzeitung.

Biblia. — A Monthly Magazine, devoted to Biblical Archaeology and Oriental Research. Vol. I—X. (Vol. XI in progress). Published monthly. Annual Subscription, 5s.

Biblical World (The) — Continuing the Old and New Testament Student. Edited by WILLIAM R. HARPER. New Series. Vol. I—X. (Vol. XI and XII in progress). Published monthly. Annual Subscription, 10s. 6d.

"The Biblical World makes a faithful record and helpful critic of present Biblical Work, as well as an efficient practical and positive independent force in stimulating and instructing the student, preacher and teacher"

Bibliographical List of Books on Africa and the East. Published in England. 2 Vols. Vol. I. Containing the Books published between the Meetings of the Eighth Oriental Congress at Stockholm, in 1889, and the Ninth Congress in London in 1892. Vol. II. Containing the Books published between the Meetings of the Ninth Oriental Congress in London, in 1892, and the Tenth Oriental Congress at Geneva, in 1894. Systematically arranged, with Preface and Author's Index, by C. G. Luzac. 12mo. each Vol. 1s.

Bibliotheca Indica. — Messrs Luzac & Co. are agents for the sale of this important series and keep most of the numbers in stock.

Blackden (M. W.) and G. W. Frazer. — Collection of Hieratic Graffiti, from the Alabaster Quarry of Hat-Nub, situated near Tell El Amarna. Found December 28th. 1891, copied September, 1892. Obl. pp. 10. 10s.

Buddhaghosuppatti; or, Historical Romance of the Rise and Career of Buddaghosa. Edited and translated by JAMES GRAY, Professor of Pali. Rangoon College. Two Parts in one. Demy 8vo. Cloth. pp. VIII, 75 and 36. 6s.

Budge (E. A. Wallis) — The Laughable Stories collected by Bar-Hebraeus. The Syriac Text with an English Translation, by E. A. WALLIS BUDGE, Litt. D., F. S. A., Keeper of the Department of Egyptian and Assyrian Antiquities, British Museum. 8vo. Cloth. 21s. net. [Luzac's Semitic Texts and Translation Series, Vol. I].

"Dr. BUDGE's book will be welcome as a handy reading book for advanced students of Syriac, but in the mean time the stories will be an addition to the literature of gnomes and proverbs, of which so many are found in India, and in Persian, Hebrew and Arabic, although not yet published. We are happy to say that Dr. BUDGE's new book is well edited and translated as far as we can judge". — *Athenæum*.

"The worthy Syrian Bishops idea of humour may excite admiration when we hear that he collected his quips in the grey dawn of the middle ages". — *Pall Mall Gazette*.

"Man sieht, das Buch ist in mehr als einer Hinsicht interessant, und wir sind Budge für die Herausgabe aufrichtig dankbar. — *Lit. Centralb*.

"Sous le titre de *Récits amusants*, le célèbre polygraphe syrien Barhébraeus a réuni une collection de sept cent vingt-sept contes, divisés en vingt chapitres et renfermant des aphorismes, des anecdotes et des fables d'animaux ayant un caractère soit moral, soit simplement récréatif. Le livre nous était connu par quelques spécimens publiés précédement. M. BUDGE, qui a déja rendu tant de services aux lettres syriaques, vient d'éditer l'ouvrage entier avec une traduction anglaise..... En tous cas, M. B. a eu raison de ne pas faire un choix et de donner l'ouvrage en son entier.... Les aphorismes, écrits dans un style concis et avec, une pointe dont la finesse n'est pas toujours sensible, présentent des difficultés de traduction dont M. B. a généralement triomphé." — *Revue Critique.*

"È questo un libro singolare, appartemente ad un genere assai scarso nella letteratura siriaca, quantunque così ricca, cioè a quello dell'amena letteratura. Bar Ebreo scrisse questo libro nella vecchiaia, o forse allora mise insieme e ordinò estr atti che avea prese nelle lunghe letture da lui fatte, di tanto opere e cosi svariate.... I cultori degli studi siriaci saranno assai grati al Dr. Budge per questo suo novello contributo; l'edizione per carte e per tipi è veramente bellissima." — *La Cultura.*

Budge, see Luzac's Semitic Text and Translation Series. Vols. I, III, V and VII.

Cappeller (Carl) — A Sanskrit-English Dictionary. Based upon the St. Petersburg Lexicons. Royal 8vo. Cloth. pp. VIII, 672 [Published £ 1. 1*s*]. Reduced to 10*s*. 6*d*.

"Linguistic and other students should hail with satisfaction the publication of a cheap and handy Sanskrit-English Dictionary, such as is now to be found in the new English edition of Prof. CAPPELLER's Sanskrit-German 'Wörterbuch,' recently published by Messrs. Luzac. The book is well adapted to the use of beginners, as it specially deals with the text usually read in commencing Sanskrit; but it will be of use also to philological students — or such as have mastered the Nāgari character — as it includes most Vedic words, a great desideratum in many earlier dictionaries, especially such as were founded on native sources. The basis of the present work is, on the contrary, the great lexicon of Boethlingk and Roth with the addition of compound forms likely to be of service to beginners." — *Athenæum.*

"The English edition of Prof. CAPPELLER's Sanskrit Dictionary is some thing more than a mere translation of the German edition. It includes the vocabulary of several additional texts; many compounds have been inserted which are not given in the Petersburg lexicons; and some improvements have been made in the arrangement. The errors enumerated by the reviewer of the *Academy* have for the most part been corrected, though a few still remain. .... The book is certainly the cheapest, and, for a beginner, in some respects the best, of existing Sanskrit-English dictionaries." — *Academy.*

"Professor CAPPELLER furnishes the Student of Sanskrit, if not with a complete Lexicon, — for that he tells us, was not his object, — still with a handy and yet very full vocabulary of all the words occurring in the texts which are generally studied in that language. His plan is to avoid all unnecessary complications, to give each word in such a manner as to show its formation, if it is not itself a stem. It is not merely an English version of the author's Sanskrit-German Dictionary, nor merely an enlarged edition of the same; it is a new work, with a distinct plan and object of its own. We can recommend it to the Sanskrit student as a sufficient dictionary for all practical purposes, which will enable him to dispense with larger and more costly and complicated Lexicons till he has acquired a considerable proficiency in this difficult and scientific language." — *Asiatic Quarterly Review.*

Ceylon. A Tale of Old..... See: Sinnatamby.

Chakrabarti (J. Ch.) — The Native States of India. 8vo. Cloth. pp. XIV, 274. With Map. 5s. net.

Cool (W.) — **With the Dutch in the East.** An Outline of the Military Operations in Lombock, 1894, Giving also a Popular Account of the Native Characteristics, Architecture, Methods of Irrigations, Agricultural Pursuits, Folklore, Religious Customs and a History of the Introduction of Islamism and Hinduism into the Island. By Capt. W. COOL (Dutch Engineer), Knight of the Order of Orange Nassau; decorated for important War Services in the Dutch Indies; Professor at the High School of War, the Hague. Translated from the Dutch by E. J. Taylor. Illustrated by G. B. HOOYER. Late Lieut. Col. of the Dutch Indian Army; Knight of the Military Order of William; decorated for important War Services in the Dutch Indies. Roy. 8vo. Cloth. 21s.

"There are, it is to be feared, but few books published in this country from which English readers can obtain information as to the doings of the Dutch in their Eastern colonies. — For this reason we are glad that Capt. Cool's account of the Lombock expedition has been translated." — *Athenæum.*

"The book contains an interesting account of the Balinese and Sassak customs, and throws some light on the introduction of the Mahomedan and Hindu religions into Lombock... The translation by Miss E. J. Taylor is satisfactory, and some of the illustrations are excellent." — *The Times.*

"Lombock forms a small link in the long chain of volcanic lands... To folklorists and students of primitive religions it has always presented many attractive features... They will be much interested in the local traditions recorded in the volume before us. Miss Taylor's version deserves a word of recognition, and the general equipment of the book is creditable to the Amsterdam press. There is a good index." — *Academy.*

"The author not only describes the military operations, but gives a full history of Lombock and its people. Much curious information as to a land very much out of the way and little known to English readers is given. In addition the account of the actual warfare is full of incident. The book is freely illustrated." — *Yorkshire Daily Post.*

"This is a work which will no doubt attract considerable attention, both in the West and throughout the East. Miss Taylor has acquitted herself as a translator with rare ability and taste, and the comprehensive and excellent way in which the work is illustrated adds an additional charm to what is at once the most entertaining and most attractive chapter of Netherlands Indian history." — *European Mail.*

"Besides containing a great deal of information concerning this hitherto very slightly known island and its inhabitants, Captain Cool's volume is profusely and excellently illustrated ... Miss Taylor's translation of it is fluent and thoroughly readable." — *Glasgow Herald.*

Cowell, E. B., See: Bāna's Harsa Carita.

Cowper (B. H.) Principles of Syriac Grammar. Translated and abridged from the work of Dr. HOFFMANN. 8vo. Cloth. pp. 184. 7s. 6d.

Cust (R. N.) — The Gospel Message or Essays, Addresses, Suggestions and Warnings of the different aspects of Christian Missions to Non Christian Races and peoples. 8vo. pp. 494. Paper 6s. 6d. Cloth. 7s. 6d.

".... There are few objects of controversy in missionary matters which are not very fully discussed by Dr. CUST, and if we not infrequently differ from him we gladly thank him for copious information and the benefits of his long experience" — *Guardian.*

"It is a big book, it ranges over a very wide field, and it is never dull or dry". — *Expository Times.*

"The scheme is so comprehensive as to include almost every detail of the missionary enterprise. Every essay is stamped, of course with the personality of its author, whose views are expressed with characteristic force and clearness". — *The Record.*

Cust (R. N.) — Essay on the Common Features which appear in all Forms of Religious belief. Post 8vo. Cloth. pp. XXIV, 194. 5s.

"Dr. CUST has put his very considerable knowledge to excellent purposes in this modest little publication. He seems most at home with the faiths of the East, but even the most elementary of savage creeds have not escaped him". — *Pall Mall Gazette.*

Cust (R. N.) — Essay on Religious Conceptions. Post 8vo. Cloth. pp. V, 148. 5s.

Cust (R. N.) — **Linguistic and Oriental Essays.** Fourth Series. From 1861 to 1895. 8vo. pp. XXV, 634. Paper Covers. 16s., Cloth. 17s. 6d.

Dawlatshah's Lives of the Persian Poets. Edited by EDWARD G. BROWNE, Lecturer in Persian in the University of Cambridge. Vol. 1. Tadhkiratu'sh Sh'arā. 8vo. Cloth. 18s. net.

Edkins (Joseph) — **China's Place in Philology.** An Attempt to show that the Languages of Europe and Asia have a common Origin. Demy 8vo. Cloth. pp. XXIII, 403. (Published 10s. 6d.) 7s. 6d.

Edkins (Joseph) — **Introduction to the Study of the Chinese Characters.** Royal 8vo. Boards. pp. XIX, 211, 101. (Published 18s.) 12s. 6d.

Edkins (Joseph) — **Nirvana of the Northern Buddhists.** 8vo. pp. 21. Reprint. 6d.

Edkins (Joseph) — **Chinese Architecture.** Contents. — 1. Classical Style. — 2. Post-Confucian Style. — 3. Buddhist Style. — 4. Modern Style. 8vo. pp. 36. 1s.

Edkins (Joseph) — **Chinese Currency.** Roy. 8vo. pp. 29. 1s.

Edkins (Joseph) — **Ancient Symbolism among the Chinese.** Cr. 8vo. pp. 26. 6d.

Efes Damîm. — A Series of Conversations at Jerusalem between a Patriarch of the Greek Church and a Chief Rabbi of the Jews, concerning the Malicious Charge against the Jews of using Christian Blood. By J. B. LEVINSOHN. Translated from the Hebrew by Dr. L. LOEWE. Roy. 8vo. Cloth. pp. XVI, 208. (Published 8s.) Reduced Price 2s. 6d.

Eitel (E. J.) — **Europe in China. The History of Hongkong.** From the Beginning to the year 1882. 8vo. Cloth. pp. VII, 575. With Index. 15s. net.

"His work rises considerably above the level commonly attained by colonial histories written from a colonial point of view". — *Times.*

"His painstaking volume is really a detailed history of the colony and of the adminstration of successive governors from 1841 down to the present day" — *Daily Telegraph*.

"This is an interesting book. The subject is full of matter, and Dr. EITEL has, as a rule, treated it successfully. — *Athenæum*.

".... The student will find Dr. EITEL's book a very storehouse of information .... has told it with a mastery of fact that vouches for his industry and perseverance" — *Saturday Review*.

Gladstone (Right Hon. W. E.) — Archaic Greece and the East. 8vo. pp. 32. 1s.

Gribble (J. D. B.) — A History of the Deccan. With numerous Illustrations, Plates, Portraits, Maps and Plans. Vol. I. Roy. 8vo. Cloth. 21s.

"In a style easy and pleasant the author tells the story of the Mohammedan occupation of the Deccan .... the general style of the book and the admirable photographs and drawings with which it is enriched leave nothing to be desired". — *Athenæum*.

"Mr. J. D. B. GRIBBLE has accomplished a difficult task. He has constructed from original materials a continuous narrative of one of the most confused periods of Indian history. He has also presented it with a lucidity of style which will go far to render it acceptable to the reading public.... The book is illustrated by a number of interesting reproductions of scenery and architecture in Southern India. These and the maps, plans, and clear genealogical tables reflect credit both upon the author and the publisher" — *Times*.

"Mr. GRIBBLE has brought great industry and knowledge of the country to this compilation .... The work is of some historical importance". — *Saturday Review*.

Gray (James). See Buddhaghosuppatti.

Gray (James). See Jinalankara.

Guide to the Dutch East Indies. By Dr. J. F. van BEMMELEN and G. B. HOOYER. Trans. from the Dutch by the Rev. B. J. BERRINGTON B.A., with 16 Plates, 13 Maps and Plans, and a copious index. Sm. 8vo. pp. 202. 1s. 6d.

"For any one going in that direction this remarkably complete little work is indispensable". — *Pall Mall Gazette*.

"The guide book omits nothing needed by the traveller. It describes the necessary outfit, customs afloat and ashore, mode of living, how to dress, how often to bathe, who to tip, and how much" — *The Shipping World*.

Guirandon (F. G. de) — Manuel de la langue foule, parlée dans la Sénégambie et le Soudan. Grammaire textes, vocabulaire. 8vo. Cloth. pp. 144. 6s.

Halcombe (Charles J. H.) — **The Mystic Flowery Land.** A Personal Narrative. By CHARLES J. H. HALCOMBE. Late of Imperial Customs. China, 8vo. Cloth. gilt. pp. 226. 16s.

"This valuable and handsome volume contains thirty long chapters, a frontispiece of the Author and his wife — the latter in her Oriental costume — numerous fine reproductions from photographs, and several beautiful coloured pictures representing many scenes and phases of Chinese life, etchings and comprehensive notes by the Author.

"His pages are full of incident and his narrative often vivid and vigorous". — *Times.*

"The illustrations are good and numerous. Many are facsimiles of coloured Chinese drawings showing various industrial occupations: others are photogravures representing buildings and scenery". — *Morning Post.*

"Handsomely attired in red, yellow and gold, with Chinese characters to give further appropriateness to the outer garb, is this volume of freely illustrated personal experience in China.... Mr. HALCOMBE gives a graphic description of places and peoples, with their manners and customs". — *Liverpool Courier.*

"The illustrations are all good, and the Chinese pictures reproduced in colours interesting. We have not seen any of them before". — *Westminster Review.*

Hansei Zasshi. Monthly. Vol. I—XII. (Vol. XIII in progress). Annual subscription. 6s.

Hardy (R. Spence) — **The Legends and theories of the Buddhists.** Compared with History and Science. 8vo. Cloth. pp. 244. 7s. 6d.

Harîri. — The Assemblies of al Harîri. Translated from the Arabic with an Introduction and notes, Historical and Grammatical, by TH. CHENERY and F. STEINGASS. With Preface and Index, by F. F. ARBUTHNOT, 2 Vols. 8vo. Cloth. pp. X, 540 and XI, 395. £1.10s.

Harper (Robert Francis) — **Assyrian and Babylonian Letters,** belonging to the K. Collection of the British Museum. By ROBERT FRANCIS HARPER, of the University of Chicago. Vols. I to IV. Post 8vo. Cloth. Price of each Vol. £1. 5s. net.

"The Assyriologist, will welcome them with gratitude, for they offer him a mass of new material which has been carefully copied and well printed, and which cannot fail to yield important results." — *Athenæum*.

"The book is well printed, and it is a pleasure to read the texts given in it, with their large type and ample margin." — *Academy*.

Hebraica. — A Quarterly Journal in the Interests of Semitic Study. Edited by WILLIAM R. HARPER and the Staff of the Semitic Department of the University of Chicago. Vol. I—XI. Published quarterly. Annual Subscription. 14s.

See American Journal of Semitic Languages, etc.

India. (The Native States of). See: Chakrabarti.

India. (The Armenians in). See: Seth.

Indian Antiquary (The) — A Journal of Oriental Research in Archaeology, Epigraphy, etc. etc. Edited by R. C. TEMPLE. Vol. I—XXVI. (Vol. XXVII in progress). Annual Subscription, £ 1. 16s.

Indian Terms. (A Glossary of). See: Temple.

Indian Wisdom. See: Monier-Williams.

Jastrow's Dictionary of the Targumim, the Talmud Babli and Yerushalmi, and the Midrashic Literature. Compiled by M. JASTROW, Ph. D. Parts I to IX. 4to. pp. 480. 5s. each Part.

"This is the only Talmudic dictionary in English, and all students should subscribe to it. The merits of this work are now too well known to need repetition." — *Jewish Chronicle*.

Jinalankara or **"Embellishments of Buddha"**, by Buddharakkhita. Edited with Introduction, Notes and Translation, by JAMES GRAY. Two Parts in one. Demy 8vo. Cloth. 6s.

"The commendable care with which the volume has been prepared for the use of students is evident throughout its pages. — *Athenæum*.

Johnson (Capt. F. N). — The Seven Poems etc. See: Muallakat.

Johnston (C.) Useful Sanskrit Nouns and Verbs. In English Letters. Compiled by CHARLES JOHNSTON,

Bengal Civil Service, Dublin University Sanskrit Prizeman, India Civil Service Sanskrit Prizeman. Small 4to. Boards. pp. 30. 2s. 6d.

Johnston (C.) — The Awakening to the Self.
Translated from the Sanskrit of Shankara the Master. Oblong 8vo. Paper covers. 2s.

Journal of the Buddhist Text Society of India.
Edited by Sarat Candra Das, C. J. E. Vols. I to IV. 8vo. Calcutta, 1893—1897. £ 1. 10s.

Messrs. Luzac & Co. are the English agents for the above and can supply the Continuation. Subscription. 10s. each Vol.

Judson (A.) — English-Burmese Dictionary.
Fourth Edition. Royal 8vo. Half bound. pp. 1752. £ 1. 12s.

Judson (A.) — Burmese-English Dictionary. Revised and enlarged by ROBERT C. STEVENSON. Royal 8vo. Paper covers. pp. 1192.

Kathákoça. See Tawney.

King (Leonard W.) — Babylonian Magic and Sorcery. Being "The Prayers of the Lifting of the Hand". The Cuneiform Texts of a Group of Babylonian and Assyrian Incantations and magical Formulae, edited with Transliterations, Translations, and full Vocabulary from Tablets of the Kuyunjik Collection preserved in the British Museum. By LEONARD W. KING, M. A., Assistant in the Department of Egyptian and Assyrian Antiquities, British Museum. Roy. 8vo. Cloth. 18s. net.

"We cannot pretend to form an adequate judgment of the merits of Mr. KING's work, but it is manifestly conceived and executed in a very scholarly spirit." — *Times.*

"Mr. KING's book, will, we believe be of great use to all students of Mesopotamian religions, and it marks an era in Assyriological studies in England.... A word of special praise is due to Mr. KING for the excellence of his autograph plates of text." — *Athenæum.*

"The work will be found a valuable addition to our knowledge of Babylonian history, and to the study of comparative philology."
Morning Post.

King, L. W. See: Luzac's Semitic Text and Translation Series, Vols. II, IV and VI.

Kittel (Rev. F.) — **A Kannada-English Dictionary.** By Rev. F. KITTEL, B. G. E. M. Royal 8vo. Half-Bound. pp. L. 1725. £ 1. 12s.

Korean Repository. Vols. I to III. Annual Subscription 15s. Post free.

Land (J. P. N.) — **The Principles of Hebrew Grammar.** By J. P. N. LAND, Professor of Logic and Metaphysics in the University of Leyden. Translated from the Dutch by REGINALD LANE POOLE, Balliol College, Oxford. Demy 8vo. Cloth. pp. XX, 219 (Published 7s. 6d.) Reduced price 5s.

Lives of the Persian Poets Series. See Dawlatshah.

Loewe (L.) — **A Dictionary of the Circassian Language.** In two Parts. English—Circassian—Turkish, and Circassian—English—Turkish. 8vo. Cloth. (Published 21s.) Reduced price 6s.

Loewe (L.) Efes Damim. See: Efes.

Luzac's Oriental List. — Containing Notes and News on, and a Bibliographical List of all new Publications on Africa and the East. Published Monthly. Annual Subscription, 3s. Vols. I to VIII (1890—1897) are still to be had (with Index, half-bound), at £ 2. 15s.

Vols. I to IV are nearly out of print and can only be sold in the set. Vols V to VIII are still to be had at 5s. each vol.

"It deserves the support of Oriental students. Besides the catalogue of new books published in England, on the Continent, in the East, and in America, it gives, under the heading of "Notes and News" details about important Oriental works, which are both more full and more careful than anything of the sort to be found elsewhere." — *Academy*.

"A bibliographical monthly publication which should be better known." *The Record*.

Luzac's Semitic Text and Translation Series. Vol. I: See: Budge.

Vol. II. The Letters and Despatches of Hammurabi king of Babylon about B. C. 2250, to Sin-idinnam, King of Larsa, together with other royal and official correspondence of the same period: the Cuneiform texts edited with an Introduction and short descriptions by L. W. King, M. A.

This volume will contain about 100 letters relating to a variety of official subjects, and their contents are of great importance for the study of the history of Babylonia, Elam and the neighbouring districts about the time of the patriarch Abraham. These letters reveal the system by which Hammurabi maintained his rule in the remote provinces of his newly acquired empire, and contain some of the orders and directions which he issued for the movements of troops, for the building of canals and waterways, for the food-supply of his capital, and for the regulation of legal tribunals. The letters of Hammurabi are the oldest Babylonian despatches extant. — *Ready in June.*

Vol. III. The History of the Blessed Lady Mary the Virgin, and the History of the Image of Christ, which the men of Tiberias made to mock at; the Syriac text edited, with an English translation, by E. A. WALLIS BUDGE, Litt. D., D. Lit., etc. — *Ready in October.*

This Life of the Virgin is the fullest known to exist in Syriac, and varies in many important particulars from the versions of which fragments have already been published. The Life has been copied from an ancient Nestorian MS., to the text of which have been added all the variants found in the XVIth century MS. in the possession of the Royal Asiatic Society of Great Britain.

Vol. IV. The Letters and Despatches of Hammurabi together with other official and private correspondence of the same period, by L. W. KING, M. A.

This volume will contain a number of transliterations and translations of the texts of the 100 letters and despatches which are printed in volume 2; to these will be added indexes of proper names etc. and a List of Characters. An attempt will be made to give a description of the circumstances under which these letters were written, and short notes on points of grammar, history, etc. will be added. — *In the Press.*

Vol. V. The History of Rabban Hormizd by Mâr Simon, the disciple of Mâr Yôzâdhâk; the Syriac text edited, with an English translation by E. A. WALLIS BUDGE, Litt. D., D. Lit., etc.

The text describes the life of this famous Nestorian anchorite, the building of his monastery, and the struggle which went on in the VIIth century between the rival sects of Jacobites and Nestorians in Mesopotamia. This prose version of the life of Rabban Hormizd is, probably, the source from which the metrical versions were drawn; and it is of great importance for the study of the second great development of monasticism in Mesopotamia. — *In the Press.*

Vol. VI. Babylonian Private Letters written during the period of the First Dynasty of Babylon; the Cuneiform texts edited with Introduction and short descriptions by L. W. KING, M. A.

This volume will contain about 200 letters of a private nature which reveal the social condition of the country and incidentally throw much light upon the civilization of the period. From grammatical and lexicographical points of view these texts are of considerable importance, for they afford numerous examples of unusual words and forms of expression. — *In the Press.*

Vol. VII. The Life of Rabban Bar-Idtâ by John his disciple; The Syrac text edited, with an English translation, by E. A. WALLIS BUDGE, Litt. D., D. Lit., etc.

Bar-Idtâ was the founder of a famous rule and monastery in Mesopotamia in the VIIth century, and the author of a very valuable work on monastic history which is quoted with respect by Thomas, Bishop of Margâ. He was a contemporary of Babhai of Mount Izlâ, and of Jacob of Bêth Abbê.

Volumes 5, 6, and 7 will, it is hoped be ready early next year.

Macnaghten (Sir W. Hay) — Principle of Hindu and Mohammedan Law. Republished from the Principles and Precedences of the same. Edited by the late H. H. WILSON. 8vo. Cloth. pp. 240. 6s.

Margoliouth (D. S.) — Arabic Papyri of the Bodleian Library reproduced by the Collotype Process. With Transcription and Translation. Text in 4to. pp. 7 and 2 Facsimiles in large folio. 5s.

Margoliouth (D. S.) — Chrestomathia Baidawiana. The Commentary of El-Baidâwi on Sura III. Translated and explained for the Use of Students of Arabic. By D. S. MARGOLIOUTH, M. A., Laudian Professor of Arabic in the University of Oxford, etc. etc. Post 8vo. Cloth. 12s.

"The book is as scholarly as it is useful. Of particular importance are the numerous grammatical annotations which give the beginner an insight into the method of the Arabic national grammarians, and which form an excellent preparatory study for the perusal of these works in the original..... The introduction and the remarks in particular show how well Mr. MARGOLIOUTH has mastered the immense literatures of Moslim Tradition, Grammar and Kalaim.... The perusal of the book affords pleasure from beginning to end." — *Journal Royal Asiatic Society.*

Mirkhond. — The Rauzat-us-Safa; or, Garden of Purity. Translated from the Original Persian by E. REHATSEK; edited by F. F. ARBUTHNOT. Vols. I to V. 10s. each Vol.

Vols. 1 and 2 contain: The Histories of Prophets, Kings and Khalifs.
Vols. 3 and 4 contain: The life of Muhammad the Apostle of Allah.
Vol. 5 contains: The Lives of Abû Bakr, O'mar, O'thmàn, and Ali', the four immediate successors of Muhammad the Apostle.

Monier-Williams (Sir Monier) — Indian Wisdom; or Examples of the religious, philosophical, and ethical Doctrines of the Hindus, with a brief History of the chief Departments of Sanskrit Literature, and some account of the past and present Condition of India, moral and intellectual. By Sir MONIER MONIER-WILLIAMS, K. C. I. E., M. A., Hon. D. C. L., Oxford. Fourth Edition, enlarged and improved. Post 8vo. Cloth. pp. 575. £ 1. 1s.

"His book .... still remains indispensable for the growing public, which seeks to learn the outline of Indian literature and thought in a simple and readable form. We are glad to welcome the fourth edition of this eminently readable book." — *Daily Chronicle.*

"The learned professor's thorough mastery of his subject enables him to deal effectively with his difficult task..... He omits nothing that enters the scope of his work : he is choice in his selections and accurate in his comments, and the result is a work as instructive and sound as it is pleasant to read." — *Asiatic Quarterly Review.*

"For all students of the philosophy of religion, as well as for all especially interested in Indian literature and thought, the work is one of very great value." — *Glasgow Herald.*

"It is a fine volume and contains valuable additions by the author.... this edition will be more than ever prized by students of Indian lore." *Scotsman.*

Muallakat. — **The Seven Poems suspended in the Temple at Mecca.** Translated from the Arabic. By Capt. F. E. JOHNSON. With an Introduction by Shaikh Taizullabhai. 8vo. pp. XXIV, 238. 7s. 6d.

"This handy volume decidedly supplies a great want for those who make a serious study of Arabic.... The grammatical, historical, geographical and other notes comments and explanations are ample and thorough". — *Imperial and Asiatic Quarterly Review.*

Müller (F. Max) — **Address** delivered at the Opening of the Ninth International Congress of Orientalists, held in London, Sept. 5, 1892, 8vo. pp. 66. 1s. 6d.

Mystic Flowery Land. See: Halcombe.

Oriental Translation Fund (New), See: Mirkhond, Tawney, Bana, and Hariri.

Oudemans Jzn. (A. C.) — The Great Sea-Serpent. An historical and critical Treatise. With the Reports of 187 Appearances (including those of the Appendix), the Suppositions and Suggestions of scientific and non-scientific Persons, and the Author's Conclusions. With 82 Illustrations. Royal 8vo. Cloth. pp. XV, 592. £ 1. 5s. net.

"The volume is extremely interesting". *Athenaeum.*

Reis Sidi Ali. The Travels and Adventures of the Turkish Admiral. In India, Afghanistan, Central Asia and Persia 1553—1556. Translated from the Turkish into English with notes. By H. VAMBERY. — *In the Press.*

Ridding (C. M.) — See: Bana's Kadambari.

Rosen (F.) — A Modern Persian Colloquial Grammar, containing a short Grammar, Dialogues and Extracts from Nasir Eddin Shah's Diaries, Tales, etc. and a Vocabulary. Cr. 8vo. Cloth. pp. XIV, 400. 10s. 6d.

"Dr. ROSEN's learned work will be useful to all who have occasion to go to Persia, Baluchistan, and Afghanistan. The Vocabulary will be a boon to students, especially as it is in the same volume with the grammar and the dialogues." — *Publ. Circular.*

"Very useful to students." — *Westminster Review.*
"Excellent Guide to the acquisition of Persian." — *Asiatic Quarterly Review.*

Rosthorn (A. de) — On the Tea Cultivation in Western Ssüch'uan and the Tea Trade with Tibet via Tachienlu. 8vo. pp. 40. With Sketch Map. 2s. net.

Ruben (Paul) — Critical Remarks upon some Passages of the Old Testament, by PAUL RUBEN, Ph. D. 4to. Cloth. pp. II. 24, 14. 3s. 6d.

"It may suffice to congratulate ourselves that a scholar of vigorous mind and accurate philological training is devoting his leisure to a subject worthy of attention.... Very many of the notes are in a high degree stimulating and suggestive. The get up of the book is excellent"
Academy.

"Dr. RUBEN shows much originality, a wide knowledge of authorities, and a true grasp of critical principles". — *Jewish Chronicle.*

Sacred Books of the Old Testament. — A critical Edition of the Hebrew Text, Printed in Colours, with Notes. Prepared by eminent Biblical Scholars of Europe and America. Under the editorial direction of PAUL HAUPT, Professor in the John Hopkins Univ. Baltimore. **Edition de Luxe**, in 120 numbered Copies only. 4to. Subscription price for the complete Work (20 Parts), £ 20.

> Prospectuses sent on application. The following Parts have already been issued:
> Part 1: **Book of Genesis**, by C. J. Ball. pp. 120. London. 1896. £ 2.
> Part 3: **Leviticus**, by Prof. S. R. Driver. pp. 32. 1894. 16s.
> Part 6: **Joshua**, by Prof. W. H. Bennet. pp. 32. 1895. £ 1.
> Part 8: **Samuel**, by Prof. K. Budde. pp. 100. 1894. £ 1. 10s.
> Part 11: **Jeremiah**, by Prof. C. H. Cornill. pp. 80. 1895. £ 1..
> Part 14: **Psalms**, by J. Wellhausen, pp. 96. 1895. £ 1. 10s.
> Part 18: **Book of Daniel**, by A. Kamphausen, 4to. pp. 44. 1896. £ 1.
> Part 20: **Chronicles**, by R. Kittel. pp. 82. 1895. £ 1. 10s.

A valuable "Edition de Luxe" in 120 numbered copies only, and which may be described as the most splendidly got up Hebrew work in existence.

Each single part is numbered and signed by the editor with his own hand. The single parts will be issued in highly elegant covers. After the conclusion of the work a handsome binding cover will be supplied.

Sankaranarayana (P.) — **English-Telugu Dictionary**, by P. SANKARANARAYNA M. A., M. R. A. S., Tutor to their Highnesses the Princes of Cochin. 8vo. Cloth. pp. 61, 756, 10s. 6d.

Sanskrit Phonetics. A Manual of. See: Uhlenbeck.

Sanskrit Nouns and Verbs. See: Johnston.

Sayce (A. H.) — **Address** to the Assyrian Section of the Ninth International Congress of Orientalists. 8vo. pp. 32. 1s.

Sauerwein (G.) — **A Pocket Dictionary** of the English and Turkish Languages. Small 8vo. Cloth. limp. pp. 298. 3s. 6d.

Scholia on passages of the Old Testament. By MAX JACOB Bishop of Edessa. Now first edited in the original Syriac with an English translation and notes by G. PHILLIP. DD. 8vo. Paper Covers. 5s.

Seth (Mesrovb J.) — History of the Armenians in India. From the earliest Times to the present Day. 8vo. Cloth. pp. XXIV, 199. 7s. 6d. net.

"The subject is invested with peculiar interest at the present time by recent events in Asia Minor.... his unpretending little work is a valuable repertory of original information never before accessible in print and scarcely even known to exist." — *Times.*

"The book is happily distinguished among the number of books recently issued concerning Armenia in that it deals strictly with fact..... The volume deserves the attention of every one interested in the history of India and of the hardly treated race which seems to flourish better there than in its own country." — *Scotsman.*

"Sinnatamby". Letchimey. A Tale of Old Ceylon. 8vo. pp. III, 54. With Photogr. Plates and Illustrations. *In the Press.*

Stein (M. A.) — Catalogue of the Sanskrit MSS. in the Raghunata Temple Library of His Highness the Maharaja of Jammu and Kashmir. 4to. Cloth. pp. 423. 12s.

Steele's (R.) The Discovery of Secrets, attributed to Geber from the MS Arabic text. 8vo. 1s.

Stoffel (C.) Studies in English, Written and Spoken. For the Use of continental Students. With Index. First Series. Roy. 8vo. Cloth. pp. XII, 332. 7s. 6d.

Suhrillekha (The); or "Friendly Letter;" written by Lung Shu (Nàgàrjuna), and addressed to King Sadvaha. Translated from the Chinese Edition of I-Tsing, by the late Rev. SAMUEL BEAL, with the Chinese Text. 8vo. pp. XIII, 51. 5s.

Swami Vivekananda's Addresses. See: Vivekananda.

Tawney (C. H.) — The Kathákoça; or Treasury of Stories. Translated from Sanskrit Manuscripts. With Appendix, containing Notes, by Prof. ERNST LEUMANN. 8vo. Cloth. pp. XXIII, 260. 10s.

Temple (G.) — A Glossary of Indian Terms relating to Religion, Customs, Government, Land, and other Terms and Words in Common Use. To which is added a Glossary of Terms used in District Work in the N. W. Provinces and Oudh., and also of those applied to Labourers. With an Appendix giving Computation of Time and Money, and Weights and Measures, in British India, and Forms of Address. Roy. 8vo. Cloth. pp. IV, 332. 7s. 6d.

"The book is moderate in price and clear in print." — *Athenæum*.

"The book is handy, well printed and well got up and no student of Indian subjects should be without it." — *Asiatic Quarterly Review*.

"Students of Oriental travel may find something serviceable in its pages; and those who are engaged in trade in the East Indies might occasionally turn to the volume, with profit, if it were on the office shelf." — *The Nation*.

Temple (Major R. C.) — **Notes on Antiquities in Ramannadesa.** (The Talaing Country of Burma.) 4to. pp. 40. With 24 Plates and a Map. 18s.

Thomas, F. W., See: Bāna, Harsa Carita.

Tiele (C. P.) — **Western Asia,** according to the Most Recent Discoveries. Rectorial Address on the Occasion of the 318th Anniversary of the Leyden University, 8th February, 1893. Translated by ELIZABETH J. TAYLOR. Small 8vo. Bound. pp. 36. 2s. 6d.

"An authoritative summary of the results of recent Oriental research and discovery." — *The Times*.

"The address presents a graphic picture of the political situation in Western Asia in the fifteenth and fourteenth centuries B. C."
Morning Post.

"The professor's grasp of his subject is very evident, and his deductions from the materials commented on worthy of all attention."
Imperial and Asiatic Quarterly Review.

T'oung Pao. — **Archives pour servir à l'étude de l'histoire,** des langues, de la géographie et de l'ethnographie de l'Asie orientale. (Chine, Japon, Corée, Indo-Chine, Asie Centrale et Malaise.) Rédigées par MM. G. SCHLEGEL et H. CORDIER. Vol. I—VIII. Vol. IX in progress). Annual Subscription. £ 1.

Transactions of the Ninth International Congress of Orientalists. London, 5th to 12th September, 1892.) Edited by E. DELMAR MORGAN. 2 Vols. Roy. 8vo. Cloth. £1. 15s.

Vol. I. contains: Indian and Aryan Sections. £1. 1s.

Vol. II. contains: Semitic, Egypt and Africa, Geographical, Archaic Greece and the East, Persia and Turkey, China, Central Asia and the Far East, Australasia, Anthropology and Mythology Sections. £1. 1s.

Uhlenbeck. (C. C.). A Manual of Sanskrit Phonetics. In comparison with the Indogermanic mother-language, for students of Germanic and classical philology. 8vo. pp. 115. 6s.

Ummagga Yataka. See: Yatawara.

Usha. — The Dawn. A Vedic Periodical, edited by Pandit Satya Vrata Samasrami. 8vo. Published monthly. Annual subscription. £1. 1s.

Valmiki. — The Ramayan of Valmiki. Translated into English Verse, by R. T. H. GRIFFITH, M. A., C. I. E. Complete in one Volume. 8vo. Cloth. pp. IX, 576. 7s. 6d.

Vambery, see: Reis Sidi Ali.

Vivekânanda (Swami). — Lectures delivered in London. Nos. 1—12. 6d. each.

Vivekânanda (Swami). — Madras Lectures. 8vo. 1s. 6d.

Vizianagram Sanskrit Series. — Under the Superintendence of ARTHUR VENIS, M.A., Oxon, Principal, Sanskrit College, Benares. Different Prices.

West (Sir Raymond) — Higher Education in India: Its Position and Claims. 8vo. pp. 61. 1892. 1s.

Wildeboer (G.) — The Origin of the Canon of of the Old Testament. An historico-critical Enquiry. Translated by WISNER BAÇON. Edited with

Preface by Prof. GEORGE F. MOORE. Royal 8vo. Cloth. pp. XII, 182. 7s. 6d.

"We will only add that we cordially echo the professor's hope that his book may not only be read by professed students but that it may come also into the hands of such as have already left the University."
Guardian.

"The method adopted is that of historical investigation: the student is thus enabled to see how the results of critical inquiry have been obtained.... he accompanies a guide who is familiar with the way which leads to them." — *Academy.*

"The first thing to notice is the translation. This is how a book ought to be translated.... The book must be used, not read merely... it is independent, painstaking, farseeing." — *Expository Times.*

Winckler (H.) — The Tell-El-Amarna Letters. Transliteration, English Translation, Vocabulary, etc. Roy. 8vo. Cloth. pp. XLII, 416, and Registers 50 pages. £ 1. 1s. net.
The same. In Paper Covers. £ 1.

With the Dutch in the East. See: Cool.

Wright (W.) — The Book of Jonah in four Semitic versions. Chaldee, Syriac, Aethiopic and Arabic. With corresponding glossaries. 8vo. Cloth. pp. 148. 4s.

Wynkoop (J. D.) — Manual of Hebrew Syntax. Translated from the Dutch by C. VAN DEN BIESEN. 8vo. Cloth. pp. XXII, 152 and Index. 2s. 6d. net.

"It is a book, which every Hebrew student should possess,.... we recommend it for general usefulness, and thank Dr. van den Biesen for giving it to the English reader." — *Jewish World.*

"It is one of those books which will become indispensable to the English student who will desire to become acquainted with the construction of Hebrew syntax.... this takes a high rank and will undoubtedly become a general text book on the subject in many colleges and universities."
American Hebrew News.

Wynkoop (J. D.) — Hebrew Grammar. Translated from the Dutch by C. VAN DEN BIESEN. 8vo. Cloth. 2s. 6d. net.

Yatawara (J. B.) — The Ummaga Yataka, translated into English. *In the Press.*

FOREIGN AND ORIENTAL BOOKS.

Messrs. LUZAC & Co. having Agents in all the principal Towns of the Continent, America and the East, are able to supply any Books not in stock at the shortest notice and at the most reasonable terms.

Subscriptions taken for all Foreign, American and Oriental Periodicals.

LIST OF
INDIAN GOVERNMENT PUBLICATIONS.

Messrs. LUZAC & Co. are Official Agents for the sale ot the Indian Government Publications.

Acts of the several Governments in India. Different dates and prices.
Aden Gazetteer. By Captain F. M. Hunter. 1877. 5s.
Adi Granth. By E. Trumpp. 1877. £1.
Agriculture, Report on Indian. By J. A. Voelcker, Ph. D. 1893. 3s. 6d.
Annals of the Calcutta Botanic Gardens:
    I. Monograph on Ficus. Part 1. 1887. £1 5s.
    "   "   Part 2. 1888. £2.
    "   "   Appendix. 1889. 10s. 6d.
    II. Species of Artocarpus, &c. 1889. £1 12s 6d.
    III. Species of Pedicularis, &c. 1891. £3 10s.
    IV. Anonaceæ of British India. 1893. £3 10s.
    V., Part 1. A Century of Orchids. Memoir of W. Roxburgh. 1895. £3 3s. coloured, £1 12s. 6d. uncoloured.
    V., Part 2. A Century of New and Rare Indian Plants. 1896. £1 12s. 6d.
    VI., Part 1. Turgescence of Motor Organs of Leaves. Parasitic species of Choanephora. 1895. £1 10s.
    VII. Bambuseæ of British India. 1896. £2.
Anwar-i-Soheli. By Colonel H. S. Jarrett. 1880. 15s.
Archæological Survey of India. (New Series):
    IX. South Indian Inscriptions. By E. Hultzsch, Ph.D. Vol. I. 1890. 4s.
    X.   "   "   "   " Vol. II, Part. 1. 1891. 3s. 6d.

South Indian Inscriptions. By E. Hultzsch, Ph.D. Vol. II, Part 2. 1892. 3s. 6d.
South Indian Inscriptions. By E. Hultzsch, Ph.D. Vol. II, Part 3. 1895. 5s. 6d.
XI. Sharqî Architecture of Jaunpur. By A. Führer, Ph.D. 1889. £1 1s. 6d.
XII. Monumental Antiquities in the North-West Provinces. By A. Führer, Ph.D. 1891. 13s. 6d.
XV. South Indian Buddhist Antiquities. By A. Rea. 1894. 12s. 6d.
XVII. Architectural, &c. Remains in Coorg. By A. Rea. 1894. 2s.
XVIII. The Moghul Architecture of Fatehpur Sikri. By E. W. Smith. Part 1. 1894. £1 5s.
The Moghul Architecture of Fatehpur Sikri By E. W. Smith. Part 2. 1896. 17s. 6d.
XXI. Châlukyan Architecture. By A. Rea. 1896. £1 2s.
XXIII. Muhammadan Architecture in Gujarat. By J. Burgess, C.I.E., LL.D. 1896. £1.

Army List, The Indian. Quarterly. 4s.
Art Ware, Photographs of Madras and Burmese. 1886. £1 15s.
Arzis: Bengali, Canarese, Hindi, Mahratta, Malayalam, Tamil, Telugu, and Urdu. 7s. 6d. each.
Translations of the above (except Hindi). 7s. 6d. each.

Beer Casks, Destruction of, by a Boring Beetle. By W. F. H. Blandford. 1893. 6d.
Bibliographical Index of Indian Philosophical Systems. By F. Hall. 1859. 9s.
Bihar Peasant Life. By G. A. Grierson, Ph.D., C.I.E. 1885. 6s. 6d.
Bihari Language, Seven Grammars of. By G. A. Grierson, Ph.D. C.I.E. (8 parts). 1883—87. £1.
Bihari, The Satsaiya of. Edited by G. A. Grierson, Ph.D., C.I.E. 1896. 7s. 6d.
Bombay Gazetteer, Edited by J. M. Campbell, LL.D., C.I.E.;
  I. (Not yet published). — II. Surat and Broach. 1877. 5s. 6d. — III. Kaira and Panch Mahals. 1879. 2s. 6d. — IV. Ahmedabad. 1879. 3s. — V. Cutch, Palanpur, and Mahi Kantha. 1880. 4s. — VI. Rewa Kantha, Narukot, Cambay, and Surat States. 1880. 3s. — VII. Baroda. 1883. 5s. — VIII. Kathiawar. 1884. 6s. 6d. — IX. (Not yet published). — X. Ratnagiri and Savantvadi. 1880. 5s. — XI. Kolaba and Janjira. 1883. 5s. — XII. Khandesh. 1880. 6s. — XIII. Thana. (2 parts) 1882. 8s. — XIV. Thana: places of interest. 1882. 5s. — XV. Kanara. (2 parts). 1883. 7s. 6d. — XVI. Nasik. 1883. 6s. 6d. — XVII. Ahmadnagar. 1884. 7s. — XVIII. Poona. (3 parts). 1885. 15s. 6d. — XIX. Satara. 1885. 6s. 6d. — XX. Sholapur. 1884. 5s. — XXI. Belgaum. 1884. 6s. — XXII. Dharwar. 1884. 7s. 6d. — XXIII. Bijapur. 1884. 6s. 6d. — XXIV. Kolhapur. 1886. 5s. — XXV. Botany of the Presidency. 1886. 4s. 6d. — XXVI. Materials for a Statistical of Bombay Town and Island, Parts I., II., and III. 1893—94. 5s. each.
British Burma Gazetteer. Edited by H. R. Spearman. (2 vols.) 1879—80. £1 13s. 6d.
Buddha Gaya; the Hermitage of Sakya Muni. By Rajendralal Mitra. 1878. £3.
Burmese, Tables for the Transliteration of, into English. 1896. 1s.

Catalogue of the India Office Library, Vol. I (with Index). 1888. 10s. 6d.
" " " (Supplement). 1895. 5s.
" of the Arabic MSS. in the India Office Library. By O. Loth. 1877. 15s.
" of the Mandalay MSS. in the India Office Library. By V .Fausböll. 1897. 2s.
" of the Pali MSS. in the India Office Library. By H. Oldenberg. 1882. 5s.
" of the Sanskrit MSS. in the India Office Library. By Dr. J. Eggeling. (Parts I to V). 1887—96. 10s. 6d. each.
" of Sanskrit MSS., Bikanir. By Rajendralal Mitra. 1880. 3s.
" " Tanjore. By A. C. Burnell. 1880. £1 11s. 6d.
" of MSS. in Oudh. By A. Sprenger 1854. 15s.
Chestnuts, Papers on Spanish. With Introduction by Sir George Birdwood, K. C. I., C. S. I. 1892. 1s.
Cholera, What can the State do to prevent is? By Dr. J. M. Cunningham. 1884. 3s.
Coorg Gazetteer. 1884. 5s.
Corpus Inscriptionum Indicarum:
 I. Inscriptions of Asoka. By Major-General Sir A. Cunningham, K. C. I. E., C. S. I. 1877. 9s. 6d.
 II. (Not yet published.)
 III. Inscriptions of the early Gupta King. By J. F. Fleet, C. I. E. 1889. £1 13s. 6d. with plates. £1 without plates.
Covenanted Civil Servants, Manual of Rules applicable to. Second edition. 1891. 2s. 6d.
Dictionary of Indian Economic Products. By Dr. Geo Watt, C. I. E. (6 vols. in 9). 1889—93. £3 3s.
Ditto, Index to. 1896. 3s.
Durga puja. By Pratapa Chandra Ghosha. 1871. 6s.
English-Sanskrit Dictionary. By Sir M. Monier-Williams, K. C. I. E. 1851. £1 10s.
Fibres. Report on Indian. By C. F. Cross, E. J. Bevan, &c. 1887. 5s.
Finance and Revenue Accounts of the Government of India. Annual volumes. 2s. 6d. each.
Forest Working Plans. By W. E. D'Arcy. (Second edition). 1892. 1s. 6d.
Fort St. George Diary and Consultation Books: 1681 (Selection) 1893. 3s. 6d. — 1682. 1894. 4s. — 1683. 1894. 5s. 6d. — 1684. 1895. 5s. 6d. — 1685. 1895. 7s.
Geological Survey Department Publications.
Glossary of Indian Terms. By H. H. Wilson. 1855. £1 10s.
Hastings, Warren, Selections from the Records of the Foreign Department relating to the Administration of. Edited by G. W. Forrest, B. A. (3 vols.) 1890. 16s.
" " The Administration of. (A reprint of the Introduction to the foregoing.) By G. W. Forrest, B. A. 1892. 5s. 6d.
India Office Marine Records, List of. 1896. 5s.
Kachin Language, Handbook of the. By H. F. Hertz. 1895. 1s.

Lansdowne, Lord, The Administration of. By G. W. Forrest, B. A. 1894. 2s. 6d.
Lepcha Grammar. By Colonel G. P. Mainwaring. 1876. 3s.
Lighthouse Construction and Illumination, Report on. By F. W. Ashpitel. 1895. £1 9s. 6d.

Madras District Manuals (revised issues:)
South Canara (2 vols.) 1894. 4s.
North Arcot (2 vols.) 1895. 6s.
Malabar Manual. By W. Logan. (3 vols.) 1891. £1 2s. 6d.
Manava-Kalpa-Sutra. By Th. Goldstücker. 1861. £3.
Manual of Hydraulics. By Captain H. D. Love, R. E. 1890. 5s.
Marathi Dictionary. By J. T. Molesworth. 1857. 16s.
Marathi Grammar. By the Rev. Ganpatrao R. Navalkar. (Third edition.) 1894. 10s. 6d.
Meteorological Department Publications.
Muntakhabat-i-Urdu. (Second edition.) 1887. 1s. 10d.
Mutiny, the Indian, Selections from the Records of the Military Department relating to. Edited by G. W. Forrest, B. A. Vol. I. 1893. 12s. 6d.

North-East Frontier of Bengal, Relations of the Government with the Hill Tribes of the. By Sir Alexander Mackenzie, K. C. S. I. 1884. 6s. 6d.
North-West Provinces Gazetteer:
I. Bundelkhand, 1874. 8s. 6d. — II. Meerut Part. I. 1875. 6s. 6d. — III. Meerut, Part. II. 1876. 8s. 6d. — IV. Agra, Part. I. 1876. 8s. 6d. — V. Rohilkhand. 1879. 8s. 6d. — VI. Cawnpore, Gorakhpur and Basti. 1881. 9s. — VII. Farukhabad and Agra. 1884. 8s. — VIII. Muttra, Allahabad and Fatehpur. 1884. 10s. — IX. Shahjahanpur, Moradabad and Rampur Native State. 1883. 8s. — X. Himalayan Districts, Part. I. 1882. 13s. — XI. Himalayan Districts, Part. II. 1884. 12s.¹ 6d. — XII. Himalayan Districts Part. III. 1886. 12s. — XIII. Azamgarh, Ghazipur and Ballia' 1883. 8s. — XIV. Benares, Mirzapur and Jaunpur. 1884. 10s.

Oudh Gazetteer. (3 vols.) 1877—78. £1.

Paintings, &c. in the India Office, Descriptive Catalogue of. By W. Forster. 1893. 1s.
Prakrita Prakasa. By E. B. Cowell. 1854. 9s.
Prem Sagar. By E. B. Eastwick. 1851. 15s.

Rajputana Gazetteer. (3 vols.) 1879—80. 15s.
Rigveda Sanhita. Vols. IV to VI. By Professor Max Müller. 1862—74. £2 12s. 6d. per volume.
Index to ditto. £2 5s.
Rigveda Translations. By H. H. Wilson. Vols I, III and IV. 1850—66. 13s. 6d. per volume.
Vols. V and VI. 1888. 18s. per volume.

Sanskritt MSS. in S. India, First and Second Reports on. By Dr. Hultzsch. 1895—96. 1s. 8d. each.
Scientific Memoirs by Medical Officers of the Indian Army:
Part I. 1885. 2s. 6d. — Part II. 1887. 2s. 6d. — Part III. 1888.

4*s.* — Part IV. 1889. 2*s.* 6*d.* — Part V. 1890. 4*s.* — Part VI. 1891. 4*s.* — Part VII. 1892. 4*s.* — Part VIII. 1893. 4*s.* — Part IX. 1895. 4*s.*
Selections from the Records of the Burmese Illuttaw. 1889. 6*s.*
Sikkim Gazetteer. By H. H. Risley, C. I. E., and others. 1894. 12*s.* 6*d.*
Specimens of Languages in India. By Sir G. Campbell, K. C. S. I. 1874. £ 1. 16*s.*
Survey Department Publications.
Surveys 1875—90, Memoir on the Indian. By C. E. D. Black. 1891. 7*s.* 6*d.*
Tamil Papers. By Andrew Robertson. 1890. 4*s.*
Technical Art Series of Illustrations of Indian Architectural Decorative Work for the use of Art Schools and Craftsmen:
1886—87. (6 plates.) 2*s.* — 1888—89. (18 plates.) 6*s.* — 1890. (12 plates.) 4*s.* — 1891. (18 plates.) 6*s.* — 1892. (13 plates.) 4*s.* 6*d.* — 1893. (12 plates) 4*s.* — 1894. (14 plates.) 5*s.* — 1895. (12 plates.) 4*s.* — 1896. (15 plates.) 4*s.*
Telegu Reader. By C. P. Brown. (2 vols.) 1852. 14*s.*
Textile Manufactures and Costumes of the People of India. By Dr. Forbes Watson. 1866. £ 1. 1*s.*
Tibetan-English Dictionary. By H. A. Jaeschke. 1881. £ 1.
Timber, Mensuration of. By P. J. Carter. 1893. 1*s.*
Tobacco. Cultivation and Preparation of, in India. By Dr. Forbes Watson. 1871. 5*s.*
Tombs or Monuments in Bengal, Inscriptions on. Edited by C. R. Wilson, M.A. 1896. 3*s.* 6*d.*
Vikramarka, Tales of. By Ravipati Gurumurti. 1850. 1*s.*
Yield tables of the Scotch Pine. By W. Schlich, Ph. D. 1889. 1*s.*

N.B. In addition to the above, a large number of departmental reports, &c., are on sale at the various Government presses in India. These publications are not kept in stock at the India Office; but should copies of them be required, they will be furnished (on payment), as far as possible, from the supply received for official purposes.

In all cases applications for publications must be made through the official agents.

INDEX OF PRIVATE NAMES.

Apte, M. C., 1
Arbuthnot, F. F., 10, 15
D'Arcy, W. E. D., 25
Ashpitel, F. W.; 26
Aston, W. G., 2

Bacon, Wisner, 21
Ball, C. J., 18
Beal, S., 19
Bemmelen, J. F. van, 9
Bennet, W. H., 18
Berrington, B. J., 9
Bevan, E. J., 25
Bezold, C., 3
Biesen, C. van den, 22
Birdwood, Sir G., 25
Black, C. E. D., 27
Blackden, M. W., 4
Blandford, W. F. H., 24
Brown, C. P., 27
Browne, Edward G., 9
Budde, K., 18
Budge, E. A. Wallis 4, 14, 15
Burgess, J., 24
Burnell, A. C., 25

Campbell, J. M., 24
Campbell, Sir G., 27
Cappeller, Carl, 5
Carter, P. J., 27
Chakrabarti J. C., 6
Chenery, J., 10
Cool, W., 6
Cordier, H., 20
Cornill, C. H., 18
Cowell, E. B., 2, 26
Cowper, B. H., 7
Cross, C. J., 25
Cunningham, J. M., 25.

Cunningham, Sir A., 25
Cust, R. N., 7, 8

Das, Sarat Candra, 13
Driver, S. R., 18

Eastwick, E. B., 26
Edkins, J., 8
Eggeling, J., 25
Eitel, E. J., 8

Fausböll, V., 25
Fleet, J. F., 25
Forrest, G. W., 25, 26
Forster, W., 26
Frazer, G. W., 4
Führer, A., 24

Ghosha, P. C., 25
Gladstone (W. E.), 9
Goldstücker, J., 26
Gray, J., 4, 11
Gribble, J. D. B., 9
Grierson, G. A., 24
Griffith, R. J. H., 21
Guirandon, F. G. de, 10
Gurumurti, R., 27

Halcombe C. J. H., 10
Hall, F. 24
Hardy, R. S., 10
Harper, W. R., 1, 3, 11
Harper, R. F., 10
Haupt, P., 17.
Hertz, H. F., 25
Hirschfeld, H., 2
Hooyer, G. B., 6, 9
Hultzsch, E., 23, 26
Hunter, F. M., 23

Jacob, Max, 18
Jaeschke, H. A., 27
Jarrett, H. S., 23
Jastrow, M., 11
Johnson, F. E., 16
Johnston, C., 11, 12
Judson, A., 13

Kamphausen, A., 18
King, L. W., 12, 14
Kittel, F., 13
Kittel, R., 18

Lacouperie, T. de, 2
Land, J. P. N., 13
Leumann, E., 19
Levinsohn, J. B., 8
Loewe, L., 8, 13
Logan, W., 26
Loth, O., 25
Love, H. D., 26
Luzac, C. G., 3

Mackenzie, Sir A., 26
Macnaghten, (Sir W. Hay), 15
Mainwaring, G. P., 26
Margoliouth, D. S., 15
Mitra, R., 24, 25
Molesworth, J. T. 26
Monier-Williams, Sir M., 16, 25
Moore, G. F., 22
Morgan, E. Delmar, 21
Müller, F. Max, 16, 26

Navalkar, G. R., 26

Oldenberg, H., 25
Oudemans, A. C., 17

Poole, R. Lane, 13

Rea, A., 24.
Rehatsek, E., 15
Ridding, C. M., 2
Risley, H. H., 27
Robertson, A., 27

Rosen, F., 17
Rosthorn, A. de, 17
Ruben, P., 17

Samasrami, S. V., 21
Sankaranarayna, P., 18
Sauerwein, G., 18.
Sayce, A. H. 18
Schlegel, G., 20.
Schlich, W. , 27.
Seth, Mesrovb J., 19
Smith, E. W., 24
Sprenger, A., 25
Steele, R., 19
Stein, M. A., 19
Steingass, F., 10
Stoffel, C., 19
Swâmi Vivekânanda, 21

Taylor, E. J., 6, 20
Tawney, C. H., 19
Temple, G., 20
Temple, R. C., 11, 20
Thomas, F. W., 2
Tiele, C. P., 20
Trumpp, E., 23

Uhlenbeck, C. C., 21

Vambery, H., 17
Venis, A., 21
Vivekânanda Swâmi, 21
Voelcker, J. A., 23

Watson, F., 27
Watt, G. 25
Wellhausen, J., 18
West, Sir R., 21
Wildeboer, G., 21
Wilson, C. R., 27
Wilson, H. H., 15, 25, 26
Winckler, H., 22
Wright, W., 22
Wynkoop, J. D., 22

Yatawara, J. B., 22

LUZAC'S ORIENTAL LIST.

NOTICE TO OUR READERS.

With this number we enter upon the eighth year of the publication of our «Oriental List." Four years ago in the first number of our fourth volume we thanked our readers for the generous support we had received from various quarters, including some flattering notices in our contemporaries referring to the value of our «List", and we now tender our thanks to an extended circle of readers. Within recent years the number of works on oriental subjects has increased enormously, and our «List" was started with the object of furnishing a record of such works which should be published at regular intervals. Our aim has therefore been to give each month a complete list of oriental books published in England, on the Continent, in the East and in America, while under the heading «Notes and News" we have endeavoured to give a faithful account of the progress made during the month in the various branches of oriental learning, literature and archaeology. The encouragement we have continuously received from the beginning of the undertaking emboldens us to believe that the «List" has really supplied a want on the part of those who from taste or profession are interested in the languages, literatures and antiquities of the East, and we therefore venture to appeal to our readers who are in the habit of consulting our «List" when making out their orders to send them to us direct.

LONDON, Jan. '98.   LUZAC & Co.

PRINTED BY E. J. BRILL., LEYDEN (HOLLAND).

www.ingramcontent.com/pod-product-compliance
Lightning Source LLC
Chambersburg PA
BHW030819230426
3667CB00008B/1291